CONTENTS

T0019964

Top to bottom: Plan #F09-101D-0050 on page 270; Plan #F09-155D-0027 on page 31; Plan #F09-011D-0342, on page 232; Plan #F09-155D-0070 on page 229; Plan #F09-011D-0347 on page 156; Plan #F09-051D-0981 on page 256.

what's the right
PLAN for you?

Choosing a house design is exciting, but can be a difficult task. Many factors play a role in what home plan is best for you and your family. To help you get started, we have pinpointed some of the major factors to consider when searching for your dream home. Take the time to evaluate your family's needs and you will have an easier time sorting through all of the house designs offered in this book.

BUDGET is the first thing to consider. Many items take part in this budget, from ordering the blueprints to the last doorknob purchased. When you find the perfect house plan, visit houseplansandmore.com and get a cost-to-build estimate to ensure that the finished home will be within your cost range. A cost-to-build report is a detailed summary that gives you the total cost to build a specific home in the zip code where you're wanting to build. It is interactive allowing you to adjust labor and material costs, and it's created on

demand when ordered so all pricing is up-to-date. This valuable tool will help you know how much your dream home will cost before you buy plans (see page 282 for more information).

FAMILY LIFESTYLE After your budget is deciphered, you need to assess you and your family's lifestyle needs. Think about the stage of life you are in now, and what stages you will be going through in the future. Ask yourself questions to figure out how much room you need now and if you will need room for expansion. Are you married? Do you have children? How many children do you plan on having? Are you an empty-nester? How long do you plan to live in this home?

Incorporate into your planning any frequent guests you may have, including elderly parents, grandchildren or adult children who may live with you.

Does your family entertain a lot? If so, think about the rooms you will need to do so. Will you need both formal and informal spaces? Do you need a gourmet kitchen? Do you need a game room and/ or a wet bar?

FLOOR PLAN LAYOUTS When looking through these home plans, imagine yourself walking through the house. Consider the flow from the entry to the living, sleeping and gathering areas. Does the layout ensure privacy for the master bedroom? Does the garage enter near the kitchen for easy unloading? Does the placement of the windows provide enough privacy from any neigh-

boring properties? Do you plan on using furniture you already have? Will this furniture fit in the appropriate rooms? When you find a plan you want to purchase, be sure to picture yourself actually living in it.

EXTERIOR SPACES With many different home styles throughout ranging from Traditional to Contemporary, flip through these pages and find which best-selling home design appeals to you the most and think about the neighborhood in which you plan to build. Also, think about how the house will fit on your site. Picture the landscaping you want to add to the lot. Using your imagination is key when choosing a home plan.

Choosing a house design can be an intimidating experience. Asking yourself these questions before you get started on the search will help you through the process. With our large selection of sizes and styles, we are certain you will find your dream home in this book.

MAKE A LIST!

Experts in the field suggest that the best way to determine your needs is to begin by listing everything you like or dislike about your current home.

BEST-SELLING
HOUSE PLANS

Note: The homes as shown in the photographs and renderings in this book may differ from the actual blueprints. When studying the house of your choice, please check the floor plans carefully. All plans appearing in this publication are protected under copyright law.

Reproduction of the illustrations or working drawings by any means is strictly prohibited. The right of building only one structure from the plans purchased is licensed exclusively to the buyer and the plans may not be resold unless by express written authorization.

The homes on the cover are: Top, Plan #F09-155D-0101 on page 180; Bottom, left to right: Plan #F09-007D-0140 on page 152; Plan #F09-011D-0660 on page 93; Plan #F09-141D-0013 on page 119.

The home featured on page 1 is Plan #F09-056D-0120 on page 33.

10 steps to BUILDING your dream home

1 talk to a lender

If you plan to obtain a loan in order to build your new home, then it's best to find out first how much you can get approved for before selecting a home design. Knowing the financial information before you start looking for land or a home will keep you from selecting something out of your budget and turning a great experience into a major disappointment. Financing the home you plan to build is somewhat different than financing the purchase of an existing house. You're going to need thousands of dollars for land, labor, and materials. Chances are, you're going to have to borrow most of it. Therefore, you will probably need to obtain a construction loan. This is a short-term loan to pay for building your house. When the house is completed, the loan is paid off in full, usually out of the proceeds from your long-term mortgage loan.

2 determine needs

Selecting the right home plan for your needs and lifestyle requires a lot of thought. Your new home is an investment, so you should consider not only your current needs, but also your future requirements. Versatility and the potential for converting certain areas to other uses could be an important factor later on. So, although a home office may seem unnecessary now,

in years to come, the idea may seem ideal. Home plans that include flex spaces or bonus rooms can really adapt to your needs in the future.

3 choose a home site

The site for your new home will have a definite impact on the design you select. It's a good idea to select a home that will complement your site. This will save you time and money when building. Or, you can then modify a design to specifically accommodate your site. However, it will most likely make your home construction more costly than selecting a home plan suited for your lot right from the start. For example, if your land slopes, a walk-out basement works perfectly. If it's wooded, or has a lake in the back, an atrium ranch home is a perfect style to take advantage of surrounding backyard views.

SOME IMPORTANT CRITERIA TO CONSIDER WHEN SELECTING A SITE:

- Improvements will need to be made including utilities, sidewalks and driveways
- Convenience of the lot to work, school, shops, etc.
- Zoning requirements and property tax amounts
- Soil conditions at your future site
- Make sure the person or firm that sells you the land owns it free and clear

---

4 select a home design

We've chosen the "best of the best" of the home plans found at houseplansandmore.com to be featured in this book. With over 18,000 home plans from the best architects and designers across the country, this book includes the best variety of styles and sizes to suit the needs and tastes of a broad spectrum of homeowners.

5 get the cost to build

If you feel you have found "the" home, then before taking the step of purchasing house plans, order an estimated cost-to-build report for the exact zip code where you plan to build. Requesting this custom cost report created specifically for you will help educate you on all costs associated with building your new home. Simply order this report and gain knowledge of the material and labor cost associated with the home you love. Not only does the report allow you to choose the quality of the materials, you can also select options in every aspect of the project from lot condition to contractor fees. This report will allow you to successfully manage your construction budget in all areas, clearly see where the majority of the costs lie, and save you money from start to finish.

A COST-TO-BUILD REPORT WILL DETERMINE THE OVERALL COST OF YOUR NEW HOME INCLUDING THESE 5 MAJOR EXPENSE CATEGORIES:

- Land
- Foundation
- Materials
- General Contractor's fee - Some rules-of-thumb that you may find useful are: (a) the total labor cost will generally run a little higher than your total material cost, but it's not unusual for a builder or general contractor to charge 15-20% of the combined cost for managing the overall project.
- Site improvements - don't forget to add in the cost of your site improvements such as utilities, driveway, sidewalks, landscaping, etc.

6 hire a contractor

If you're inexperienced in construction, you'll probably want to hire a general contractor to manage the project. If you do not know a reputable general contractor, begin your search by contacting your local Home Builders Association to get references. Many states require building contractors to be licensed. If this is the case in your state, its licensing board is another referral source. Finding a reputable, quality-minded contractor is a key factor in ensuring that your new home is well constructed and is finished on time and within budget. It can be a smart decision to discuss the plan you like with your builder prior to ordering plans. They can guide you into choosing the right type of plan package option especially if you intend on doing some customizing to the design.

7 customizing

Sometimes your general contractor may want to be the one who makes the mod-

ifications you want to the home you've selected. But, sometimes they want to receive the plans ready to build. That is why we offer home plan modification services. Please see page 285 for specific information on the customizing process and how to get a free quote on the changes you want to make to a home before you buy the plans.

8 order plans

If you've found the home and are ready to order blueprints, we recommend ordering the PDF file format, which offers the most flexibility. A PDF file format will be emailed to you when you order, and it includes a copyright release from the designer, meaning you have the legal right to make changes to the plan if necessary as well as print out as many copies of the plan as you need for building the home one-time. You will be happy to

have your blueprints saved electronically so they can easily be shared with your contractor, subcontractors, lender and local building officials. We do, however, offer several different types of plan package depending on your needs, so please refer to page 283 for all plan options available and choose the best one for your particular situation.

Another helpful component in the building process that is available for many of the house plans in this book is a material list. A material list includes not only a detailed list of materials, but it also indicates where various cuts of lumber and other building components are to be used. This will save your general contractor significant time and money since they won't have to create this list before building begins. If a material list is available for a home, it is indicated in the plan data box on the specific plan page in this book.

9 order materials

You can order materials yourself, or have your contractor do it. Nevertheless, in order to thoroughly enjoy your new home you will want to personally select many of the materials that go into its construction. Today, home improvement stores offer a wide variety of quality building products. Only you can decide what specific types of windows, cabinets, bath fixtures, etc. will make your new home yours. Spend time early on in the construction process looking at the materials and products available.

10 move in

With careful planning and organization, your new home will be built on schedule and ready for your move-in date. Be sure to have all of your important documents in place for the closing of your new home and then you'll be ready to move in and start living your dream.

Browse the pages of Best-Selling House Plans and discover over 360 designs offered in a huge variety of sizes and styles to suit many tastes. From Craftsman and Country, to Modern and Traditional, there is a home design here for everyone with all of the amenities and features homeowners are looking for in a home today. Start your search right now for the perfect home!

Top, left: Plan #F09-150D-0007 on page 99; top, right: Plan #F09-051D-0670 on page 28; bottom, left: Plan #F09-056D-0120 on page 33; bottom, right: Plan #F09-170D-0003, on page 49.

Plan #F09-167D-0008

Dimensions:	62'4" W x 50'7" D
Heated Sq. Ft.:	3,328
Bedrooms: 4	Bathrooms: 3½
Exterior Walls:	2" x 6"

Foundation: Crawl space standard;
slab for an additional fee

See index for more information

Images provided by designer/architect

Detached Garage

garage 21'x19'

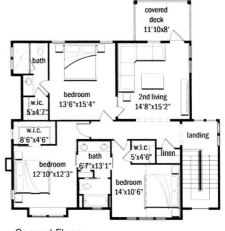

Features

- Classic American Farmhouse style with a Modern Farmhouse twist makes this a perfect home with a simple, yet stylish feel
- The first floor plan has a living room, large dining area, and kitchen completely open to one another
- Handy laundry and mud rooms offer an opportunity for great organizing
- Two doors off the living area lead to a private home office
- The vaulted owner's suite has two walk-in closets, a private bath with a huge walk-in shower and freestanding tub, and access to a deck
- The second floor has another living area with covered deck access
- 2-car detached side entry garage

© Copyright by designer/architect

First Floor
2,046 sq. ft.

Second Floor
1,282 sq. ft.

Plan #F09-032D-1134

Dimensions:	40' W x 34'4" D
Heated Sq. Ft.:	2,652
Bedrooms: 4	Bathrooms: 2
Exterior Walls:	2" x 6"
Foundation:	Basement

See index for more information

Features

- This stylish Craftsman home has Modern Farmhouse flair thanks to its black window panes, white vertical siding and light fixture choices
- Right off the foyer is a handy enclosed mud room for keeping the rest of the house tidy
- The living and dining rooms are open to one another and are topped with a cathedral ceiling
- The kitchen features a huge corner walk-in pantry, an oversized island with seating and is open to the dining room
- The lower level has a spacious recreation area, two additional bedrooms, a full bath and the laundry room

Lower Level
1,326 sq. ft.

© Copyright by
designer/architect

First Floor
1,326 sq. ft.

Images provided by designer/architect

Plan #F09-084D-0091

Dimensions: 59' W x 68'2" D
Heated Sq. Ft.: 1,936
Bedrooms: 3   **Bathrooms:** 2
Foundation: Slab standard; crawl space for an additional fee

See index for more information

Features

- The perfect stylish ranch home with a split bedroom layout
- Enter the dining/foyer and find a beamed ceiling for added interest and it opens to the vaulted living area with centered fireplace
- The kitchen enjoys an open feel and has an island and a mud room entrance from the garage
- The vaulted master bedroom has a built-in bench for added character plus a walk-in closet, and a private bath with an oversized tub and a walk-in shower with seat
- Two additional bedrooms share a full bath
- 2-car side entry garage

Images provided by designer/architect

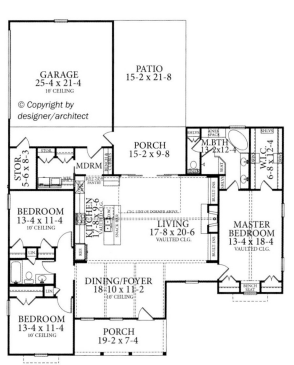

GARAGE 25-4 x 21-4 10' CEILING

© Copyright by designer/architect

PATIO 15-2 x 21-8

PORCH 15-2 x 9-8

STOR. 5-6 x 8-3

MDRM

M.BTH 13-2x12-4

W.I.C. 6-8 x 12-4

BEDROOM 13-4 x 11-4 10' CEILING

KITCHEN 17-8 x 9-6 VAULTED CLG.

LIVING 17-8 x 20-6 VAULTED CLG.

MASTER BEDROOM 13-4 x 18-4 VAULTED CLG.

DINING/FOYER 18-10 x 11-2 10' CEILING

BENCH SEAT

BEDROOM 13-4 x 11-4 10' CEILING

PORCH 19-2 x 7-4

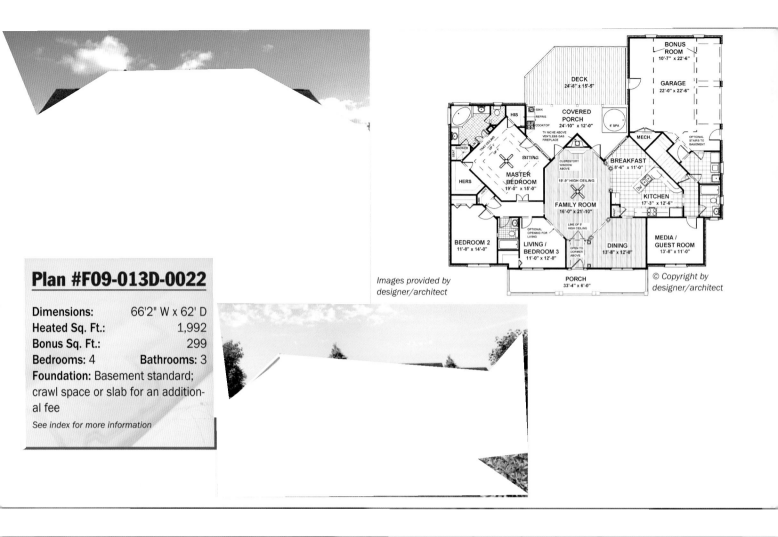

Images provided by designer/architect

© Copyright by designer/architect

Plan #F09-013D-0022

Dimensions: 66'2" W x 62' D
Heated Sq. Ft.: 1,992
Bonus Sq. Ft.: 299
Bedrooms: 4   **Bathrooms:** 3
Foundation: Basement standard; crawl space or slab for an additional fee

See index for more information

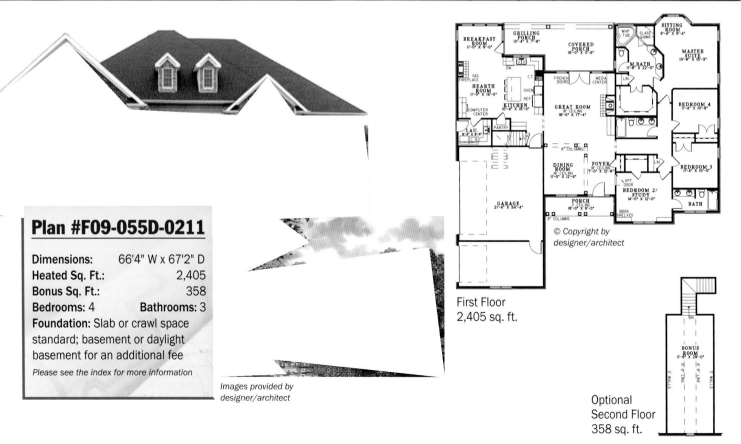

© Copyright by designer/architect

First Floor
2,405 sq. ft.

Plan #F09-055D-0211

Dimensions: 66'4" W x 67'2" D
Heated Sq. Ft.: 2,405
Bonus Sq. Ft.: 358
Bedrooms: 4   **Bathrooms:** 3
Foundation: Slab or crawl space standard; basement or daylight basement for an additional fee

Please see the index for more information

Images provided by designer/architect

Optional
Second Floor
358 sq. ft.

Optional
Second Floor
332 sq. ft.

DOWN

CLOSET
8'-8" X 5'-7"

OPTIONAL
BONUS
ROOM
12'-7" x 18'-1"
8' SLOPE CEILING

Plan #F09-170D-0015

Dimensions:	90'8" W x 59' D
Heated Sq. Ft.:	2,694
Bonus Sq. Ft.:	332
Bedrooms: 4	Bathrooms: 3

Foundation: Monolithic slab
or slab standard; crawl space,
basement or daylight basement for
an additional fee

See index for more information

PATIO

BEDROOM 4
12'-0" x 12'-0"

MASTER BEDROOM
17'-1" x 15'-2"
10' TRAY CEILING

UTILITY
8'-7"
BATH 3
6'-7"

REAR PORCH
18'-0" x 11'-6"

SCREEN PORCH

SAFE ROOM
7'-1" x 6'-9"
8' CEILING

MASTER
BATH

SIDE PORCH
4'-0"
X
14'-11"

MUDROOM

KITCHEN
20'-5" x 19'-3"
10' CEILING

CLOSET

EATING
10' CEILING

FAMILY ROOM
18'-0" x 23'-3"
11' TRAY CEILING

BEDROOM 2
11'-8" x 14'-5"

UP

PANTRY

GARAGE
24'-0" x 6'-0"

DINING
8'-5" x 16'-4"
11' TRAY CEILING

FOYER
10' CEILING

BEDROOM 3
11'-11" x 10'-0"

BATH 2

FRONT PORCH
31'-0" x 6'-0"
11' CEILING

First Floor
2,694 sq. ft.

Plan #F09-028D-0097

Dimensions:	60' W x 53' D
Heated Sq. Ft.:	1,908
Bedrooms: 3	Bathrooms: 2
Exterior Walls:	2" x 6"
Foundation:	Slab

See index for more information

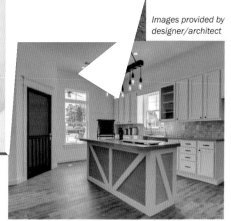

MASTER
BEDROOM
18'-0" X 14'-0"

GREAT
ROOM
18'-0" X 18'-4"

MASTER
BATH
13'-6" X 9'6"

WIC

DINING AREA
14'-0" X 12'-0"

DOUBLE GARAGE
24' X 20'

BEDROOM 2
12'-6" X 12'-0"

BATH 2

FOYER

KITCHEN
16'-0" X 16'6"

BEDROOM 3
12'-6" X 12'-0"

PANTRY

6 FT. DEEP COVERED PORCH

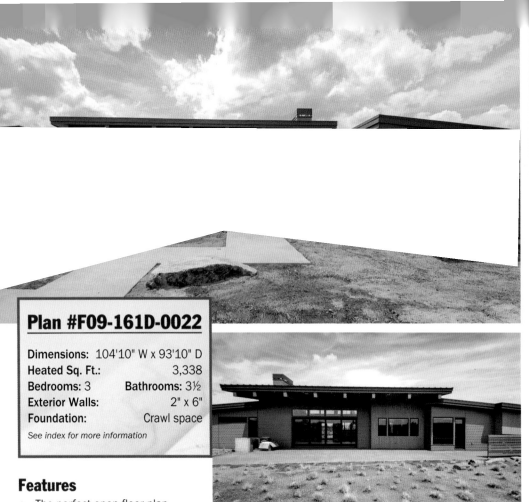

Plan #F09-161D-0022

Dimensions: 104'10" W x 93'10" D
Heated Sq. Ft.: 3,338
Bedrooms: 3   **Bathrooms:** 3½
Exterior Walls: 2" x 6"
Foundation: Crawl space

See index for more information

Features

- The perfect open floor plan for today's family focuses on plenty of windows and private bedrooms for every family member
- A massive great room, dining area, and kitchen form the main hub of this home
- A private master suite has a sun-filled bath with a free-standing tub and separate shower
- A fun game room is tucked between two secondary bedrooms, perfect for a kid's play area
- 3-car side entry garage

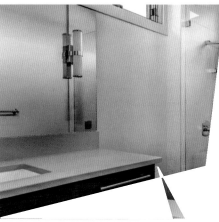

Images provided by designer/architect

Plan #F09-101D-0117

Dimensions:	98' W x 81'2" D
Heated Sq. Ft.:	2,925
Bonus Sq. Ft.:	1,602
Bedrooms: 3	**Bathrooms:** 2½
Exterior Walls:	2" x 6"

Foundation: Basement, daylight basement or walk-out basement, please specify when ordering

See index for more information

Features

- This stunning Prairie inspired rustic Modern Farmhouse has a welcoming front porch and leads into an open foyer with beautiful views of the great room
- The luxury master bedroom has covered deck access, a massive bath with a freestanding tub, and a huge walk-in closet with direct laundry and mud room access
- The kitchen maintains a feeling of openness and enjoys the added function of the large island
- Two bedrooms can be found behind the kitchen and they share a large Jack and Jill bath
- The optional lower level has an additional 1,602 square feet of living area and includes a huge rec room with fireplace, a wet bar, and two additional bedrooms each with their own bath
- 3-car side entry garage

© Copyright by designer/architect

First Floor
2,925 sq. ft.

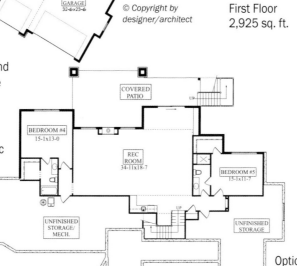

Optional Lower Level
1,602 sq. ft.

Images provided by designer/architect

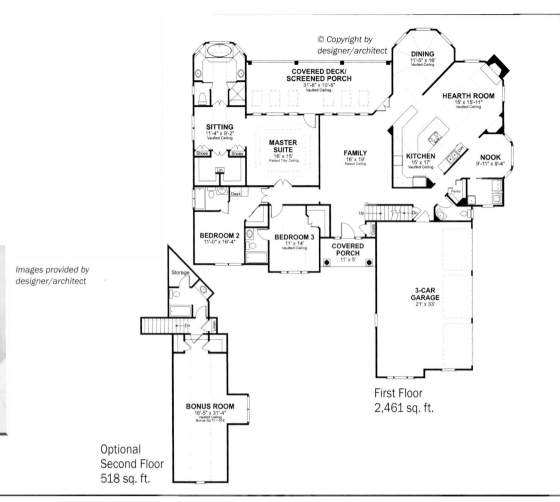

Plan #F09-013D-0053

Dimensions:	71'4" W x 74'8" D
Heated Sq. Ft.:	2,461
Bonus Sq. Ft.:	518
Bedrooms: 3	Bathrooms: 3½

Foundation: Basement standard; crawl space or slab for an additional fee

See index for more information

Images provided by designer/architect

First Floor
2,461 sq. ft.

Optional
Second Floor
518 sq. ft.

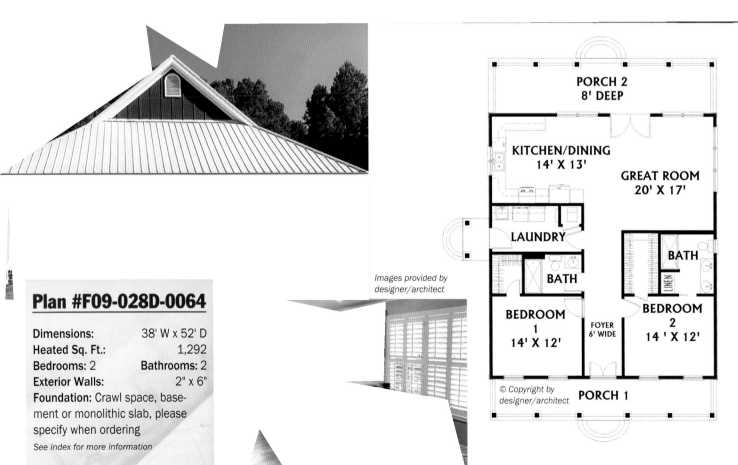

Plan #F09-028D-0064

Dimensions:	38' W x 52' D
Heated Sq. Ft.:	1,292
Bedrooms: 2	Bathrooms: 2
Exterior Walls:	2" x 6"

Foundation: Crawl space, basement or monolithic slab, please specify when ordering

See index for more information

Images provided by designer/architect

Images provided by designer/architect

Plan #F09-155D-0134

Dimensions: 70'6" W x 56'2" D
Heated Sq. Ft.:   2,031
Bonus Sq. Ft.:   406
Bedrooms: 3   Bathrooms: 2½

Foundation: Crawl space or slab standard; basement or daylight basement for an additional fee

See index for more information

Optional
Second Floor
406 sq. ft.

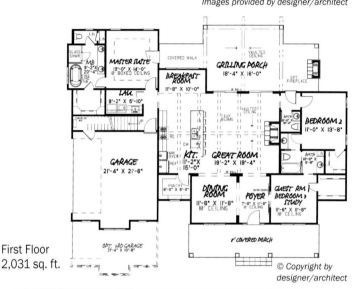

First Floor
2,031 sq. ft.

© Copyright by designer/architect

© Copyright by designer/architect

First Floor
1,793 sq. ft.

Images provided by designer/architect

Plan #F09-016D-0049

Dimensions: 69'10" W x 51'8" D
Heated Sq. Ft.:   1,793
Bonus Sq. Ft.:   779
Bedrooms: 3   Bathrooms: 2

Foundation: Crawl space or slab standard; basement for an additional fee

See index for more information

Optional
Second Floor
779 sq. ft.

Plan #F09-028D-0112

Dimensions:	56' W x 52' D
Heated Sq. Ft.:	1,611
Bedrooms: 3	Bathrooms: 2
Exterior Walls:	2" x 6"

Foundation: Slab or crawl space, please specify when ordering

See index for more information

Features

- This Craftsman one-story home has timeless farmhouse appeal
- A cozy great room with fireplace has built-ins on each side for added storage and style
- The kitchen and dining area enjoy a snack bar, great when entertaining in the great room
- The master bedroom enjoys its privacy, and its own bath and walk-in closet
- Two additional bedrooms share the full bath between them
- 2-car side entry garage

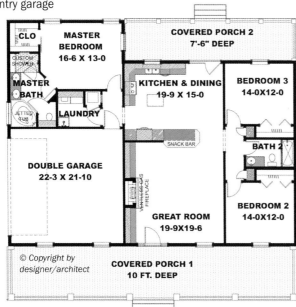

Images provided by designer/architect

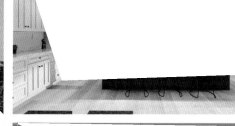

Plan #F09-0172S-0003

Dimensions:	73' W x 76' D
Heated Sq. Ft.:	4,658
Bedrooms: 6	**Bathrooms:** 4½
Exterior Walls:	2" x 6"

Foundation: Crawl space standard; monolithic slab, stem wall slab, basement, daylight basement or walk-out basement for an additional fee

See index for more information

Images provided by designer/architect

Features

- So many wonderful features fill this stylish luxury Modern Farmhouse design including a guest room, and a luxurious master suite
- The kitchen has plenty of extras like a walk-through pantry, a large mud room and an island with dining space
- The second floor features a hobby room with an outdoor balcony that could also be a wonderful and private home office
- Three bedrooms share a bath and enjoy the second floor washer and dryer being nearby
- There's also a completely separate apartment over the garage with a bedroom, kitchen, family room, bath with laundry space and an outdoor deck
- 3-car rear entry garage, and a 1-car side entry garage

First Floor
2,369 sq. ft.

Second Floor
2,289 sq. ft.

© Copyright by designer/architect

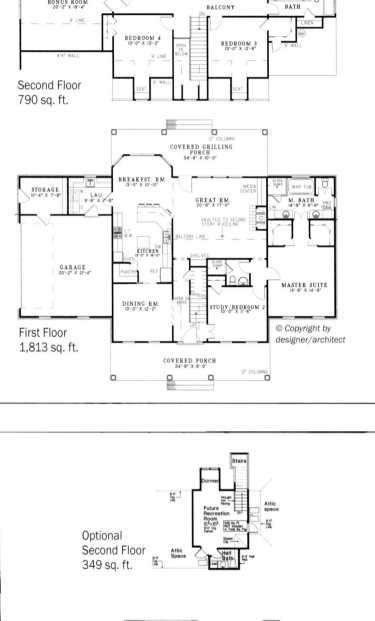

Second Floor
790 sq. ft.

First Floor
1,813 sq. ft.

© Copyright by
designer/architect

Plan #F09-055D-0212

Dimensions:	70'2" W x 53'4" D
Heated Sq. Ft.:	2,603
Bonus Sq. Ft.:	410
Bedrooms: 4	Bathrooms: 3

Foundation: Crawl space or slab
standard; basement or daylight
basement for an additional fee

See index for more information

*Images provided by
designer/architect*

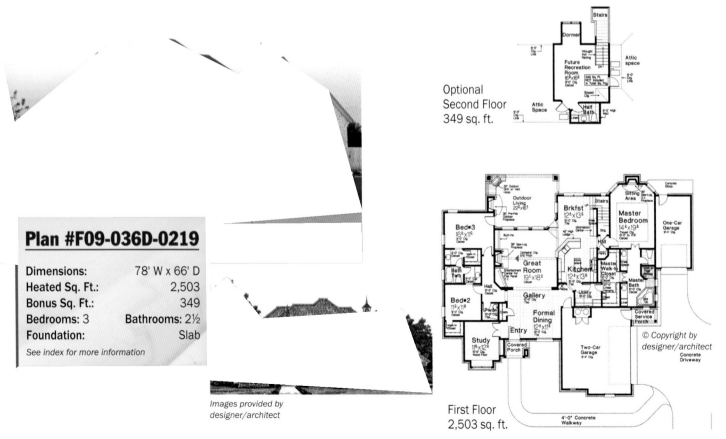

**Optional
Second Floor**
349 sq. ft.

© Copyright by
designer/architect

Plan #F09-036D-0219

Dimensions:	78' W x 66' D
Heated Sq. Ft.:	2,503
Bonus Sq. Ft.:	349
Bedrooms: 3	Bathrooms: 2½
Foundation:	Slab

See index for more information

*Images provided by
designer/architect*

First Floor
2,503 sq. ft.

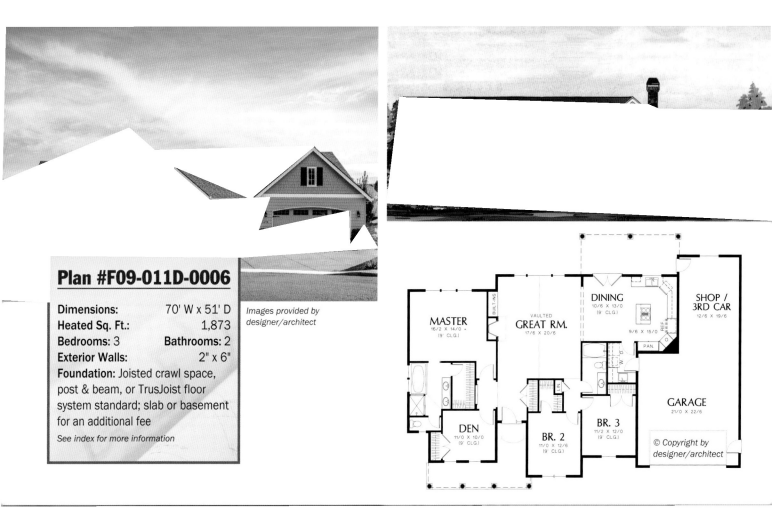

Plan #F09-011D-0006

Dimensions:	70' W x 51' D
Heated Sq. Ft.:	1,873
Bedrooms: 3	Bathrooms: 2
Exterior Walls:	2" x 6"

Foundation: Joisted crawl space, post & beam, or TrusJoist floor system standard; slab or basement for an additional fee

See index for more information

Images provided by designer/architect

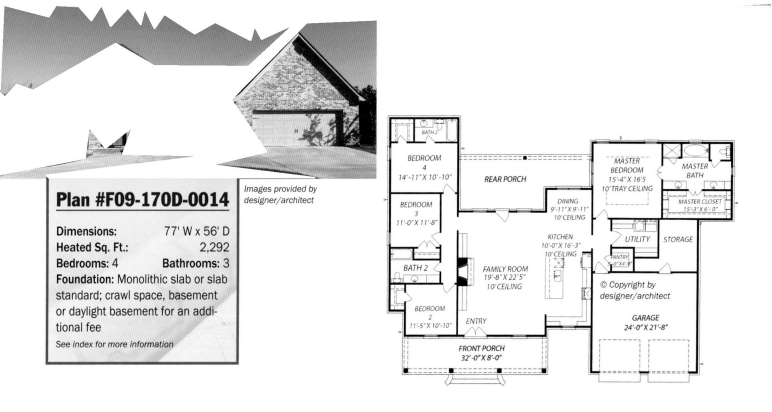

Plan #F09-170D-0014

Images provided by designer/architect

Dimensions:	77' W x 56' D
Heated Sq. Ft.:	2,292
Bedrooms: 4	Bathrooms: 3

Foundation: Monolithic slab or slab standard; crawl space, basement or daylight basement for an additional fee

See index for more information

Plan #F09-101D-0044

Dimensions:	101'6" W x 82'8" D
Heated Sq. Ft.:	3,897
Bonus Sq. Ft.:	1,678
Bedrooms: 4	Bathrooms: 3½
Exterior Walls:	2" x 6"
Foundation:	Walk-out basement

See index for more information

Images provided by designer/architect

Features

- No detail has been overlooked in this Craftsman-inspired luxury home
- The first floor offers a central gathering spot with the great room that has direct access to the open kitchen that features a huge island with food preparation space as well as casual dining
- The covered deck wraps the rear of the home and includes a spot off the master bedroom with a pergola above and an outdoor fireplace
- The garage includes a toy storage space that could be designated for children's toys, or adult toys like an ATV or sports equipment
- The optional lower level has an additional 1,678 square feet of living area and is comprised of a game area, a TV area, an exercise room, a wet bar, a guest bedroom with a full bath
- 2-car front entry garage, and a 1-car side entry garage

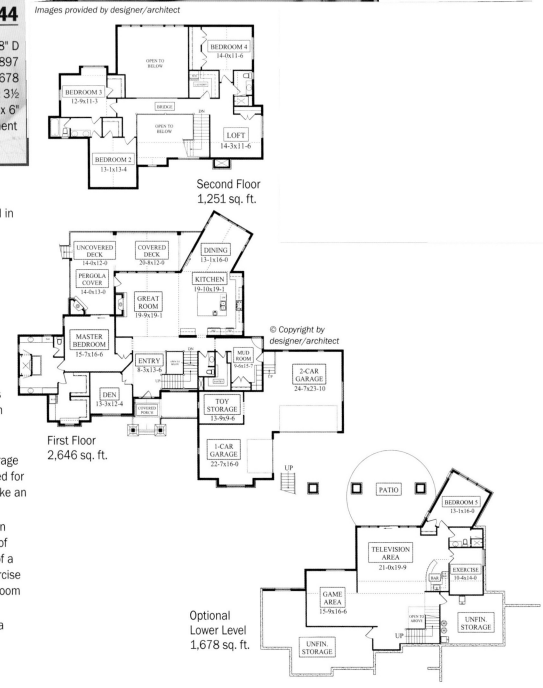

Second Floor
1,251 sq. ft.

First Floor
2,646 sq. ft.

Optional
Lower Level
1,678 sq. ft.

© Copyright by designer/architect

Plan #F09-149D-0007

Dimensions:	71' W x 48' D
Heated Sq. Ft.:	2,381
Bedrooms: 3	Bathrooms: 3½

Foundation: Slab standard; crawl space or basement for an additional fee

See index for more information

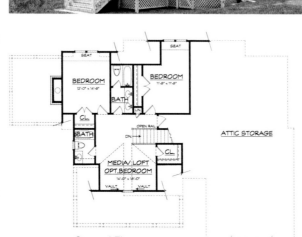

Features

- This home provides a very functional floor plan layout with the informal gathering areas open to one another, providing the ultimate in family living
- There is a formal dining room when you want to step it up a notch when entertaining
- The expansive master suite is tucked away for the ultimate in privacy and offers a bath with double vanities and separate tub, shower and toilet space
- A screened porch is perfect for enjoying the outdoors
- The second floor is an amazing retreat complete with two bedrooms, two baths and a central space for a media room or whatever your family's needs may be
- 2-car side entry garage

Second Floor
827 sq. ft.

First Floor
1,554 sq. ft.

© Copyright by designer/architect

Images provided by designer/architect

Plan #F09-055D-0748

Dimensions: 67'2" W x 55'10" D
Heated Sq. Ft.: 2,525
Bedrooms: 4   **Bathrooms:** 3
Foundation: Crawl space or slab standard; basement or walk-out basement for an additional fee
See index for more information

Features

- This expansive one-story design has the split-bedroom floor plan everyone loves
- Stunning columns frame the foyer that leads into the open great room with fireplace
- The formal dining room, casual breakfast room, and large grilling porch with fireplace provide an abundance of locations for dining opportunities
- Three bedrooms and two baths occupy one side of this home, while the master suite is secluded on the other
- 2-car front entry garage

Images provided by designer/architect

© Copyright by designer/architect

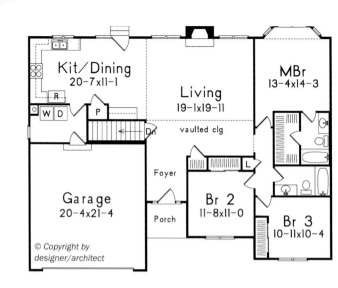

Kit/Dining
20-7x11-1

Living
19-1x19-11
vaulted clg

MBr
13-4x14-3

Garage
20-4x21-4

Foyer

Porch

Br 2
11-8x11-0

Br 3
10-11x10-4

© Copyright by
designer/architect

Plan #F09-058D-0016

Dimensions:	54' W x 42' D
Heated Sq. Ft.:	1,558
Bedrooms: 3	**Bathrooms:** 2

Foundation: Basement standard;
crawl space for an additional fee

See index for more information

*Images provided by
designer/architect*

Deck

Dining
10-0x13-6

Kit/Brk
11-8x13-6

P

MBr
13-6x13-6
tray clg

WD

Living
22-0x15-6
sloped ceiling

L

Br 2
11-6x11-8

Br 3
12-6x11-0

Foyer

First Floor
1,668 sq. ft.

Porch depth 8-0

*Images provided by
designer/architect*

Plan #F09-053D-0002

Dimensions:	56' W x 40' D
Heated Sq. Ft.:	1,668
Bonus Sq. Ft.:	780
Bedrooms: 3	**Bathrooms:** 2
Foundation:	Walk-out basement

See index for more information

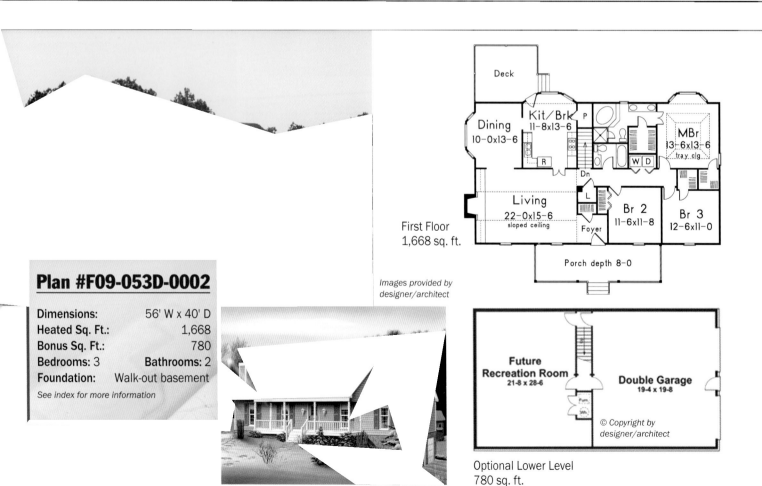

Future
Recreation Room
21-8 x 28-6

Double Garage
19-4 x 19-8

© Copyright by
designer/architect

Optional Lower Level
780 sq. ft.

Plan #F09-170D-0007

Dimensions: 61'9" W x 77'4" D
Heated Sq. Ft.: 2,323
Bedrooms: 4   **Bathrooms:** 3
Foundation: Monolithic slab or slab standard; crawl space, basement or daylight basement for an additional fee

See index for more information

Images provided by designer/architect

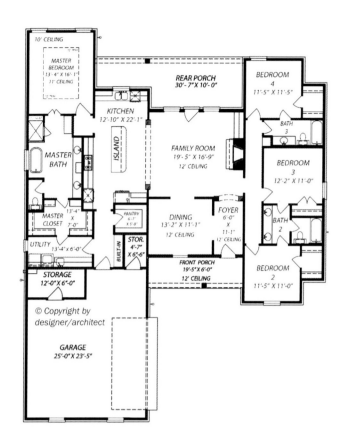

© Copyright by designer/architect

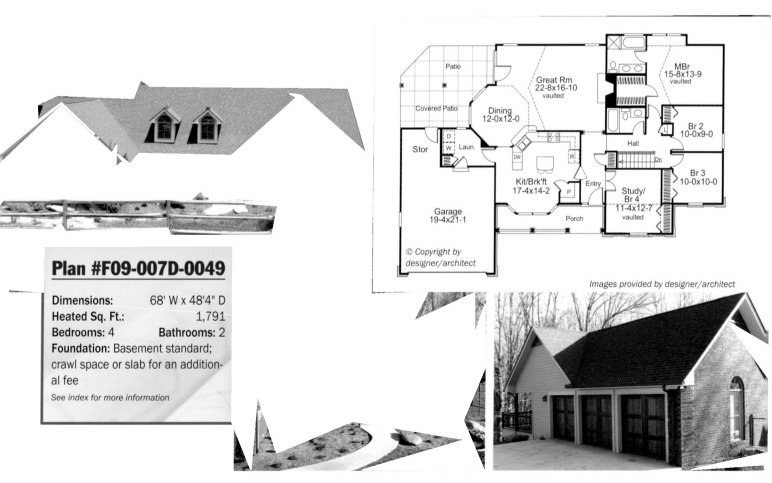

Plan #F09-007D-0049

Dimensions: 68' W x 48'4" D
Heated Sq. Ft.: 1,791
Bedrooms: 4   **Bathrooms:** 2
Foundation: Basement standard; crawl space or slab for an additional fee

See index for more information

Images provided by designer/architect

© Copyright by designer/architect

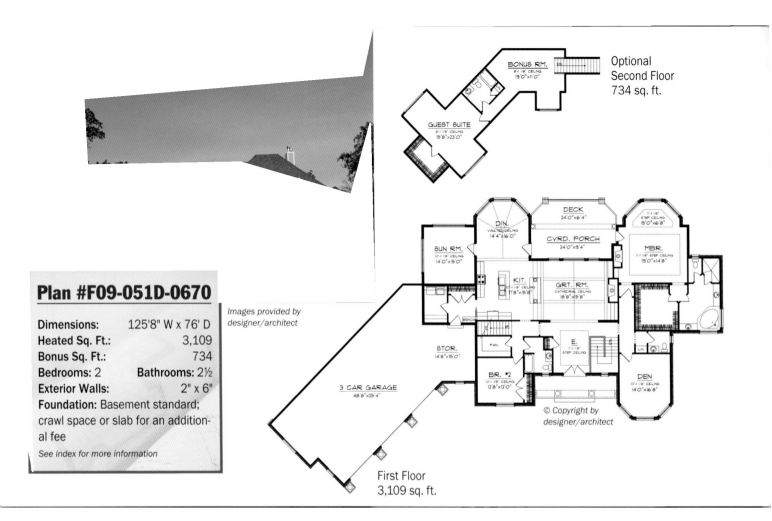

Optional
Second Floor
734 sq. ft.

Plan #F09-051D-0670

Dimensions: 125'8" W x 76' D
Heated Sq. Ft.: 3,109
Bonus Sq. Ft.: 734
Bedrooms: 2   Bathrooms: 2½
Exterior Walls: 2" x 6"
Foundation: Basement standard;
crawl space or slab for an additional fee

See index for more information

Images provided by designer/architect

© Copyright by designer/architect

First Floor
3,109 sq. ft.

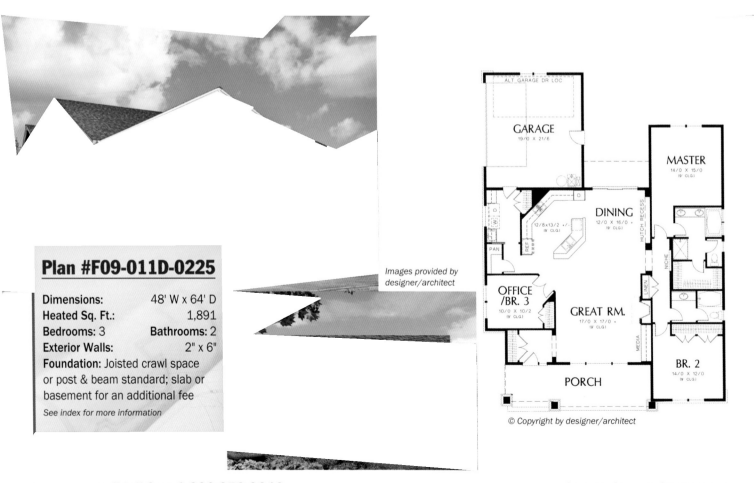

Plan #F09-011D-0225

Dimensions: 48' W x 64' D
Heated Sq. Ft.: 1,891
Bedrooms: 3   Bathrooms: 2
Exterior Walls: 2" x 6"
Foundation: Joisted crawl space
or post & beam standard; slab or
basement for an additional fee

See index for more information

Images provided by designer/architect

© Copyright by designer/architect

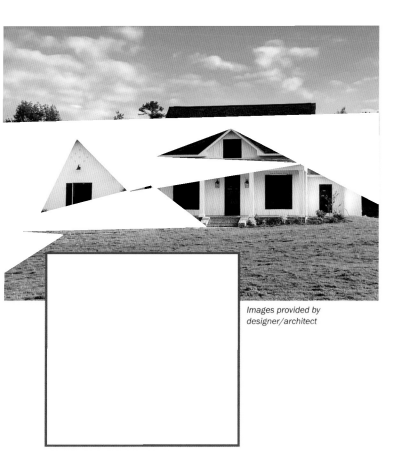

Images provided by
designer/architect

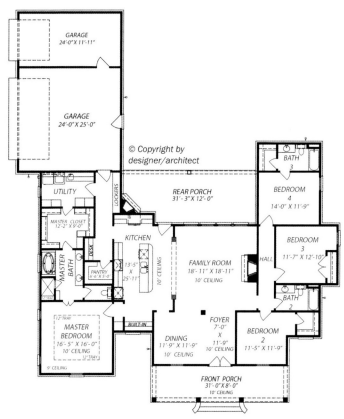

© Copyright by
designer/architect

GARAGE
24'-0" X 11'-11"

GARAGE
24'-0" X 25'-0"

UTILITY

MASTER CLOSET
12'-2" X 9'-0"

LOCKERS

DESK

MASTER
BATH

KITCHEN

PANTRY
6'-6" X 5'-0"

13'-5"
X
25'-11"

BUILT-IN

MASTER
BEDROOM
16'-5" X 16'-0"
10' CEILING

12' TRAY

12' TRAY

9' CEILING

REAR PORCH
31'-3" X 12'-0"

10' CEILING

FAMILY ROOM
18'-11" X 18'-11"
10' CEILING

DINING
11'-9" X 11'-9"
10' CEILING

FOYER
7'-0"
X
11'-9"
10' CEILING

HALL

BATH
3

BEDROOM
4
14'-0" X 11'-9"

BEDROOM
3
11'-7" X 12'-10"

BATH
2

BEDROOM
2
11'-5" X 11'-9"

FRONT PORCH
31'-0" X 8'-0"
10' CEILING

© Copyright by
designer/architect

SCREENED PORCH
14'-1" x 11'-6"

PATIO OR
DECK
14'-3" x 15'-2"

TRAY CEILING

MASTER BDRM
14'-2" x 15'-2"
11' HIGH CEILING

SITTING
6'-10" x 6'-0"
9' CEILING

BEDROOM 3
11'-0" x 13'-6"
9' CEILING

OPTIONAL
TV NICHE
ABOVE
FIREPLACE

COUNTRY
KITCHEN
14'-3" x 22'-6"
9' CEILING

Dw

UP TO BONUS

FAMILY ROOM
14'-0" x 22'-6"
12' HIGH CEILING

BEDROOM 2
11'-0" x 13'-6"
9' CEILING

LIVING
11'-0" x 12'-0"
9' CEILING

TRAY CEILING

DINING
11'-0" x 12'-0"
10' HIGH CEILING

PANTRY
7'-6" x 4'-6"

DESK

LINE OF
BONUS
ROOM

PORCH
29'-4" x 6'-0"

3 CAR GARAGE
21'-4" x 33'-2"

Images provided by
designer/architect

Plan #F09-013D-0025

Dimensions: 70'2" W x 59' D
Heated Sq. Ft.: 2,097
Bonus Sq. Ft.: 452
Bedrooms: 3   **Bathrooms:** 3
Foundation: Slab standard; crawl
space or basement for an addition-
al fee

See index for more information

Plan #F09-170D-0010

Dimensions: 58'6" W x 77'10" D
Heated Sq. Ft.: 1,824
Bedrooms: 3   **Bathrooms:** 2
Foundation: Monolithic slab or slab standard; crawl space, basement or daylight basement for an additional fee

See index for more information

Images provided by designer/architect

Plan #F09-011D-0008

Dimensions: 55' W x 48' D
Heated Sq. Ft.: 1,728
Bedrooms: 2   **Bathrooms:** 2
Exterior Walls: 2" x 6"
Foundation: Joisted crawl space, TrusJoist floor system or post & beam standard; slab or basement for an additional fee

See index for more information

Images provided by designer/architect

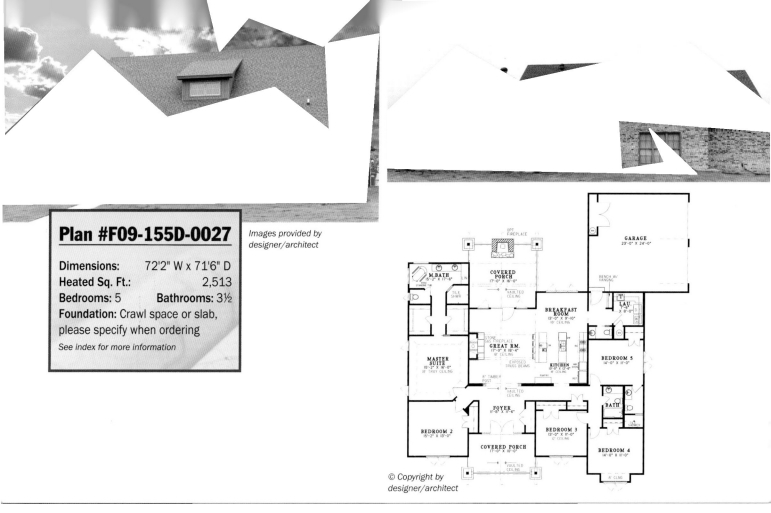

Plan #F09-155D-0027

Images provided by designer/architect

Dimensions:	72'2" W x 71'6" D
Heated Sq. Ft.:	2,513
Bedrooms: 5	Bathrooms: 3½

Foundation: Crawl space or slab, please specify when ordering

See index for more information

© Copyright by designer/architect

Plan #F09-001D-0013

Images provided by designer/architect

© Copyright by designer/architect

Dimensions:	60'10" W x 51'2" D
Heated Sq. Ft.:	1,882
Bedrooms: 3	Bathrooms: 2

Foundation: Basement standard; crawl space or slab for an additional fee

See index for more information

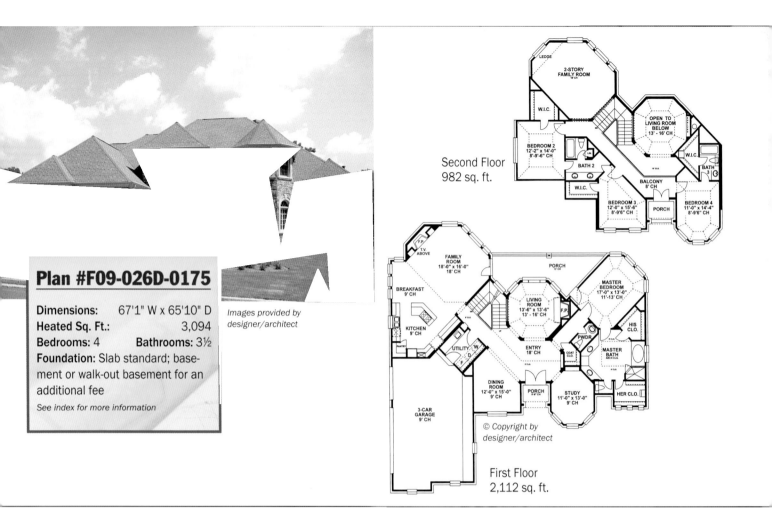

Second Floor
982 sq. ft.

Images provided by designer/architect

Plan #F09-026D-0175

Dimensions:	67'1" W x 65'10" D
Heated Sq. Ft.:	3,094
Bedrooms: 4	**Bathrooms:** 3½

Foundation: Slab standard; basement or walk-out basement for an additional fee

See index for more information

First Floor
2,112 sq. ft.

© Copyright by designer/architect

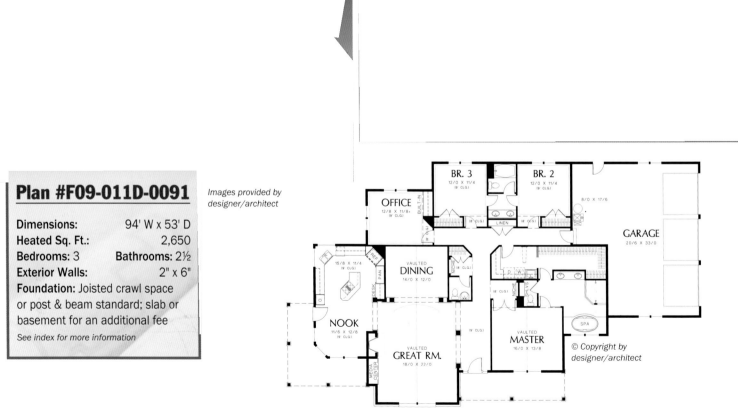

Plan #F09-011D-0091

Images provided by designer/architect

Dimensions:	94' W x 53' D
Heated Sq. Ft.:	2,650
Bedrooms: 3	**Bathrooms:** 2½
Exterior Walls:	2" x 6"

Foundation: Joisted crawl space or post & beam standard; slab or basement for an additional fee

See index for more information

© Copyright by designer/architect

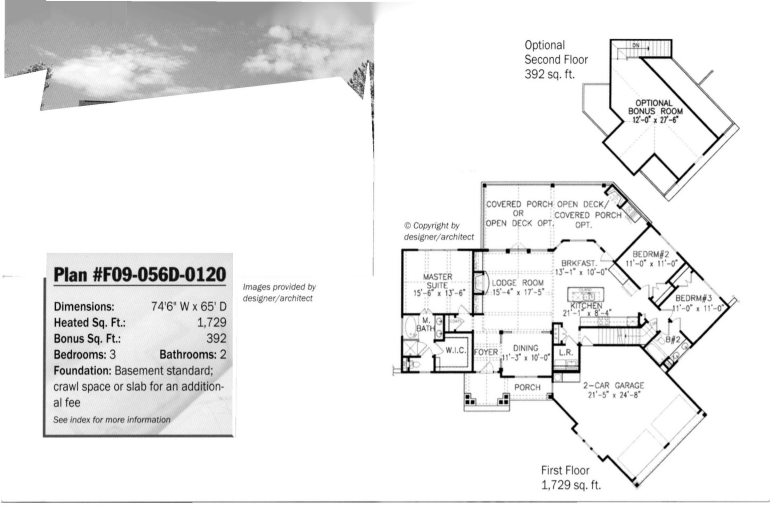

Optional
Second Floor
392 sq. ft.

OPTIONAL
BONUS ROOM
12'-0" x 27'-6"

© Copyright by
designer/architect

COVERED PORCH
OR
OPEN DECK OPT.

OPEN DECK/
COVERED PORCH
OPT.

BRKFAST.
13'-1" x 10'-0"

BEDRM#2
11'-0" x 11'-0"

MASTER
SUITE
15'-6" x 13'-6"

LODGE ROOM
15'-4" x 17'-5"

KITCHEN
21'-1" x 8'-4"

BEDRM#3
11'-0" x 11'-0"

M.
BATH

W.I.C.

FOYER

DINING
11'-3" x 10'-0"

L.R.

B#2

PORCH

2-CAR GARAGE
21'-5" x 24'-8"

First Floor
1,729 sq. ft.

Plan #F09-056D-0120

Dimensions: 74'6" W x 65' D
Heated Sq. Ft.: 1,729
Bonus Sq. Ft.: 392
Bedrooms: 3   Bathrooms: 2
Foundation: Basement standard;
crawl space or slab for an addition-
al fee

See index for more information

*Images provided by
designer/architect*

DECK

CVRD.
PORCH
15'8"x14'0"

DIN. RM.
10'-1 1/8" STEP CEILING
11'4"x11'8"

BR. #2
9'-1 1/8" CEILING
10'8"x11'8"

MBR.
10'-1 1/8" STEP CEILING
15'0"x13'4"

GRT. RM.
11'-1 1/8" CEILING
15'8"x20'4"

KIT.
11'-1 1/8" CEILING
11'4"x15'0"

E.
11'-1 1/8"
CEILING

BR. #3
9'-1 1/8" CEILING
10'8"x12'4"

HIDDEN
PANTRY

© Copyright by
designer/architect

3 CAR GARAGE
31'8"x25'8"

Plan #F09-051D-0977

Dimensions: 58' W x 64'4" D
Heated Sq. Ft.: 1,837
Bedrooms: 3   Bathrooms: 2
Exterior Walls: 2" x 6"
Foundation: Basement standard;
crawl space or slab for an addition-
al fee

See index for more information

Images provided by designer/architect

Plan #F09-170D-0005

Dimensions: 54' W x 53' D
Heated Sq. Ft.: 1,422
Bedrooms: 3   Bathrooms: 2
Foundation: Slab or monolithic slab standard; crawl space, basement or daylight basement for an additional fee

See index for more information

Images provided by designer/architect

© Copyright by designer/architect

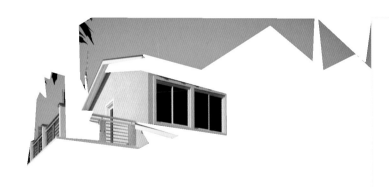

Second Floor
665 sq. ft.

First Floor
726 sq. ft.

© Copyright by designer/architect

Plan #F09-111D-0036

Dimensions: 38'6" W x 32' D
Heated Sq. Ft.: 1,391
Bedrooms: 3   Bathrooms: 2½
Foundation: Slab standard; crawl space for an additional fee

See index for more information

Images provided by designer/architect

Plan #F09-055D-0031

Dimensions:	58'6" W x 64'6" D
Heated Sq. Ft.:	2,133
Bedrooms: 3	Bathrooms: 2

Foundation: Slab or crawl space standard; basement or daylight basement for an additional fee

See index for more information

Images provided by designer/architect

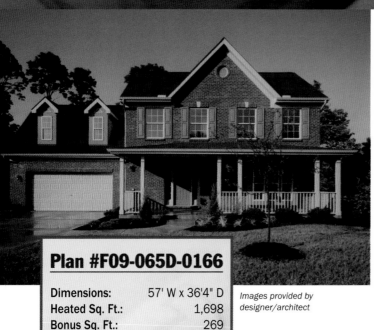

Plan #F09-065D-0166

Dimensions:	57' W x 36'4" D
Heated Sq. Ft.:	1,698
Bonus Sq. Ft.:	269
Bedrooms: 3	Bathrooms: 2½

Foundation: Basement standard; walk-out basement or crawl space for an additional fee

See index for more information

Images provided by designer/architect

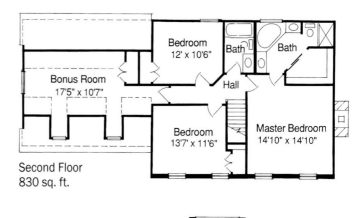

Second Floor
830 sq. ft.

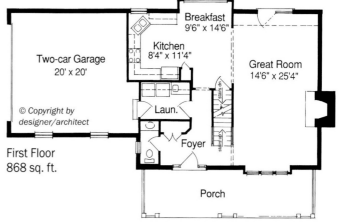

First Floor
868 sq. ft.

Plan #F09-051D-0960

Dimensions: 117' W x 50'8" D
Heated Sq. Ft.: 2,784
Bedrooms: 3   **Bathrooms:** 2
Exterior Walls: 2" x 6"
Foundation: Basement standard; crawl space or slab for an additional fee

See index for more information

Features

- This Traditional ranch home design is sure to win you over with its very classy exterior
- You are welcomed into the home with eleven-foot ceilings that top the great room and kitchen
- All three bedrooms, including the master bedroom, are located to the right in the house
- The master bedroom includes a bath with a spa style tub, dual sinks, as well as a spacious walk-in closet
- The other two bedrooms share a full bath nearby
- The three-stall garage is located on the left side of the house with a large screened-in porch behind it
- 3-car front entry garage

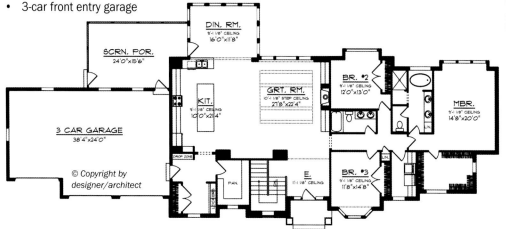

Images provided by designer/architect

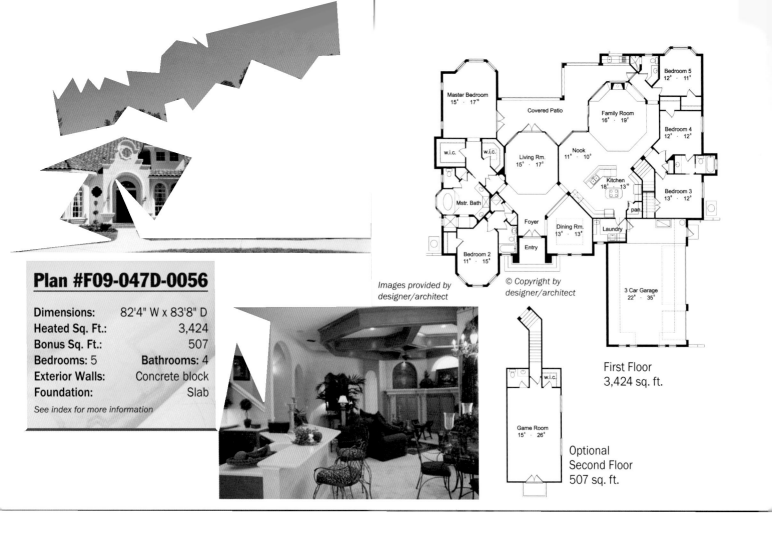

Plan #F09-047D-0056

Dimensions:	82'4" W x 83'8" D
Heated Sq. Ft.:	3,424
Bonus Sq. Ft.:	507
Bedrooms: 5	Bathrooms: 4
Exterior Walls:	Concrete block
Foundation:	Slab

See index for more information

Images provided by designer/architect

© Copyright by designer/architect

First Floor
3,424 sq. ft.

Optional
Second Floor
507 sq. ft.

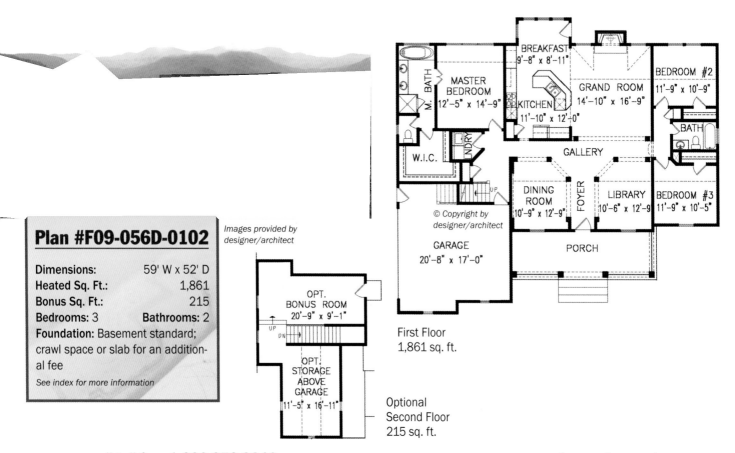

Plan #F09-056D-0102

Dimensions:	59' W x 52' D
Heated Sq. Ft.:	1,861
Bonus Sq. Ft.:	215
Bedrooms: 3	Bathrooms: 2
Foundation: Basement standard; crawl space or slab for an additional fee	

See index for more information

Images provided by designer/architect

© Copyright by designer/architect

First Floor
1,861 sq. ft.

Optional
Second Floor
215 sq. ft.

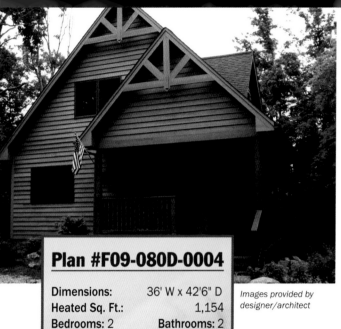

© Copyright by designer/architect

Plan #F09-080D-0004

Dimensions:	36' W x 42'6" D
Heated Sq. Ft.:	1,154
Bedrooms: 2	Bathrooms: 2
Exterior Walls:	2" x 6"
Foundation:	Crawl space

See index for more information

Images provided by designer/architect

First Floor
672 sq. ft.

Second Floor
482 sq. ft.

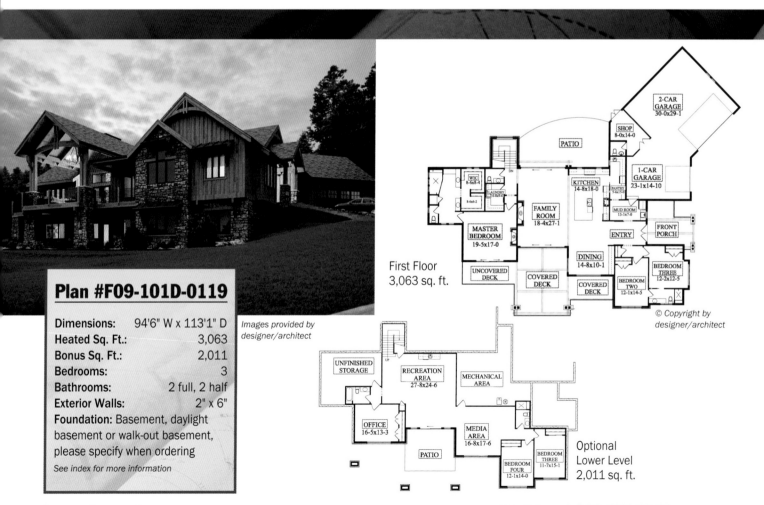

First Floor
3,063 sq. ft.

© Copyright by designer/architect

Plan #F09-101D-0119

Dimensions:	94'6" W x 113'1" D
Heated Sq. Ft.:	3,063
Bonus Sq. Ft.:	2,011
Bedrooms:	3
Bathrooms:	2 full, 2 half
Exterior Walls:	2" x 6"
Foundation:	Basement, daylight basement or walk-out basement, please specify when ordering

See index for more information

Images provided by designer/architect

Optional
Lower Level
2,011 sq. ft.

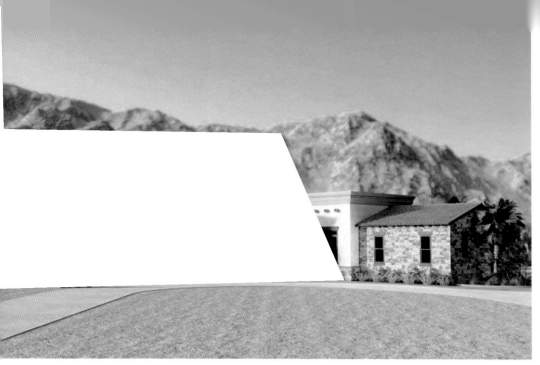

Plan #F09-019D-0046

Dimensions: 125'5" W x 76'1" D
Heated Sq. Ft.: 2,413
Bedrooms: 3 **Bathrooms:** 2½
Foundation: Slab standard; crawl space or basement for an additional fee

See index for more information

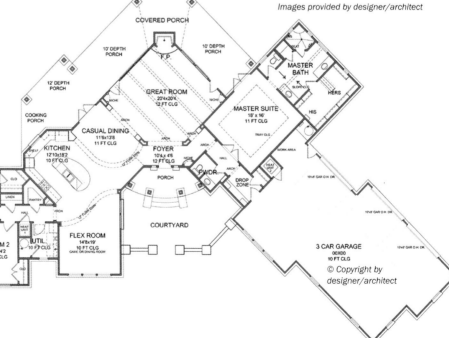

Images provided by designer/architect

Features

- This stunning Southwestern inspired home combines stone and stucco to create a home with tons of style and curb appeal

- The courtyard front entry offers a private escape for enjoying morning coffee or a cocktail at happy hour

- The grand great room is the main focal point as you enter the home thanks to its centered fireplace and tall ceilings with beams

- Off the kitchen is a handy flex room that could become a great home office, formal dining room or kid's play space

- The private master bedroom offers a luxurious environment for relaxing at the end of the day

- 3-car rear entry garage

© Copyright by designer/architect

Plan #F09-056D-0096

Dimensions:	91'6" W x 70' D
Heated Sq. Ft.:	2,510
Bonus Sq. Ft.:	2,510
Bedrooms: 3	**Bathrooms:** 2½

Foundation: Walk-out basement standard; crawl space or slab for an additional fee

See index for more information

Images provided by designer/architect

Features

- This wonderful home is designed in the popular Modern Farmhouse style
- A vaulted lodge room is connected to the kitchen and breakfast area
- Both mud and laundry rooms make this home highly efficient
- The split bedroom floor plan has the master suite separated from the other bedrooms for privacy
- The optional lower level has an additional 2,510 square feet of living area with three additional bedrooms for guests, a wine cellar, a wet bar, a cards room, and a theater
- 2-car side entry garage

© Copyright by designer/architect

First Floor
2,510 sq. ft.

Optional Lower Level
2,510 sq. ft.

Plan #F09-055D-0194

Dimensions: 38'4" W x 68'6" D
Heated Sq. Ft.: 1,379
Bedrooms: 3   **Bathrooms:** 2
Foundation: Crawl space or slab, please specify when ordering

See index for more information

Images provided by designer/architect

© Copyright by designer/architect

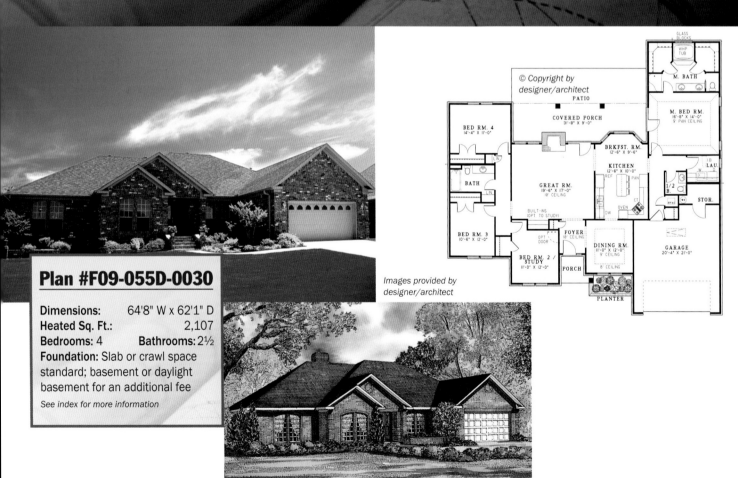

Plan #F09-055D-0030

Dimensions: 64'8" W x 62'1" D
Heated Sq. Ft.: 2,107
Bedrooms: 4   **Bathrooms:** 2½
Foundation: Slab or crawl space standard; basement or daylight basement for an additional fee

See index for more information

Images provided by designer/architect

© Copyright by designer/architect

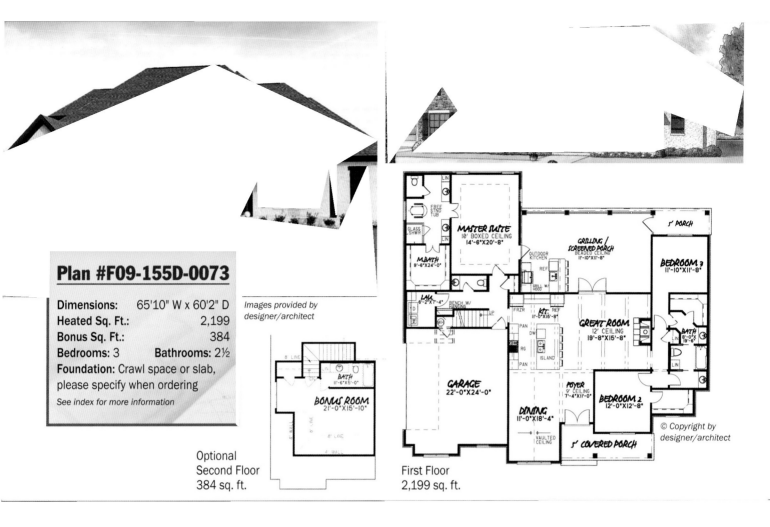

Plan #F09-155D-0073

Dimensions:	65'10" W x 60'2" D
Heated Sq. Ft.:	2,199
Bonus Sq. Ft.:	384
Bedrooms: 3	Bathrooms: 2½

Foundation: Crawl space or slab, please specify when ordering

See index for more information

Images provided by designer/architect

© Copyright by designer/architect

Optional
Second Floor
384 sq. ft.

BONUS ROOM
21'-0"X15'-10"

BATH
11'-6"X5'-0"

First Floor
2,199 sq. ft.

MBr
16-0x15-6
vaulted

Br 2
10-10x11-4

Br 4
12-10x10-0

Br 3
10-10x 13-3

Second Floor
1,108 sq. ft.

Plan #F09-027D-0005

Dimensions:	48' W x 34' D
Heated Sq. Ft.:	2,135
Bedrooms: 4	Bathrooms: 2½
Foundation:	Basement

See index for more information

Images provided by designer/architect

Family
16-0x15-6

Brk
10-2x 13-6

Kit
9-7x11-4

Dining
13-6x13-0

Living
15-4x11-6

Garage
19-4x19-6

Porch depth 6-0

© Copyright by designer/architect

First Floor
1,027 sq. ft.

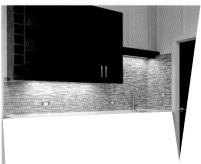

Plan #F09-011D-0351

Dimensions:	50' W x 58'8" D
Heated Sq. Ft.:	3,242
Bedrooms: 4	**Bathrooms:** 4
Exterior Walls:	2" x 6"
Foundation:	Walk-out basement

See index for more information

Features

- Angled roof lines and an open floor plan make this Mid-Century modern house plan an architectural masterpiece
- The great room has a sleek, modern feel with a vaulted ceiling and clerestory windows
- The open kitchen has an island surveying an open space ideal for dining with a view
- The master suite enjoys its own private bath with an oversized spa tub and a walk-in shower
- The lower level is comprised of a game room with fireplace and a wet bar with patio access, two additional bedrooms, a full bath, plus tons of extra storage
- 2-car front entry garage

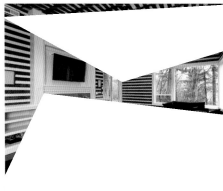

Lower Level
1,349 sq. ft.

First Floor
1,893 sq. ft.

Images provided by designer/architect

Plan #F09-032D-0368

Dimensions:	36' W x 36' D
Heated Sq. Ft.:	1,625
Bedrooms: 3	**Bathrooms:** 2
Exterior Walls:	2" x 6"

Foundation: Basement standard; crawl space, floating slab or monolithic slab for an additional fee

See index for more information

Images provided by designer/architect

Features

- The great room features an awesome two-story tall vaulted ceiling
- A fireplace and a large balcony create an enchanting atmosphere in the great room
- Plenty of cabinets and counterspace are found throughout the spacious kitchen
- The first floor master bedroom enjoys a walk-in closet and a large bath nearby
- Two spacious bedrooms share a bath on the second floor, and are able to take in impressive views from the balcony overlooking the great room below

© Copyright by designer/architect

First Floor
1,108 sq. ft.

Second Floor
517 sq. ft.

Plan #F09-032D-0656

Dimensions:	36' W x 40' D
Heated Sq. Ft.:	1,184
Bedrooms: 2	Bathrooms: 1
Exterior Walls:	2" x 6"

Foundation: Basement standard; crawl space, floating slab or monolithic slab for an additional fee

See index for more information

Images provided by designer/architect

© Copyright by designer/architect

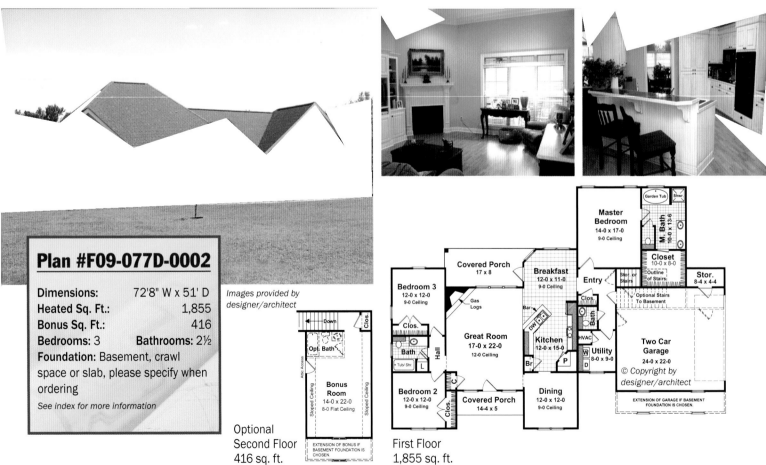

Plan #F09-077D-0002

Dimensions:	72'8" W x 51' D
Heated Sq. Ft.:	1,855
Bonus Sq. Ft.:	416
Bedrooms: 3	Bathrooms: 2½

Foundation: Basement, crawl space or slab, please specify when ordering

See index for more information

Images provided by designer/architect

Optional Second Floor
416 sq. ft.

First Floor
1,855 sq. ft.

© Copyright by designer/architect

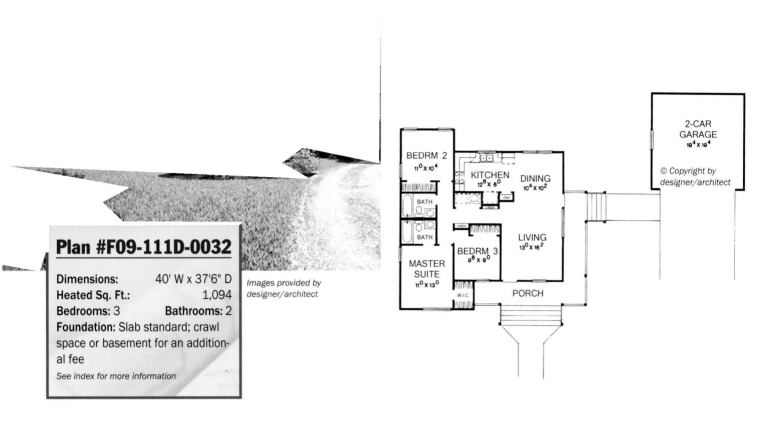

Plan #F09-111D-0032

Dimensions: 40' W x 37'6" D
Heated Sq. Ft.: 1,094
Bedrooms: 3   **Bathrooms:** 2
Foundation: Slab standard; crawl space or basement for an additional fee

See index for more information

Images provided by designer/architect

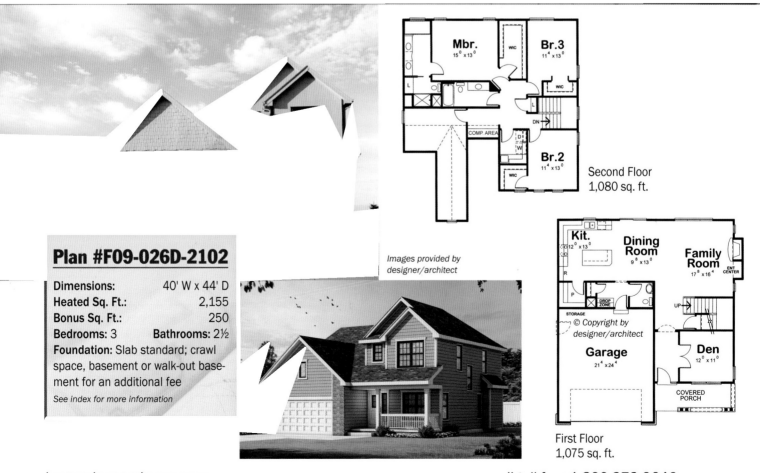

Plan #F09-026D-2102

Dimensions: 40' W x 44' D
Heated Sq. Ft.: 2,155
Bonus Sq. Ft.: 250
Bedrooms: 3   **Bathrooms:** 2½
Foundation: Slab standard; crawl space, basement or walk-out basement for an additional fee

See index for more information

Images provided by designer/architect

Second Floor
1,080 sq. ft.

First Floor
1,075 sq. ft.

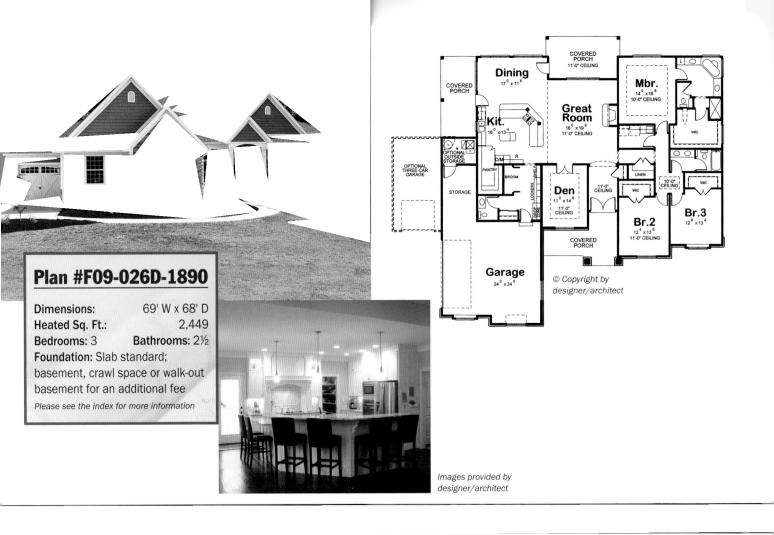

© Copyright by
designer/architect

Images provided by
designer/architect

Plan #F09-026D-1890

Dimensions: 69' W x 68' D
Heated Sq. Ft.:   2,449
Bedrooms: 3   Bathrooms: 2½
Foundation: Slab standard;
basement, crawl space or walk-out
basement for an additional fee

Please see the index for more information

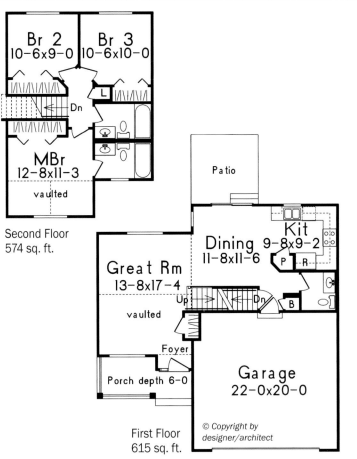

Images provided by
designer/architect

Plan #F09-041D-0006

Dimensions: 36' W x 35'8" D
Heated Sq. Ft.:   1,189
Bedrooms: 3   Bathrooms: 2½
Foundation: Basement

See index for more information

Second Floor
574 sq. ft.

First Floor
615 sq. ft.

© Copyright by
designer/architect

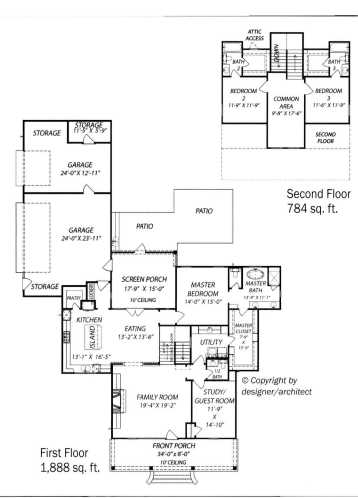

Second Floor
784 sq. ft.

ATTIC ACCESS

BATH
BEDROOM 2
11'-9" X 11'-9"
COMMON AREA
9'-8" X 17'-6"
BEDROOM 3
11'-6" X 11'-9"
BATH 3

SECOND FLOOR

STORAGE
STORAGE
11'-5" X 5'-9"

GARAGE
24'-0" X 12'-11"

GARAGE
24'-0" X 23'-11"

STORAGE

PATIO
PATIO

PANTRY
LOCKER
KITCHEN
ISLAND
13'-1" X 16'-5"

SCREEN PORCH
17'-9" X 15'-0"
10' CEILING

EATING
13'-2" X 13'-8"

MASTER BEDROOM
14'-0" X 15'-0"

MASTER BATH
13'-9" X 11'-1"

MASTER CLOSET
7'-9" X 15'-9"

UTILITY

1/2 BATH

FAMILY ROOM
19'-4" X 19'-2"

STUDY/ GUEST ROOM
11'-9" X 14'-10"

FRONT PORCH
34'-0" X 8'-0"
10' CEILING

First Floor
1,888 sq. ft.

© Copyright by designer/architect

Plan #F09-170D-0003

Images provided by designer/architect

Dimensions:	70'9" W x 91' D
Heated Sq. Ft.:	2,672
Bedrooms: 4	**Bathrooms:** 3½

Foundation: Slab or monolithic slab standard; crawl space, basement or daylight basement for an additional fee

See index for more information

Plan #F09-055D-0192

Dimensions:	69'2" W x 74'10" D
Heated Sq. Ft.:	2,096
Bedrooms: 3	**Bathrooms:** 2½

Foundation: Crawl space or slab standard; basement or daylight basement for an additional fee

Please see the index for more information

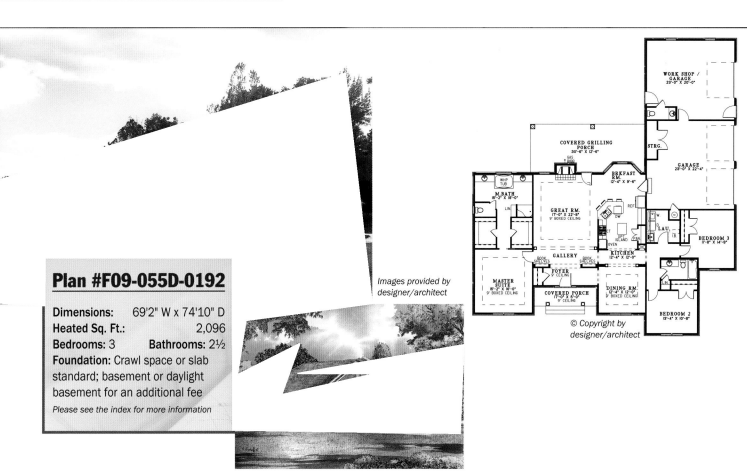

Images provided by designer/architect

WORK SHOP / GARAGE
23'-0" X 20'-0"

COVERED GRILLING PORCH
30'-6" X 12'-6"
GAS BBQ

STRG.

GARAGE
23'-0" X 22'-4"

WHP TUB
M. BATH
16'-2" X 18'-0"

LIN

BRKFAST RM.
12'-4" X 9'-6"

GREAT RM.
17'-0" X 22'-8"
9' BOXED CEILING

REF.

DW

OPT ISLAND

OVEN

LAU.
W.
D.

BEDROOM 3
11'-8" X 14'-8"

KITCHEN
12'-4" X 12'-0"

BOOK SHELVES

GALLERY

BOOK SHELVES

MASTER SUITE
16'-2" X 18'-0"
9' BOXED CEILING

FOYER
5' CEILING

COVERED PORCH
17'-0" X 6'-0"
9' CEILING

DINING RM.
12'-4" X 12'-0"
9' BOXED CEILING

BEDROOM 2
13'-4" X 10'-8"

© Copyright by designer/architect

Plan #F09-011D-0526

Dimensions:	72' W x 65'6" D
Heated Sq. Ft.:	2,735
Bonus Sq. Ft.:	379
Bedrooms: 3	Bathrooms: 2½
Exterior Walls:	2" x 6"

Foundation: Joisted crawl space or post & beam standard; slab or basement for an additional fee

See index for more information

Images provided by designer/architect

Features

- The vaulted great room with fireplace and covered porch views commands full attention when you enter this home
- A quiet home office is tucked away near the foyer
- The kitchen has an efficient angled island and breakfast bar that overlooks the great room and breakfast nook
- Two secondary bedrooms find themselves located behind the kitchen and share a full bath
- The optional second floor has an additional 379 square feet of living area
- 3-car front entry garage

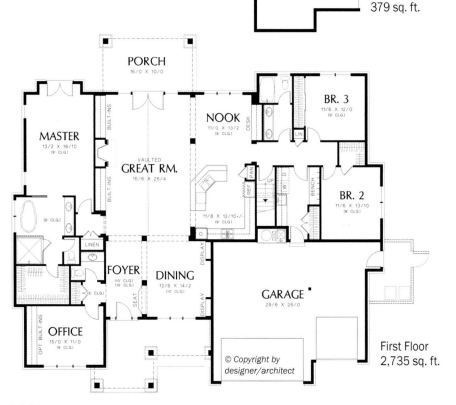

STORAGE
14/2+ X 19/0+
(8'-0" CLG.)

Optional
Second Floor
379 sq. ft.

First Floor
2,735 sq. ft.

© Copyright by designer/architect

the wow factor:
The "It" Features
home buyers want

The features found in homes today are being included for a reason; these are the things homeowners are asking for to make their lives easier! Home buyers' attitudes have shifted in recent years and today's homeowners are very practical. They are content with a smaller home featuring an open floor plan, which requires less maintenance, all while ideally being built with affordable green materials. Their need for the bells and whistles has waned, and they seek a modern, less cluttered style. Homes of yesteryear can't compete with the amazing new home designs that incorporate so many automated features and sleek open floor plans. Let's take a closer look at many of the most demanded features sought in new homes today.

go with the flow

Today's floor plans have less square footage, which means they must maximize every last square foot to the fullest. Today's homes have fewer rooms, but the rooms they do have serve many purposes. Open floor plans remain all the rage and offer the potential for a smaller home to feel larger and more functional. However, since the pandemic, the need for more compartmentalized spaces has increased with many family members working and learning from home. So, the seamless flow from the dining area, kitchen, and even the great room often seen with an open floor plan has created some issues with functionality for many families in the past year. But, many homeowners do want the interior to flow freely visually into the outdoor areas. Similar flooring color and furniture outdoors tends to visually extend the home even farther making a smaller home feel comfortably roomy and less confined. Homeowners desire outdoor spaces that mimic their home's interior and include a dedicated area for sitting and dining space. Many of these spaces include outdoor fireplaces, or calming fountains. Today's homeowners had been looking for less yard space in recent years; just enough to have an oasis to retreat to, but not enough to create additional chores and maintenance. And if there is a patio or deck, Millennials especially want exterior finishes to be as maintenance free as possible. But, many homeowners since the pandemic have moved out of more densely populated suburban areas and are seeking more yard space.

An open flow is even more important than size. So more windows and doors, and fewer walls are optimal features that add a feeling of spaciousness and volume. Formal dining and living rooms are considered spaces of the past, and in their place are flex spaces that can be converted to home offices, a guest room, or kid's playroom. With today's family, flexibility is key. Higher ceilings throughout are more popular now than attention-seeking dramatic two-story foyers.

clean living

With open, airy spaces also comes the desire for sleek interior spaces and furnishings especially in the kitchen where clutter can easily occur. Architecturally, today's homes are using simpler lines. Think less trim work and moldings, and more streamline Craftsman and Prairie style woodwork. Cabinet styles are less rounded and Traditional now, and sleek angled cabinets are popular.

Quartz countertops are being chosen more often than granite since they have more subtle surfaces. Wider plank style flooring designs are still the most popular, but the dark colors have been toned down a bit more. With the sleeker cabinets and counters, homeowners love the look of matte appliances rather than their shiny steel counterparts. Definitely a more subdued look, these appliances tend to hide scratches and fingerprints much better.

Unless noted, copyright by designer/architect; Page 54 top: Small, compact kitchen utilizes space to the fullest, istockphoto.com; middle: A great open kitchen layout, Plan #011S-0189; bottom: Sleek surfaces and cabinets are the trend, Plan #101D-0108; Page 55, top, left clockwise: Sleek and modern sink, Kohler Indio Sink, us.kohler.com; Quartz countertops look clean and fresh, Plan #101D-0052, Damon Searles, photographer; A huge kitchen island is where its at, Plan #F09-101D-0056 on page 166, Warren Diggles Photography; Matte appliances keep surfaces looking clean and free of fingerprints, kitchenaid.com. See additional photos and purchase plans at houseplansandmore.com.

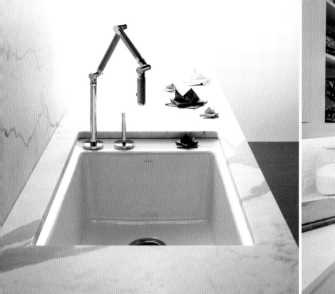

i am an island

Kitchen islands are a must-have since they offer additional prep space, storage, casual dining space, and are often steps from the dining area. Their open shelving can offer an open feel and easy access for frequently used items. Pantry sizes have increased, while the amount of cabinets has decreased. This gives the illusion of a sleeker kitchen overall.

Kitchens have become larger and more open with less clutter. Basically, today's best features in the kitchen are popular because they make it appear simpler.

peace out

Sleek, clean living continues into the bathroom, too. No longer are homeowners requesting large garden style tubs that often featured multiple steps and ornate columns. Oversized garden tubs simply take up too much bathroom real estate in today's smaller scaled homes. Instead, open walk-in showers often with practically invisible glass surrounds are trending. If the home is larger and there is space for a tub, then homeowners are requesting free-standing modern style tubs. Large floor tiles and sleek fixtures complement this Zen-like space to create a feeling of tranquility.

lite brite

When many think clean, they think bright. So, white is becoming the color of choice for both kitchen and baths. And, incorporating larger and extra windows, glass doors and skylights help to carry out the bright theme to the fullest. If a new home is being painted a color, then it's a color being called, "greige". This hybrid combines beige and gray and is a great neutral. Sleek, classic subway tile is being used everywhere. If there's anything that isn't minimalist in home design, then it's a homeowners desire for statement lighting, which are unique, often oversized fixtures that add drama to the space.

go green

Homeowners today are interested in value, environmentally sound material choices, and products that will provide lasting durability and comfort. Those building a new home realize that it's worth paying a little more for certain materials because it will result in bigger savings over the lifespan of the home. From low-E windows to high efficiency air conditioners, there are countless ways to include green building materials, and all provide an opportunity to save money on your utility bills.

Home buyers are also more interested than ever in maintaining good indoor air quality. So, green products that use zero VOCs or low VOCs are extremely popular. Practically every item in your home emits chemicals into the air. From paint and varnishes to carpeting fibers and drapery textiles, all of these things fill the air with allergens that can be harmful. Green products typically contain chemicals less harsh to our environment and offer a gentler solution overall.

smart solutions

The fastest growing trend in home design is automation. In the last few years and since the creation of smart phones, the number of products available to automate your home has flooded the market. Products that act as a "hub" can be activated with the touch of a button, and they can control and manage multiple apps devoted to maintaining your home. From monitoring your home's security, efficiency, comfort level, and inhabitants, you can virtually manage your home and everything in it all with the touch of your fingertip on your smart phone. Home buyers are also seeking more electrical outlets throughout a home in addition to high quality Wi-Fi access for every room. And, builders are hearing frequent requests for docking stations, or car charging stations in garages as the popularity of electronic cars continues to grow.

just drop it

Also, in line with making life easier is the popular feature of a drop zone. A drop zone is typically an area near the garage entrance that features lockers, cubbies, a bench, and possibly a desk with a charging station for hand held devices and smart phones. It's another practical and smart storage solution homeowners are deeming a necessity especially with families.

we are family

Our pets are becoming more a part of the family than ever before and it's dictating features being seen in home design. Built-in bowls; integrated crates and gates, and beds all make the home feel like all attention to detail was considered throughout the design process instead of these necessities appearing like an after-thought.

Thoughtful, practical, and purposeful. Today's homeowners are a unique group who want a home to feel like it was entirely designed for them. Everything in it should serve a purpose, while offering ease with life's everyday challenges for every person who dwells there right down to the family pet.

Plan #F09-152D-0060

Dimensions:	27' W x 62' D
Heated Sq. Ft.:	1,581
Bedrooms: 3	**Bathrooms: 2**
Exterior Walls:	2" x 6"
Foundation:	Pier

See index for more information

Features

- This narrow lot home is the ultimate coastal escape with covered porches front and back and a deck on the second floor for taking in surrounding views

- The living area and kitchen are open to one another creating a feeling of spaciousness on the first floor

- There are two bedrooms on the first floor, both with walk-in closets and close proximity to a full bath

- The second floor features a private bedroom with direct deck access, a walk-in closet, and a full bath with a beautiful free-standing tub in a sunny bay window

© Copyright by designer/architect

First Floor
1,185 sq. ft.

Second Floor
396 sq. ft.

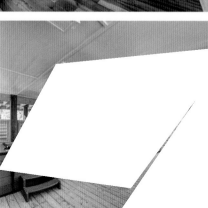

Images provided by designer/architect

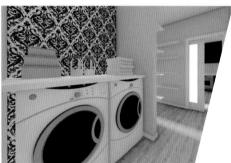

Plan #F09-144D-0023

Dimensions:	58' W x 32' D
Heated Sq. Ft.:	928
Bedrooms: 2	Bathrooms: 2
Exterior Walls:	2" x 6"

Foundation: Crawl space or slab standard; basement, daylight basement or walk-out basement for an additional fee

See index for more information

Features

- This Modern Craftsman home has an inviting entry with space for outdoor relaxation
- Enter the home and discover an open living room with a kitchen behind it
- The kitchen features a large breakfast bar with space for up to four people to dine comfortably
- To the right of the entry is the master bedroom with a large wheelchair accessible bath and walk-in closet
- A highly functional mud room/laundry area offers storage and convenience to the garage
- 2-car front entry garage

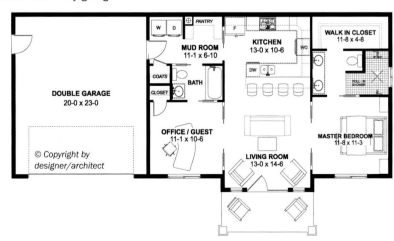

DOUBLE GARAGE
20-0 x 23-0

MUD ROOM
11-1 x 6-10

PANTRY

COATS

CLOSET

BATH

KITCHEN
13-0 x 10-6

DW

WALK IN CLOSET
11-8 x 4-8

© Copyright by
designer/architect

OFFICE / GUEST
11-1 x 10-6

LIVING ROOM
13-0 x 14-6

MASTER BEDROOM
11-8 x 11-3

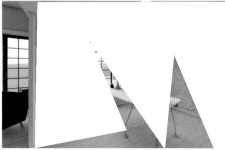

Images provided by designer/architect

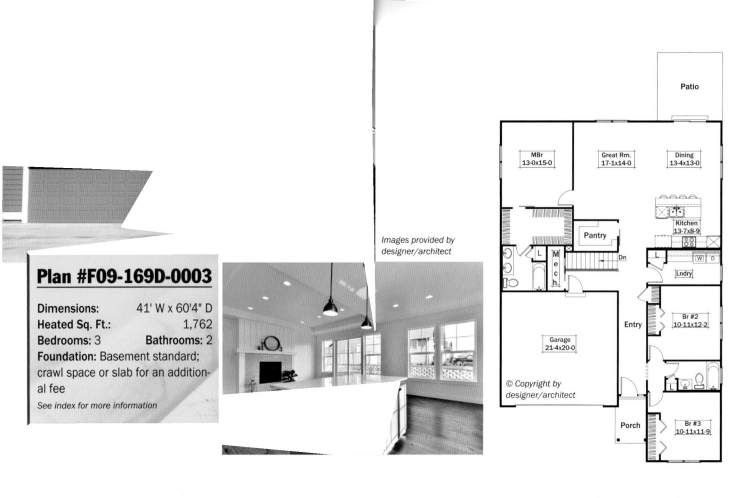

Plan #F09-169D-0003

Dimensions: 41' W x 60'4" D
Heated Sq. Ft.: 1,762
Bedrooms: 3   **Bathrooms:** 2
Foundation: Basement standard; crawl space or slab for an additional fee

See index for more information

Images provided by designer/architect

© Copyright by designer/architect

Plan #F09-128D-0017

Dimensions: 74'2" W x 46'8" D
Heated Sq. Ft.: 2,568
Bonus Sq. Ft.: 440
Bedrooms: 3   **Bathrooms:** 3½
Foundation: Crawl space or basement, please specify when ordering

See index for more information

Images provided by designer/architect

Second Floor
874 sq. ft.

First Floor
1,694 sq. ft.

© Copyright by designer/architect

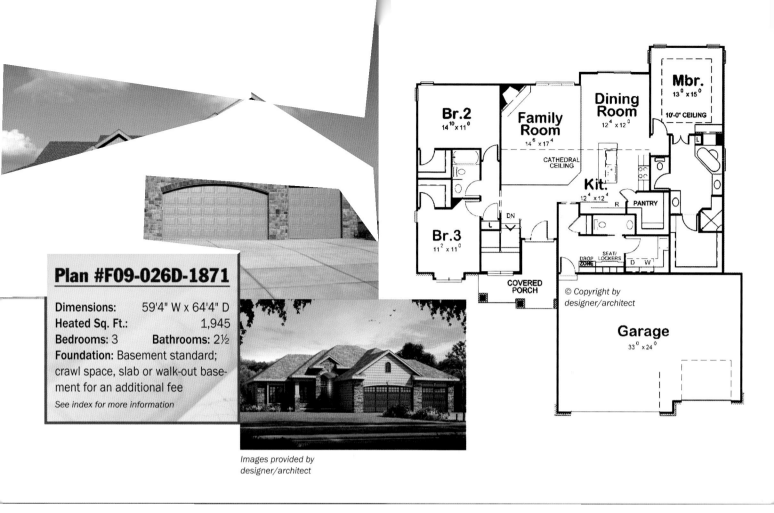

Plan #F09-026D-1871

Dimensions: 59'4" W x 64'4" D
Heated Sq. Ft.: 1,945
Bedrooms: 3   **Bathrooms:** 2½
Foundation: Basement standard; crawl space, slab or walk-out basement for an additional fee

See index for more information

Images provided by designer/architect

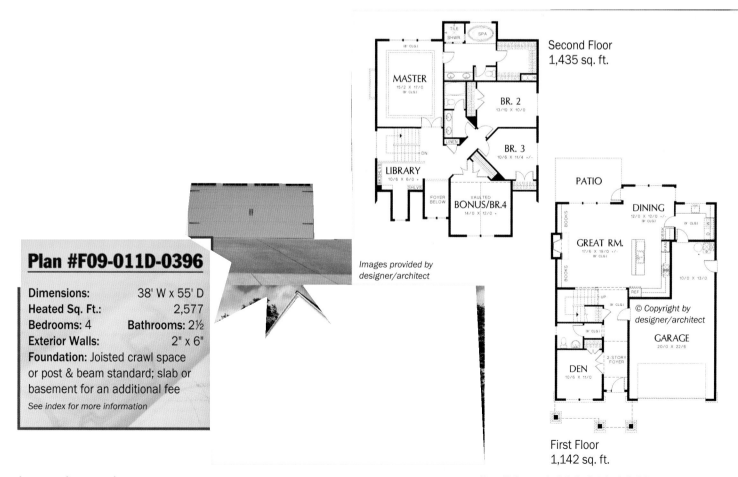

Plan #F09-011D-0396

Dimensions: 38' W x 55' D
Heated Sq. Ft.: 2,577
Bedrooms: 4   **Bathrooms:** 2½
Exterior Walls: 2" x 6"
Foundation: Joisted crawl space or post & beam standard; slab or basement for an additional fee

See index for more information

Second Floor
1,435 sq. ft.

Images provided by designer/architect

First Floor
1,142 sq. ft.

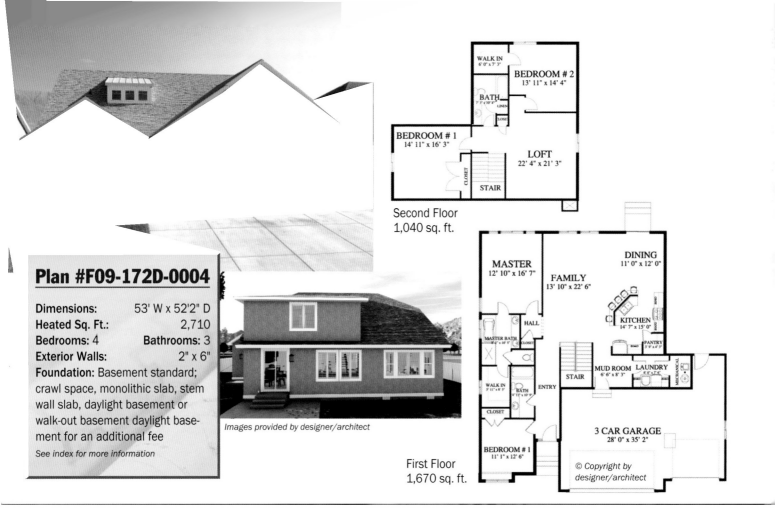

WALK IN
6' 0" x 7' 3"

BEDROOM # 2
13' 11" x 14' 4"

BATH
7' 3" x 10' 4"

LINEN

CLOSE

BEDROOM # 1
14' 11" x 16' 3"

LOFT
22' 4" x 21' 3"

CLOSET

STAIR

Second Floor
1,040 sq. ft.

Plan #F09-172D-0004

Dimensions: 53' W x 52'2" D
Heated Sq. Ft.: 2,710
Bedrooms: 4 **Bathrooms:** 3
Exterior Walls: 2" x 6"
Foundation: Basement standard; crawl space, monolithic slab, stem wall slab, daylight basement or walk-out basement daylight basement for an additional fee

See index for more information

Images provided by designer/architect

MASTER
12' 10" x 16' 7"

DINING
11' 0" x 12' 0"

FAMILY
13' 10" x 22' 6"

HALL

KITCHEN
14' 7" x 15' 0"

MASTER BATH
8' 4" x 10' 3"

CLOSET

PANTRY
3' 9" x 4' 3"

WALK IN
5' 11" x 6' 0"

BATH
6' 11" x 10' 0"

MUD ROOM
6' 6" x 8' 3"

LAUNDRY

MECHANICAL

ENTRY

STAIR

CLOSET

BEDROOM # 1
11' 1" x 12' 6"

3 CAR GARAGE
28' 0" x 35' 2"

© Copyright by designer/architect

First Floor
1,670 sq. ft.

Plan #F09-028D-0120

Images provided by designer/architect

Dimensions: 56' W x 52' D
Heated Sq. Ft.: 2,096
Bedrooms: 4 **Bathrooms:** 2
Exterior Walls: 2" x 6"
Foundation: Slab

See index for more information

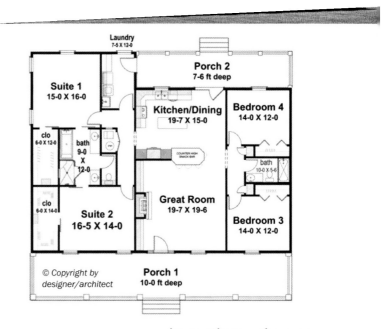

Laundry
7-5 X 12-0

Suite 1
15-0 X 16-0

Porch 2
7-6 ft deep

Kitchen/Dining
19-7 X 15-0

Bedroom 4
14-0 X 12-0

clo
6-0 X 12-0

bath
9-0 X 12-0

COUNTER HIGH SNACK BAR

bath
10-0 X 5-6

clo
6-0 X 14-0

Suite 2
16-5 X 14-0

Great Room
19-7 X 19-6

Bedroom 3
14-0 X 12-0

© Copyright by designer/architect

Porch 1
10-0 ft deep

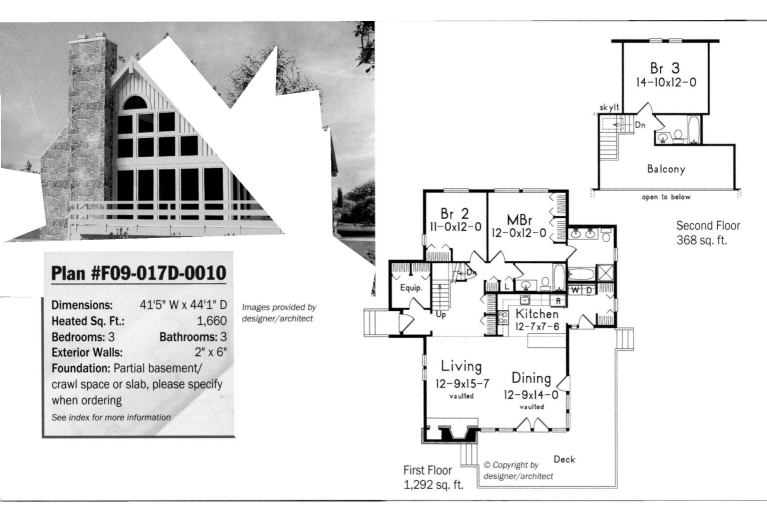

Plan #F09-017D-0010

Dimensions: 41'5" W x 44'1" D
Heated Sq. Ft.: 1,660
Bedrooms: 3   **Bathrooms:** 3
Exterior Walls: 2" x 6"
Foundation: Partial basement/crawl space or slab, please specify when ordering

See index for more information

Images provided by designer/architect

Br 3
14-10x12-0

skylt   Dn

Balcony

open to below

Second Floor
368 sq. ft.

Br 2
11-0x12-0

MBr
12-0x12-0

Equip.

Up

Kitchen
12-7x7-6

L   W D   R

Living
12-9x15-7
vaulted

Dining
12-9x14-0
vaulted

Deck

© Copyright by designer/architect

First Floor
1,292 sq. ft.

Plan #F09-156D-0006

Dimensions: 25' W x 28' D
Heated Sq. Ft.: 550
Bedrooms: 1   **Bathrooms:** 1
Foundation: Slab standard; crawl space for an additional fee

See index for more information

Images provided by designer/architect

Bath
8' x 10'-8"

WD

Kitchen
10' x 10'-8"

Closet
6'-4" x 3'

Closet
6'-4" x 2'

Living Room
13'-8" x 10'-4"

Bedroom
10'-4" x 10'-7"

Porch
11'-10" x 4'-8"

© Copyright by designer/architect

First Floor
1,532 sq. ft.

Plan #F09-172D-0008

Images provided by designer/architect

Dimensions: 78' W x 47' D
Heated Sq. Ft.: 3,016
Bonus Sq. Ft.: 1,515
Bedrooms: 4   Bathrooms: 2½
Exterior Walls: 2" x 6"
Foundation: Basement standard; crawl space, monolithic slab, stem wall slab, daylight basement or walk-out basement for an additional fee

See index for more information

Second Floor
1,484 sq. ft.

© Copyright by designer/architect

Optional Lower Level
1,515 sq. ft.

© Copyright by designer/architect

Plan #F09-020D-0015

Dimensions: 44'6" W x 59' D
Heated Sq. Ft.: 1,191
Bedrooms: 3   Bathrooms: 2
Exterior Walls: 2" x 6"
Foundation: Slab standard; crawl space or basement for an additional fee

See index for more information

Images provided by designer/architect

Plan #F09-077D-0043

Dimensions:	64' W x 45'10" D
Heated Sq. Ft.:	1,752
Bedrooms: 3	**Bathrooms:** 2

Foundation: Slab, basement or crawl space, please specify when ordering

See index for more information

Images provided by designer/architect

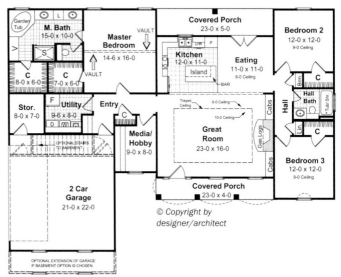

© Copyright by designer/architect

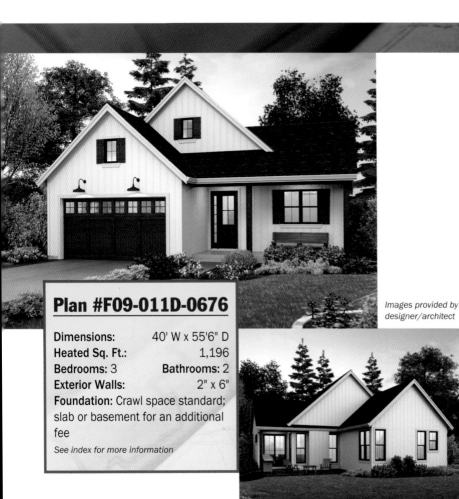

Plan #F09-011D-0676

Dimensions:	40' W x 55'6" D
Heated Sq. Ft.:	1,196
Bedrooms: 3	**Bathrooms:** 2
Exterior Walls:	2" x 6"

Foundation: Crawl space standard; slab or basement for an additional fee

See index for more information

Images provided by designer/architect

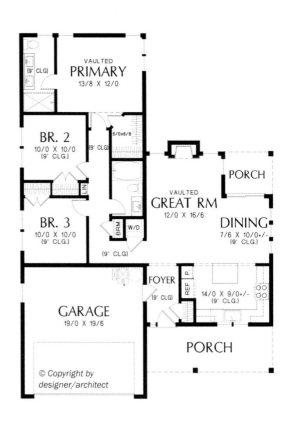

© Copyright by designer/architect

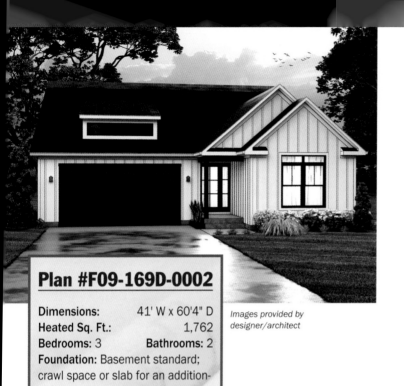

Plan #F09-169D-0002

Dimensions: 41' W x 60'4" D
Heated Sq. Ft.: 1,762
Bedrooms: 3   **Bathrooms:** 2
Foundation: Basement standard; crawl space or slab for an additional fee

See index for more information

Images provided by designer/architect

© Copyright by designer/architect

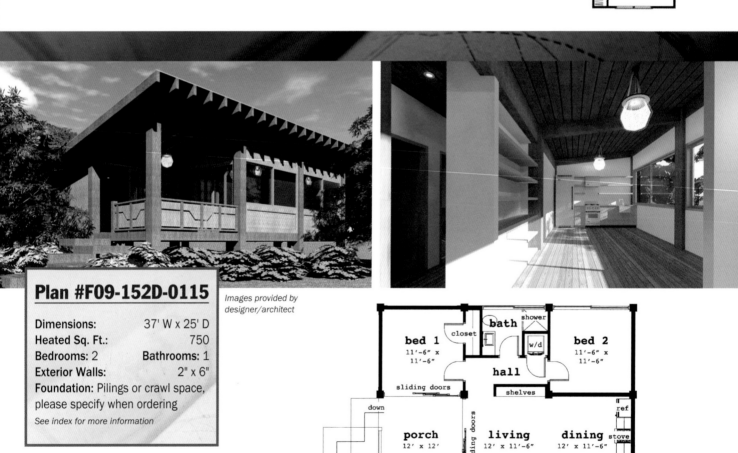

Plan #F09-152D-0115

Dimensions: 37' W x 25' D
Heated Sq. Ft.: 750
Bedrooms: 2   **Bathrooms:** 1
Exterior Walls: 2" x 6"
Foundation: Pilings or crawl space, please specify when ordering

See index for more information

Images provided by designer/architect

© Copyright by designer/architect

Plan #F09-084D-0082

Dimensions: 59'8" W x 54'3" D
Heated Sq. Ft.: 1,599
Bedrooms: 3   **Bathrooms:** 2
Foundation: Slab standard; crawl space for an additional fee

See index for more information

Images provided by designer/architect

PORCH
14-2 x 16-5
10' ceiling

GARAGE
24-4 x 23-3
10' ceiling

© Copyright by designer/architect

BEDROOM
11-3 x 11-3
10' ceiling

KITCHEN/DINING
21-8 x 11-4
10' ceiling

REF.

SNCK BAR

LAUN.
6-7 x 7-6

TUB   SHOWER

M.BATH
12-4 x 10-10
10' ceiling

DESK   STOR.

PANTRY

BATH

LIN.

LIVING
19-4 x 19-6
12' ceiling

MASTER
BEDROOM
16-3 x 13-4
10' ceiling

M.Closet
6-8 x 10-0

BEDROOM
11-3 x 11-4
10' ceiling

PORCH
35-0 x 6-3

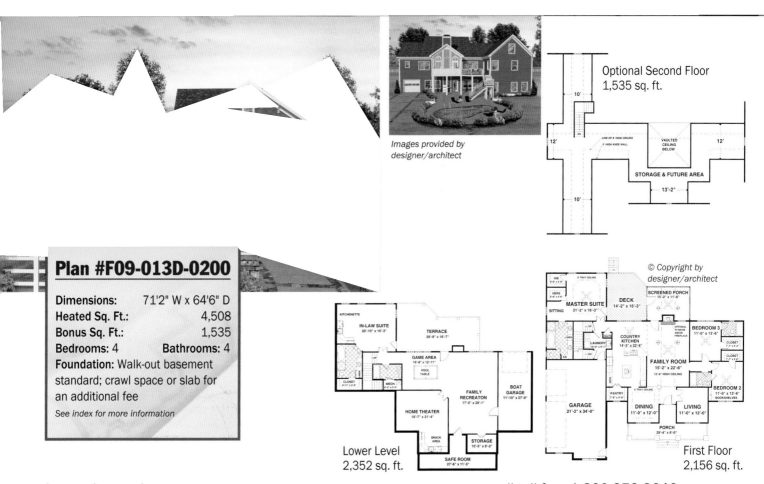

Images provided by designer/architect

Optional Second Floor
1,535 sq. ft.

VAULTED CEILING BELOW

STORAGE & FUTURE AREA
13'-2"

Plan #F09-013D-0200

Dimensions: 71'2" W x 64'6" D
Heated Sq. Ft.: 4,508
Bonus Sq. Ft.: 1,535
Bedrooms: 4   **Bathrooms:** 4
Foundation: Walk-out basement standard; crawl space or slab for an additional fee

See index for more information

© Copyright by designer/architect

IN-LAW SUITE
20'-10" x 16'-3"

KITCHENETTE

TERRACE
29'-6" x 16'-7"

GAME AREA
16'-6" x 12'-11"
POOL TABLE

FAMILY RECREATON
17'-6" x 26'-1"

BOAT GARAGE
11'-10" x 27'-0"

HOME THEATER
18'-7" x 21'-4"

SNACK AREA

STORAGE
10'-5" x 6'-2"

SAFE ROOM
27'-6" x 11'-6"

MASTER SUITE
21'-2" x 16'-3"
SITTING

DECK
14'-2" x 16'-3"

SCREENED PORCH
15'-2" x 11'-6"

COUNTRY KITCHEN
14'-3" x 22'-6"

BEDROOM 3
11'-0" x 13'-6"

FAMILY ROOM
15'-2" x 22'-6"
13'-6" HIGH CEILING

LAUNDRY

BEDROOM 2
11'-0" x 13'-6"

PANTRY

GARAGE
21'-2" x 34'-0"

DINING
11'-0" x 12'-0"

LIVING
11'-0" x 12'-0"

PORCH
29'-4" x 6'-0"

Lower Level
2,352 sq. ft.

First Floor
2,156 sq. ft.

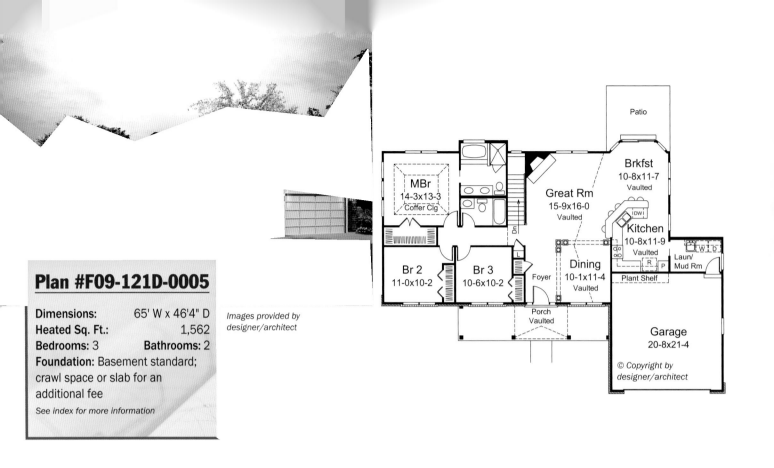

Images provided by designer/architect

MBr
14-3x13-3
Coffer Clg

Great Rm
15-9x16-0
Vaulted

Brkfst
10-8x11-7
Vaulted

Kitchen
10-8x11-9
Vaulted

Br 2
11-0x10-2

Br 3
10-6x10-2

Dining
10-1x11-4
Vaulted

Br 2

Foyer

Porch
Vaulted

Patio

DW

R

P

Laun/
Mud Rm

W D

Plant Shelf

Garage
20-8x21-4

© Copyright by
designer/architect

Plan #F09-121D-0005

Dimensions: 65' W x 46'4" D
Heated Sq. Ft.: 1,562
Bedrooms: 3   **Bathrooms:** 2
Foundation: Basement standard;
crawl space or slab for an
additional fee

See index for more information

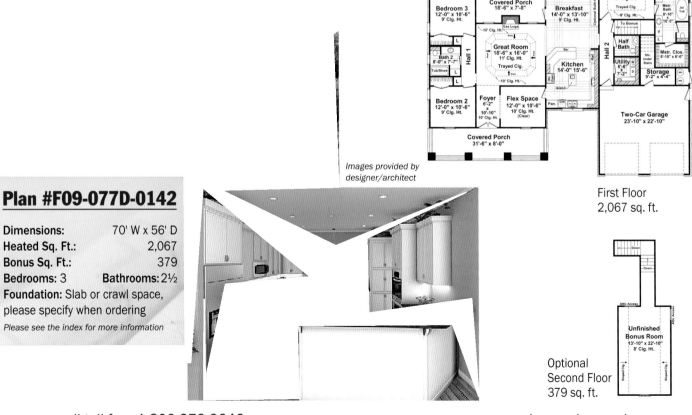

© Copyright by
designer/architect

Images provided by
designer/architect

Bedroom 3
12'-0" x 10'-6"
9' Clg. Ht.

Covered Porch
18'-6" x 7'-8"

Breakfast
14'-0" x 13'-10"
9' Clg. Ht.

Master Bedroom
14'-8" x 15'-0"
10' Clg. Ht.
Trayed Clg.

Mstr. Clos.

Great Room
18'-6" x 16'-0"
11' Clg. Ht.
Trayed Clg.

Gas Logs

Hall 1

Bath 2
8'-0" x 7'-7"
Tub/Shwr

Kitchen
14'-0" 15'-6"

Bar

Hall 2

Half
Bath

Mstr.
Bath
8'-10"
15'-0"

Jet
Tub

Mstr. Clos.
5'-10" x 6'-0"

Utility
6'-6"
x
7'-2"

Sto.
Under
Stairs

Bedroom 2
12'-0" x 10'-6"
9' Clg. Ht.

Foyer
6'-2"
x
10'-10"

Flex Space
12'-0" x 10'-6"
10' Clg. Ht.
(Clear)

Pan.

DW

Island

Storage
9'-2" x 4'-4"

Two-Car Garage
23'-10" x 22'-10"

Covered Porch
31'-6" x 8'-0"

Patio
20'-6" x 8'-10"

First Floor
2,067 sq. ft.

Attic Access

**Unfinished
Bonus Room**
13'-10" x 22'-10"
8' Clg. Ht.

Down

**Optional
Second Floor**
379 sq. ft.

Plan #F09-077D-0142

Dimensions: 70' W x 56' D
Heated Sq. Ft.: 2,067
Bonus Sq. Ft.: 379
Bedrooms: 3   **Bathrooms:** 2½
Foundation: Slab or crawl space,
please specify when ordering

Please see the index for more information

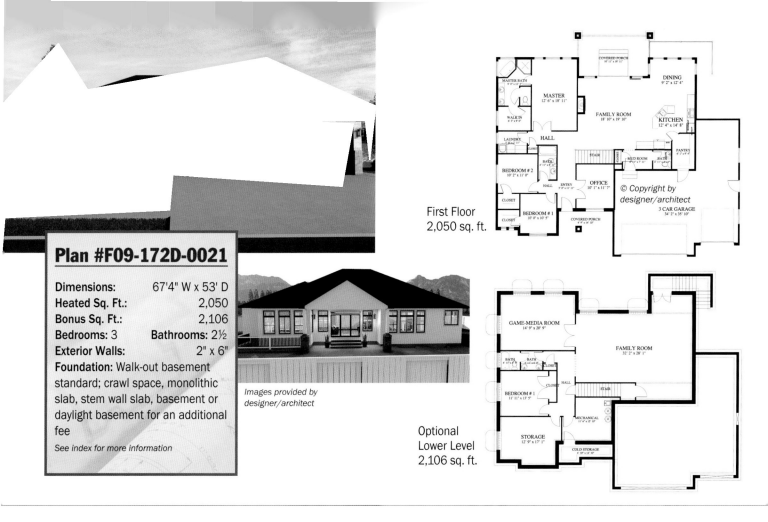

First Floor
2,050 sq. ft.

© Copyright by designer/architect

Optional Lower Level
2,106 sq. ft.

Plan #F09-172D-0021

Dimensions:	67'4" W x 53' D
Heated Sq. Ft.:	2,050
Bonus Sq. Ft.:	2,106
Bedrooms: 3	Bathrooms: 2½
Exterior Walls:	2" x 6"

Foundation: Walk-out basement standard; crawl space, monolithic slab, stem wall slab, basement or daylight basement for an additional fee

See index for more information

Images provided by designer/architect

Plan #F09-070D-0748

Dimensions:	58' W x 54'4" D
Heated Sq. Ft.:	1,959
Bedrooms: 3	Bathrooms: 2½
Exterior Walls:	2" x 6"
Foundation:	Basement

See index for more information

© Copyright by designer/architect

Images provided by designer/architect

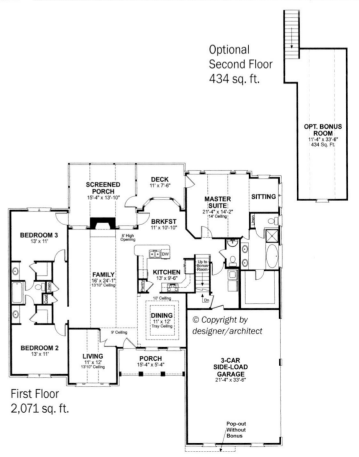

Plan #F09-001D-0067

Dimensions: 48' W x 37'8" D
Heated Sq. Ft.: 1,285
Bedrooms: 3   **Bathrooms:** 2
Foundation: Crawl space standard; basement or slab for an additional fee

See index for more information

Images provided by designer/architect

© Copyright by designer/architect

Storage
D
W
R
MBr 12-0x14-5
Furn
L
P
Kit 9-10x 10-11
Dining 10-3x 10-11
Br 2 15-6x10-8
Br 3 10-1x10-8
Living 18-10x14-2
Porch depth 6-0

Plan #F09-013D-0048

Dimensions: 63' W x 63' D
Heated Sq. Ft.: 2,071
Bonus Sq. Ft.: 434
Bedrooms: 3   **Bathrooms:** 2½
Foundation: Basement standard; crawl space or slab for an additional fee

See index for more information

Images provided by designer/architect

Optional Second Floor 434 sq. ft.

OPT. BONUS ROOM
11'-4" x 33'-6"
434 Sq. Ft.

SCREENED PORCH
15'-4" x 13'-10"

DECK
11' x 7'-6"

MASTER SUITE
21'-4" x 14'-2"
14' Ceiling

SITTING

BRKFST
11' x 10'-10"

8' High Opening

BEDROOM 3
13' x 11'

FAMILY
16' x 24'-1"
13'10" Ceiling

KITCHEN
13' x 9'-6"

Up to Bonus Room

10' Ceiling

Dn

DINING
11' x 12'
Tray Ceiling

© Copyright by designer/architect

9' Ceiling

BEDROOM 2
13' x 11'

LIVING
11' x 12'
13'10" Ceiling

PORCH
15'-4" x 5'-4"

3-CAR SIDE-LOAD GARAGE
21'-4" x 33'-6"

First Floor
2,071 sq. ft.

Pop-out Without Bonus

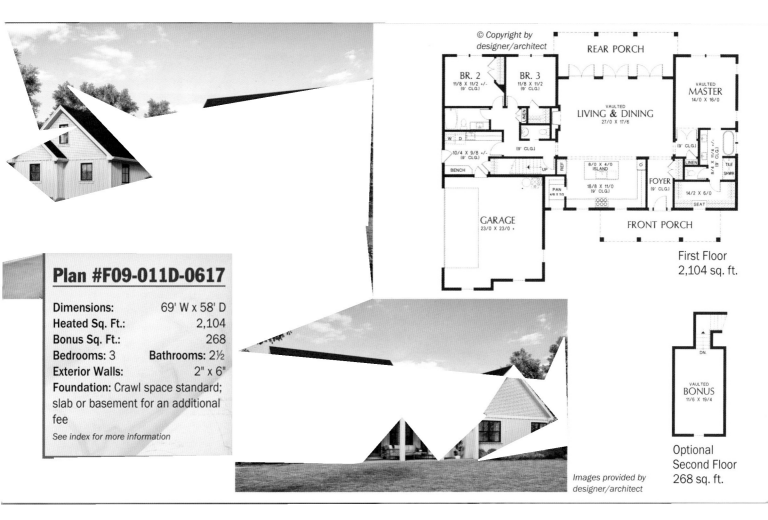

REAR PORCH

BR. 2
11/8 X 11/2
(9' CLG.)

BR. 3
11/8 X 11/2
(9' CLG.)

VAULTED
MASTER
14/0 X 16/0

VAULTED
LIVING & DINING
27/0 X 17/6

© Copyright by
designer/architect

LINEN

W D

10/4 X 9/8 +/-
(9' CLG.)

[9' CLG.]

[9' CLG.]

LINEN

TILE
SHWR

8/4 X 11/4 +/-
(9' CLG.)

BENCH

UP

REF

ISLAND
8/0 X 4/0

18/8 X 11/0
(9' CLG.)

FOYER
(9' CLG.)

14/2 X 6/0

SEAT

PAN
4/8 X 1/2

GARAGE
23/0 X 23/0 +

FRONT PORCH

First Floor
2,104 sq. ft.

Plan #F09-011D-0617

Dimensions:	69' W x 58' D
Heated Sq. Ft.:	2,104
Bonus Sq. Ft.:	268
Bedrooms: 3	Bathrooms: 2½
Exterior Walls:	2" x 6"

Foundation: Crawl space standard;
slab or basement for an additional
fee

See index for more information

DN.

VAULTED
BONUS
11/6 X 19/4

Optional
Second Floor
268 sq. ft.

*Images provided by
designer/architect*

Second Floor
845 sq. ft.

STORAGE

STORAGE

BATH

LOFT AREA
20'-0" X 17'-9"

BDRM. #3
12'-0" X 18'-1"

BDRM. #2
12'-0" X 18'-1"

STORAGE

OPEN TO BELOW

DOWN

STORAGE

Plan #F09-088D-0242

Dimensions:	53' W x 49'7" D
Heated Sq. Ft.:	2,281
Bedrooms: 3	Bathrooms: 2½
Exterior Walls:	2" x 6"
Foundation:	Walk-out basement

See index for more information

*Images provided by
designer/architect*

First Floor
1,436 sq. ft.

© Copyright by
designer/architect

COVERED ENTRY PORCH

KITCHEN
12'X13'6"

UTILITY
6'8"X10'

FOYER
6'-10" X 14'-0"

6'X5'

WIC

13'8"X10'8"

WIC

UP

DN

UP

DOWN

DINING RM.
12'-0" X 12'-5"

GREAT RM.
20'-0" X 17'-0"

MASTER SUITE
12'-0" X 15'-10"

DECK AREA

DECK AREA

UP

UNFINISHED BASEMENT

CONC. PATIO

Optional
Lower Level
1,436 sq. ft.

Plan #F09-076D-0220

Dimensions:	97'2" W x 87'7" D
Heated Sq. Ft.:	3,061
Bonus Sq. Ft.:	3,644
Bedrooms: 3	Bathrooms 3½

Foundation: Basement standard; crawl space or slab for an additional fee

See index for more information

Images provided by designer/architect

© Copyright by designer/architect

Features

- This luxury Craftsman home is loaded with curb appeal thanks to multiple gables, and a covered porch adding that undeniable charm
- The first floor is open and airy with the main gathering spaces combining perfectly maximizing the square footage
- The kitchen is open to the family room with a grilling terrace nearby
- The optional lower level has an additional 2,975 square feet of living area including a hobby room, theater, office, and a recreation area with a bar
- The optional second floor has an additional 669 square feet of living area with 277 square feet in the bedroom and 392 square feet in the recreation area
- 3-car front entry garage

First Floor
3,061 sq. ft.

Optional
Lower Level
2,975 sq. ft.

Optional
Second Floor
669 sq. ft.

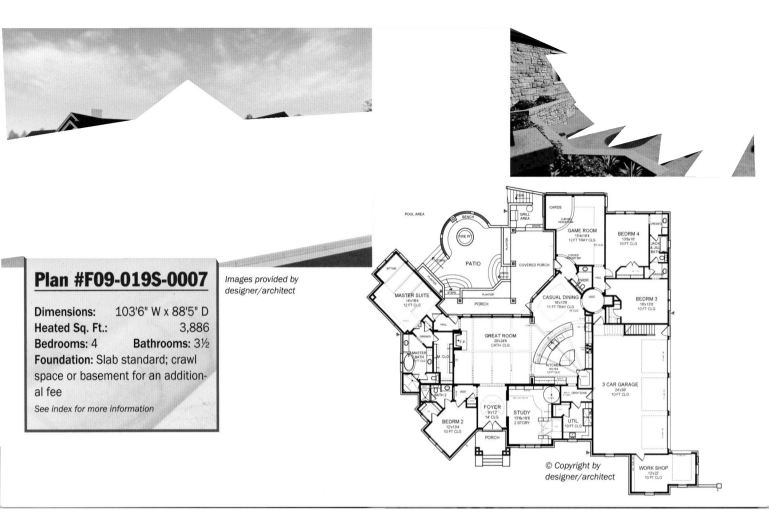

Plan #F09-019S-0007

Images provided by designer/architect

Dimensions:	103'6" W x 88'5" D
Heated Sq. Ft.:	3,886
Bedrooms: 4	**Bathrooms:** 3½

Foundation: Slab standard; crawl space or basement for an additional fee

See index for more information

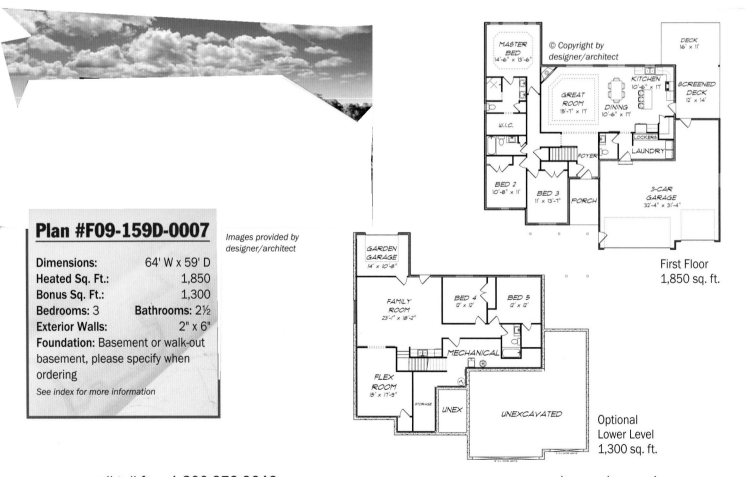

Plan #F09-159D-0007

Images provided by designer/architect

Dimensions:	64' W x 59' D
Heated Sq. Ft.:	1,850
Bonus Sq. Ft.:	1,300
Bedrooms: 3	**Bathrooms:** 2½
Exterior Walls:	2" x 6"

Foundation: Basement or walk-out basement, please specify when ordering

See index for more information

First Floor
1,850 sq. ft.

Optional
Lower Level
1,300 sq. ft.

Images provided by designer/architect

Plan #F09-058D-0240

Dimensions:	55' W x 46' D
Heated Sq. Ft.:	1,594
Bedrooms: 3	**Bathrooms:** 2
Foundation:	Basement

See index for more information

© Copyright by designer/architect

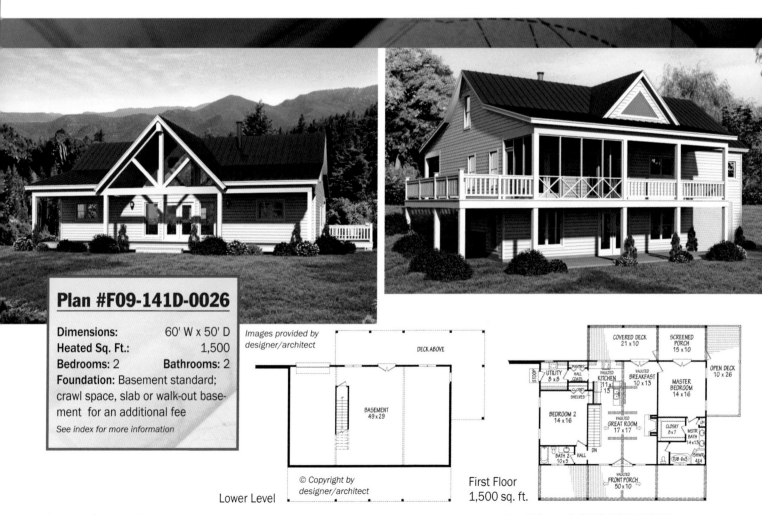

Plan #F09-141D-0026

Dimensions:	60' W x 50' D
Heated Sq. Ft.:	1,500
Bedrooms: 2	**Bathrooms:** 2
Foundation: Basement standard; crawl space, slab or walk-out basement for an additional fee	

See index for more information

Images provided by designer/architect

Lower Level

© Copyright by designer/architect

First Floor
1,500 sq. ft.

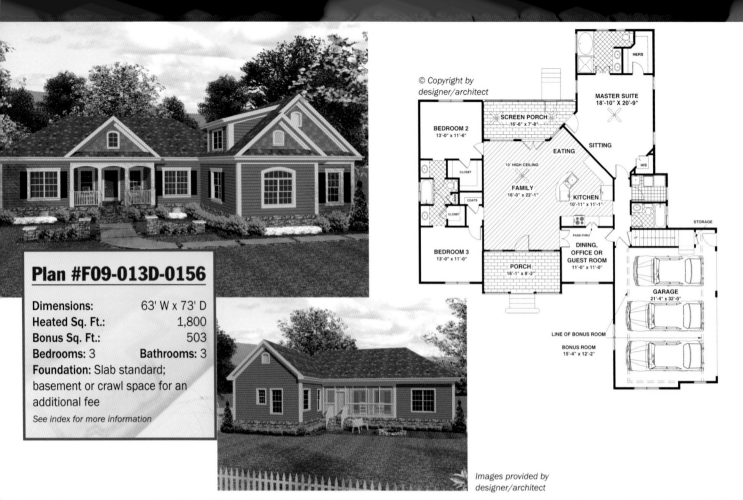

Plan #F09-013D-0156

Dimensions: 63' W x 73' D
Heated Sq. Ft.: 1,800
Bonus Sq. Ft.: 503
Bedrooms: 3 **Bathrooms:** 3
Foundation: Slab standard; basement or crawl space for an additional fee

See index for more information

Images provided by designer/architect

© Copyright by designer/architect

HERS

MASTER SUITE
18'-10" X 20'-9"

SCREEN PORCH
16'-6" x 7'-8"

BEDROOM 2
13'-0" x 11'-6"

SITTING

EATING

CLOSET

10' HIGH CEILING

HIS

FAMILY
16'-0" x 22'-1"

KITCHEN
10'-11" x 11'-1"

COATS

CLOSET

STORAGE

BEDROOM 3
13'-0" x 11'-0"

PASS-THRU

DINING, OFFICE OR GUEST ROOM
11'-0" x 11'-0"

PORCH
16'-1" x 8'-2"

GARAGE
21'-4" x 32'-0"

LINE OF BONUS ROOM

BONUS ROOM
15'-4" x 12'-2"

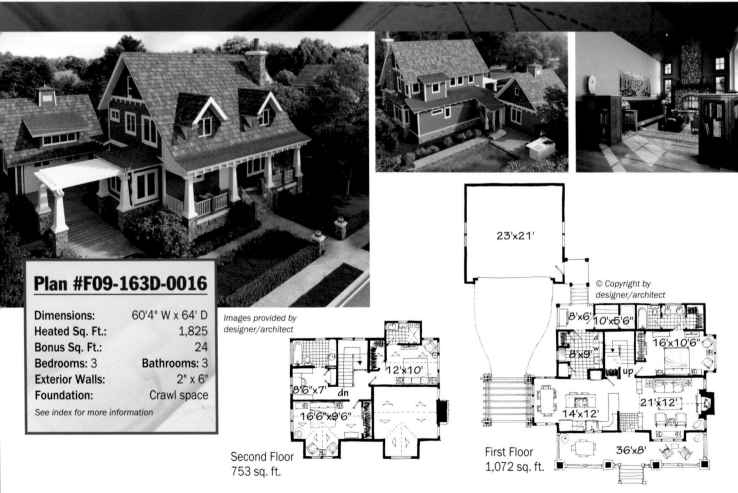

Plan #F09-163D-0016

Dimensions: 60'4" W x 64' D
Heated Sq. Ft.: 1,825
Bonus Sq. Ft.: 24
Bedrooms: 3 **Bathrooms:** 3
Exterior Walls: 2" x 6"
Foundation: Crawl space

See index for more information

Images provided by designer/architect

© Copyright by designer/architect

23'x21'

8'x6' 10'x5'6"

16'x10'6"

8'x9'

8'6"x7' dn

12'x10'

up

21'x12'

8'6"x9'6"

16'6"x9'6"

14'x12'

36'x8'

Second Floor
753 sq. ft.

First Floor
1,072 sq. ft.

Plan #F09-141D-0066

Dimensions: 30' W x 41' D
Heated Sq. Ft.: 1,050
Bedrooms: 2 **Bathrooms:** 2
Foundation: Slab standard; crawl space, basement or walk-out basement for an additional fee

See index for more information

Images provided by designer/architect

© Copyright by designer/architect

BEDRM #1
14 x 12

CLO
3 x 6

BEDRM #2
12 x 10

LIN

SHWR
3 x 3

LNDRY
6 x 8

MSTR BATH
8 x 8

CLOSET
6 x 8

HALL

BTH #2
6 x 8

STO

LIN

CTS

PAN

FAMILY ROOM
17 x 13

EAT-IN KITCHEN
12 x 16

DINING AREA

PORCH
16 x 6

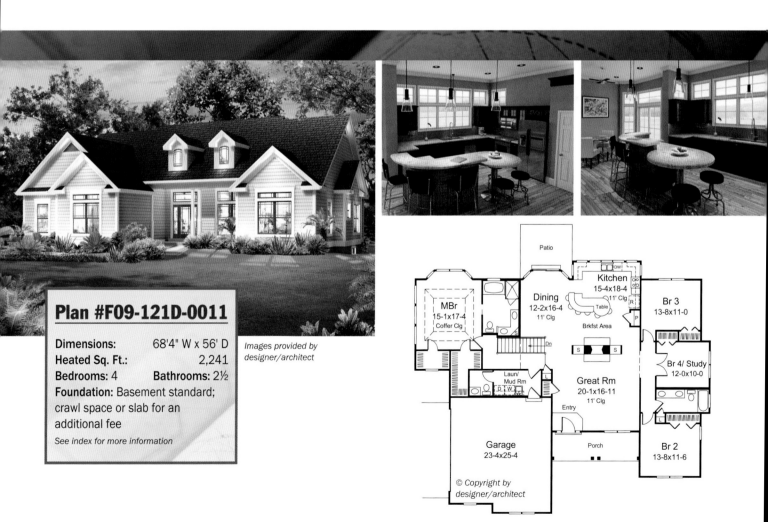

Plan #F09-121D-0011

Dimensions: 68'4" W x 56' D
Heated Sq. Ft.: 2,241
Bedrooms: 4 **Bathrooms:** 2½
Foundation: Basement standard; crawl space or slab for an additional fee

See index for more information

Images provided by designer/architect

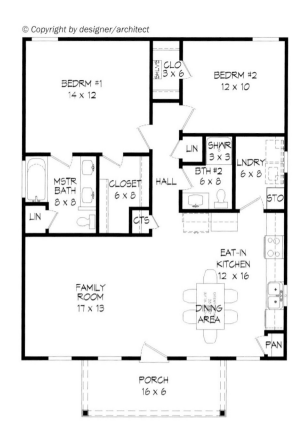

Patio

MBr
15-1x17-4
Coffer Clg

Dining
12-2x16-4
11' Clg

Kitchen
15-4x18-4
11' Clg

Brkfst Area

Br 3
13-8x11-0

Laun/ Mud Rm

Great Rm
20-1x16-11
11' Clg

Br 4/ Study
12-0x10-0

Entry

Garage
23-4x25-4

Porch

Br 2
13-8x11-6

© Copyright by designer/architect

Plan #F09-101D-0047

Dimensions:	99' W x 81' D
Heated Sq. Ft.:	2,478
Bonus Sq. Ft.:	1,795
Bedrooms: 2	**Bathrooms:** 2½
Exterior Walls:	2" x 6"
Foundation:	Walk-out basement

See index for more information

Features

- The architectural style of this home has interesting features and great curb appeal
- The master bedroom has double walk-in closets, a separate tub and shower and a double bowl vanity
- Open living at its finest with the combination of the great room, kitchen and dining for a relaxed casual atmosphere
- Directly off the foyer is a private study, perfect as a home office
- The optional lower level has an additional 1,795 square feet of living area and features a craft area, sitting area, family room, two additional bedrooms, and a bath
- Oversized 5-car front entry tandem garage, 2-car side entry garage

© Copyright by designer/architect

First Floor
2,478 sq. ft.

Optional
Lower Level
1,795 sq. ft.

Images provided by designer/architect

Plan #F09-051D-1006

Dimensions: 64'8" W x 67'4" D
Heated Sq. Ft.: 3,235
Bedrooms: 5 **Bathrooms:** 3½
Exterior Walls: 2" x 6"
Foundation: Daylight basement standard; crawl space or slab for an additional fee

See index for more information

Features

- An open concept floor plan welcomes you into this Craftsman style home with a coffered ceiling in the great room that frames the living space
- The large kitchen island overlooks the great room and the adjacent dining area to create an area that's large enough to entertain many guests
- The hidden pantry is an extra surprise with plenty of storage
- The split bedroom layout gives the master bedroom plenty of privacy
- The lower level boasts a large family room, two additional bedrooms, and a full bath
- 3-car front entry garage

First Floor
1,941 sq. ft.

Lower Level
1,294 sq. ft.

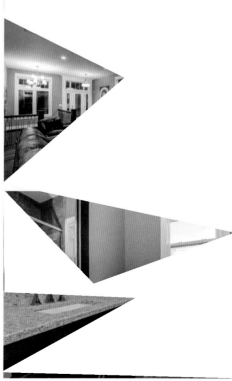

Images provided by designer/architect

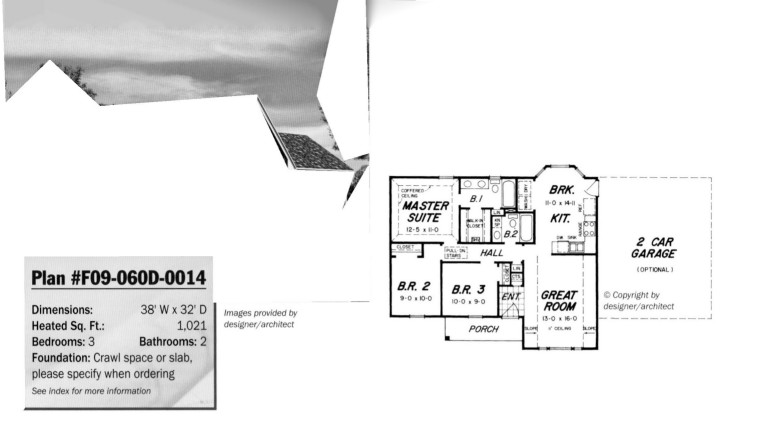

Plan #F09-060D-0014

Dimensions: 38' W x 32' D
Heated Sq. Ft.: 1,021
Bedrooms: 3 **Bathrooms:** 2
Foundation: Crawl space or slab, please specify when ordering

See index for more information

Images provided by designer/architect

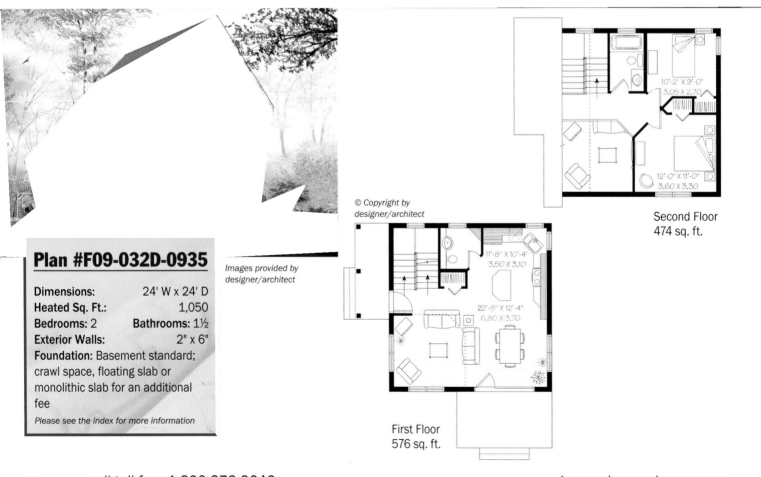

Plan #F09-032D-0935

Dimensions: 24' W x 24' D
Heated Sq. Ft.: 1,050
Bedrooms: 2 **Bathrooms:** 1½
Exterior Walls: 2" x 6"
Foundation: Basement standard; crawl space, floating slab or monolithic slab for an additional fee

Please see the index for more information

Images provided by designer/architect

Second Floor
474 sq. ft.

First Floor
576 sq. ft.

houseplansandmore.com

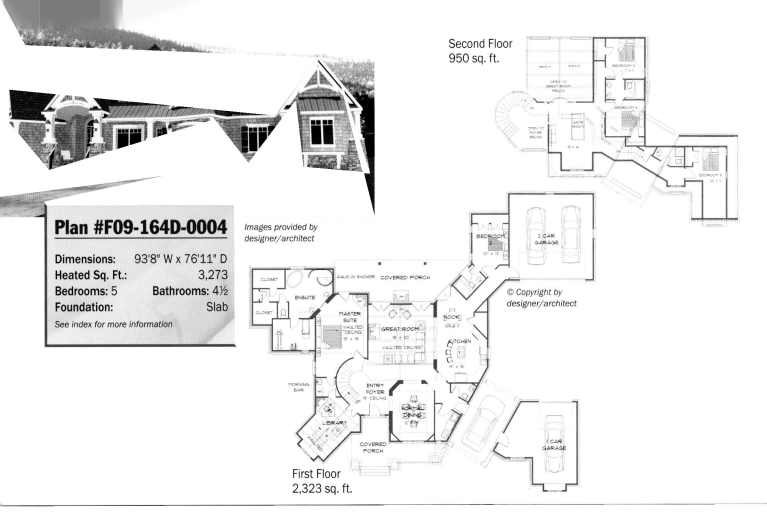

Second Floor
950 sq. ft.

Plan #F09-164D-0004

Dimensions:	93'8" W x 76'11" D
Heated Sq. Ft.:	3,273
Bedrooms: 5	Bathrooms: 4½
Foundation:	Slab

See index for more information

Images provided by designer/architect

© Copyright by designer/architect

First Floor
2,323 sq. ft.

Plan #F09-167D-0006

Dimensions:	68'11" W x 69'10" D
Heated Sq. Ft.:	2,939
Bedrooms: 4	Bathrooms: 3½
Exterior Walls:	2" x 6"
Foundation:	Slab standard; crawl space for an additional fee

See index for more information

Images provided by designer/architect

© Copyright by designer/architect

Plan #F09-101D-0057

Dimensions:	58' W x 90' D
Heated Sq. Ft.:	2,037
Bonus Sq. Ft.:	1,330
Bedrooms: 1	Bathrooms: 1½
Exterior Walls:	2" x 6"
Foundation:	Walk-out basement

See index for more information

Images provided by designer/architect

Features

- Enjoy the outdoors on both levels of this home with upper and lower covered patios and decks
- The front porch opens to an entry hall with a formal dining room and a staircase to the lower level nearby
- The large U-shaped kitchen features space for casual dining as well as a wet bar for entertaining
- The master bedroom is in a wing to itself and features a stepped ceiling, a luxurious bath, and a large walk-in closet
- The optional lower level has an additional 1,330 square feet of living area and offers two additional bedrooms with baths, an office, an open recreation space, a safe room, and unfinished storage
- 3-car side entry garage

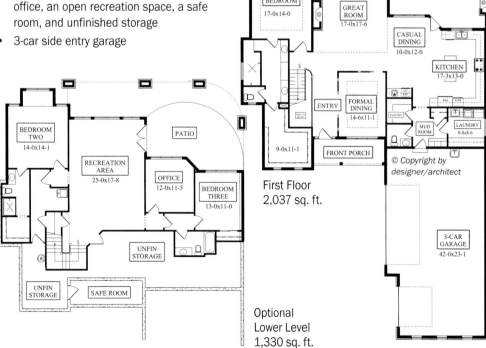

First Floor
2,037 sq. ft.

© Copyright by designer/architect

Optional
Lower Level
1,330 sq. ft.

houseplansandmore.com

Plan #F09-080D-0012

Dimensions:	36' W x 46'6" D
Heated Sq. Ft.:	1,370
Bonus Sq. Ft.:	96
Bedrooms: 3	**Bathrooms:** 2
Exterior Walls:	2" x 6"

Foundation: Basement or crawl space, please specify when ordering

See index for more information

Features

- The great room is open and bright and has an area with a two-story ceiling topped with skylights
- An enormous deck surrounds the rear of this home providing plenty of space for relaxing and dining
- The second floor vaulted master bedroom has a private covered balcony and interesting interior windows that provide additional light and distinction
- The optional lower level has an additional 96 square feet of living area

Second Floor
575 sq. ft.

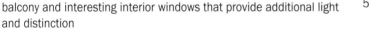

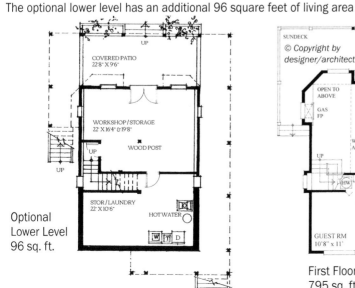

Optional Lower Level
96 sq. ft.

First Floor
795 sq. ft.

Images provided by designer/architect

Plan #F09-077D-0184

Dimensions:	73'6" W x 62' D
Heated Sq. Ft.:	2,400
Bonus Sq. Ft.:	452
Bedrooms: 4	Bathrooms: 2½

Foundation: Slab or crawl space, please specify when ordering; for basement version of this plan, see Plan #077D-0192 at houseplansandmore.com

See index for more information

Images provided by designer/architect

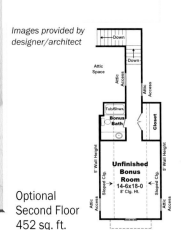

Optional Second Floor 452 sq. ft.

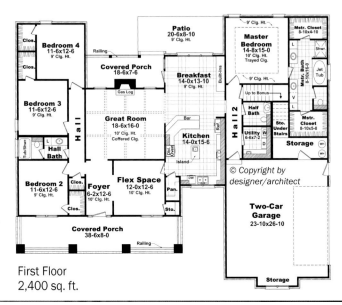

First Floor 2,400 sq. ft.

© Copyright by designer/architect

Plan #F09-007D-0134

Dimensions:	73'8" W x 32' D
Heated Sq. Ft.:	1,310
Bedrooms: 3	Bathrooms: 2

Foundation: Basement standard; crawl space or slab for an additional fee

See index for more information

Images provided by designer/architect

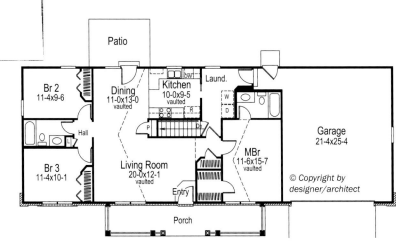

© Copyright by designer/architect

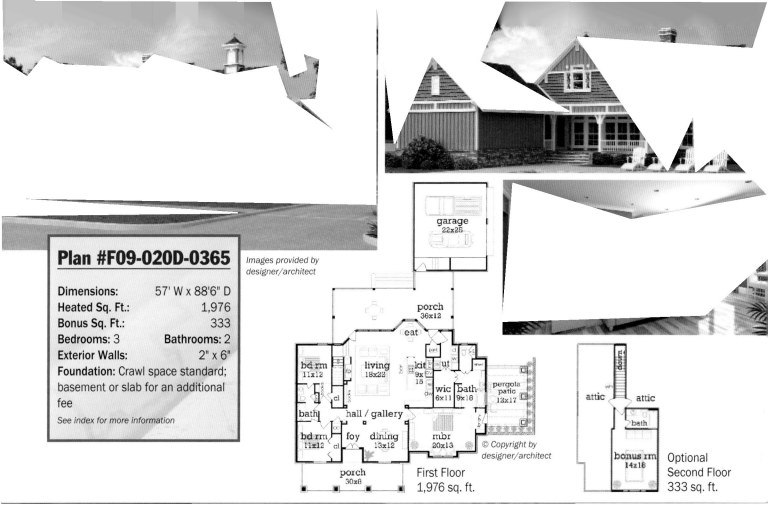

Plan #F09-020D-0365

Dimensions: 57' W x 88'6" D
Heated Sq. Ft.: 1,976
Bonus Sq. Ft.: 333
Bedrooms: 3   Bathrooms: 2
Exterior Walls: 2" x 6"
Foundation: Crawl space standard; basement or slab for an additional fee

See index for more information

Images provided by designer/architect

garage
22x25

porch
36x12

eat

bd rm
11x12

living
18x22

kit
9x18

ut

bath

bath

wic
6x11

bath
9x18

pergola
patio
12x17

hall / gallery

bd rm
11x12

foy

dining
13x12

mbr
20x13

porch
30x8

© Copyright by designer/architect

First Floor
1,976 sq. ft.

attic

down

attic

bath

bonus rm
14x18

Optional
Second Floor
333 sq. ft.

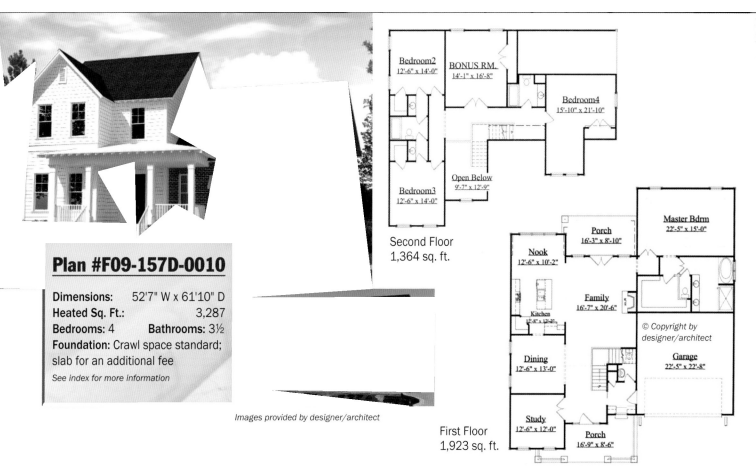

Plan #F09-157D-0010

Dimensions: 52'7" W x 61'10" D
Heated Sq. Ft.: 3,287
Bedrooms: 4   Bathrooms: 3½
Foundation: Crawl space standard; slab for an additional fee

See index for more information

Images provided by designer/architect

Bedroom2
12'-6" x 14'-0"

BONUS RM.
14'-1" x 16'-8"

Bedroom4
15'-10" x 21'-10"

Bedroom3
12'-6" x 14'-0"

Open Below
9'-7" x 12'-9"

Second Floor
1,364 sq. ft.

Porch
16'-3" x 8'-10"

Master Bdrm
22'-5" x 15'-0"

Nook
12'-6" x 10'-2"

Family
16'-7" x 20'-6"

Kitchen
12'-8" x 12'-2"

© Copyright by designer/architect

Dining
12'-6" x 13'-0"

Garage
22'-5" x 22'-8"

Study
12'-6" x 12'-0"

Porch
16'-9" x 8'-6"

First Floor
1,923 sq. ft.

Plan #F09-011D-0657

Dimensions: 26' W x 34' D
Heated Sq. Ft.: 1,394
Bedrooms: 3   **Bathrooms:** 2½
Exterior Walls: 2" x 6"
Foundation: Joisted crawl space standard; basement for an additional fee

See index for more information

Features

- Stylish Modern Farmhouse design is a great size open floor plan, perfect for today's family
- The living room and dining area are open to one another as well as the kitchen with island
- All three bedrooms are on the second floor for convenience and privacy
- The laundry room is centrally located on the first floor

© Copyright by designer/architect

PATIO

12/8 X 12/8 +/-
(9' CLG.)

DINING
9/6 X 10/6 +/-
(9' CLG.)

LIN

REF

STOR

PAN

UP

LIVING
15/0 X 14/6 +/-
(9' CLG.)

COVERED
PORCH
22/0 X 6/0

First Floor
714 sq. ft.

MASTER
13/0 X 12/8

6/4 X 5/2

LIN

DN

BR. 2
12/0 X 10/6 +/-

BR. 3
10/4 X 10/6

Second Floor
680 sq. ft.

Plan #F09-148D-0047

Dimensions:	30' W x 24' D
Heated Sq. Ft.:	720
Bonus Sq. Ft.:	720
Bedrooms: 1	Bathrooms: 1
Exterior Walls:	2" x 6"
Foundation:	Basement

See index for more information

Images provided by designer/architect

First Floor
720 sq. ft.

© Copyright by
designer/architect

Optional Lower Level
720 sq. ft.

Plan #F09-139D-0070

Images provided by designer/architect

Dimensions:	67'3" W x 78' D
Heated Sq. Ft.:	2,928
Bonus Sq. Ft.:	994
Bedrooms: 4	Bathrooms: 2½
Exterior Walls:	2" x 6"

Foundation: Crawl space standard; slab, basement, daylight basement or walk-out basement for an additional fee

See index for more information

Optional
Second Floor
994 sq. ft.

© Copyright by
designer/architect

First Floor
2,928 sq. ft.

houseplansandmore.com

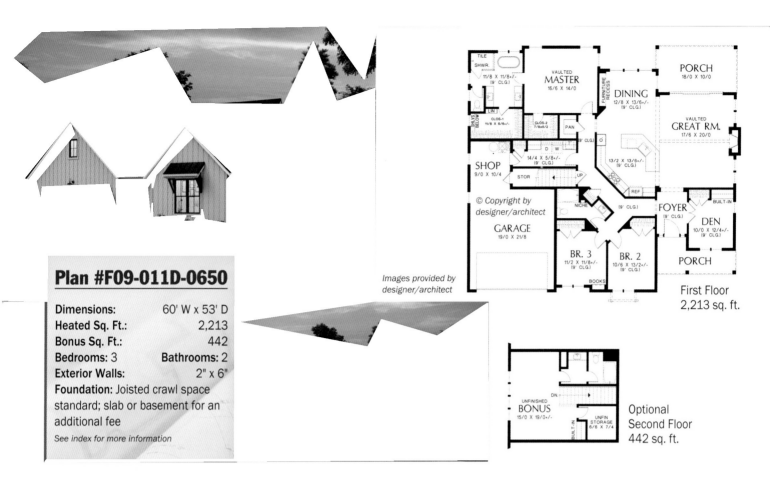

First Floor
2,213 sq. ft.

Images provided by
designer/architect

Optional
Second Floor
442 sq. ft.

Plan #F09-011D-0650

Dimensions:	60' W x 53' D
Heated Sq. Ft.:	2,213
Bonus Sq. Ft.:	442
Bedrooms: 3	**Bathrooms:** 2
Exterior Walls:	2" x 6"

Foundation: Joisted crawl space standard; slab or basement for an additional fee

See index for more information

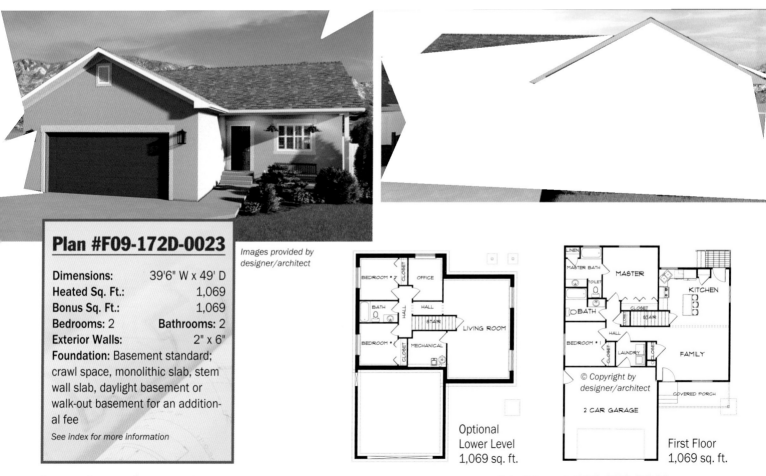

Images provided by
designer/architect

Plan #F09-172D-0023

Dimensions:	39'6" W x 49' D
Heated Sq. Ft.:	1,069
Bonus Sq. Ft.:	1,069
Bedrooms: 2	**Bathrooms:** 2
Exterior Walls:	2" x 6"

Foundation: Basement standard; crawl space, monolithic slab, stem wall slab, daylight basement or walk-out basement for an additional fee

See index for more information

Optional
Lower Level
1,069 sq. ft.

First Floor
1,069 sq. ft.

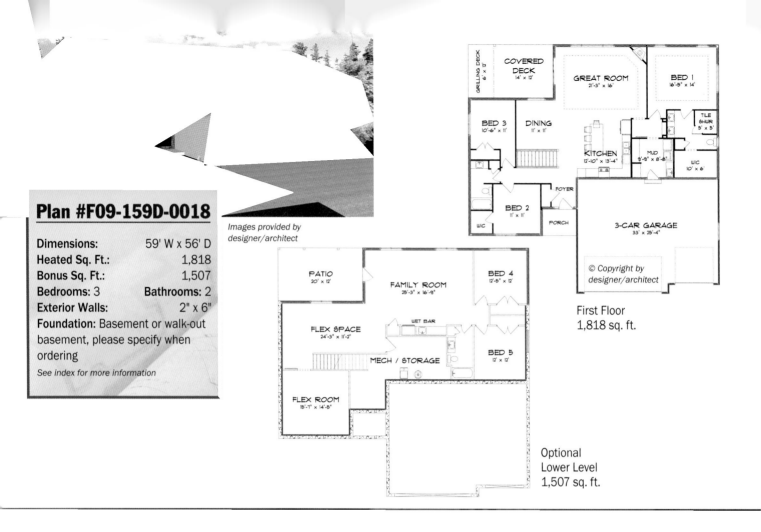

Plan #F09-159D-0018

Dimensions:	59' W x 56' D
Heated Sq. Ft.:	1,818
Bonus Sq. Ft.:	1,507
Bedrooms: 3	Bathrooms: 2
Exterior Walls:	2" x 6"

Foundation: Basement or walk-out basement, please specify when ordering

See index for more information

Images provided by designer/architect

GRILLING DECK 6' x 12'
COVERED DECK 14' x 12'
GREAT ROOM 21'-3" x 16'
BED 1 16'-5" x 14'
BED 3 10'-6" x 11'
DINING 11' x 11'
TILE SHWR 5' x 5'
KITCHEN 12'-10" x 13'-4"
MUD 9'-3" x 8'-8"
WIC 10' x 6'
FOYER
BED 2 11' x 11'
WIC
PORCH
3-CAR GARAGE 33' x 25'-4"

© Copyright by designer/architect

First Floor
1,818 sq. ft.

PATIO 20' x 12'
FAMILY ROOM 25'-3" x 16'-9"
BED 4 12'-5" x 12'
FLEX SPACE 24'-3" x 11'-2"
WET BAR
MECH / STORAGE
BED 5 12' x 12'
FLEX ROOM 15'-7" x 14'-5"

Optional Lower Level
1,507 sq. ft.

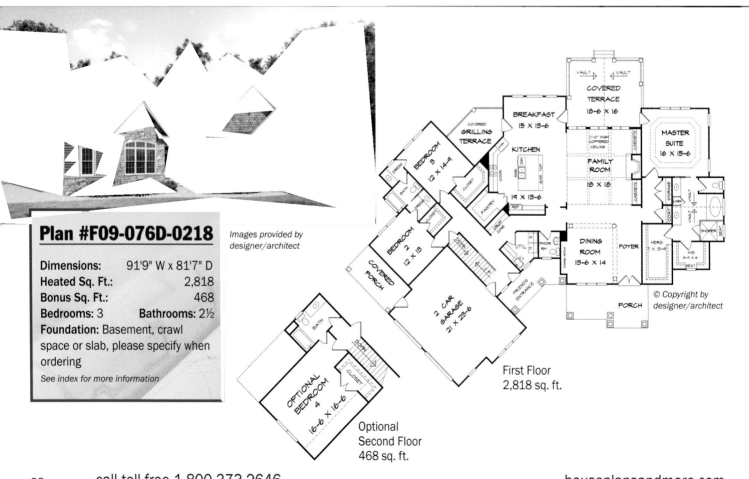

Plan #F09-076D-0218

Images provided by designer/architect

Dimensions:	91'9" W x 81'7" D
Heated Sq. Ft.:	2,818
Bonus Sq. Ft.:	468
Bedrooms: 3	Bathrooms: 2½

Foundation: Basement, crawl space or slab, please specify when ordering

See index for more information

VAULT VAULT
COVERED TERRACE 18-6 X 16
BREAKFAST 15 X 13-6
COVERED GRILLING TERRACE
KITCHEN
MASTER SUITE 16 X 15-6
11'-0" HIGH COFFERED CEILING
CABINETS
BEDROOM 3 12 X 14-9
CLOSET
PANTRY
FAMILY ROOM 18 X 18
BEDROOM 2 12 X 13
COVERED PORCH
UTIL
PWDR RM
DINING ROOM 13-6 X 14
FOYER
HERS
HIS
FRIENDS ENTRANCE
2 CAR GARAGE 21 X 23-6
PORCH

© Copyright by designer/architect

First Floor
2,818 sq. ft.

BATH
OPTIONAL BEDROOM 4 16-6 X 16-6
CLOSET

Optional Second Floor
468 sq. ft.

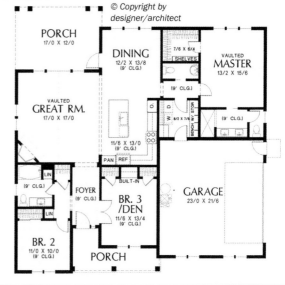

Plan #F09-011D-0660

Dimensions: 52' W x 53' D
Heated Sq. Ft.: 1,704
Bedrooms: 3   **Bathrooms:** 2½
Exterior Walls: 2" x 6"
Foundation: Joisted continuous footings or post & beam standard; slab for an additional fee

See index for more information

Images provided by designer/architect

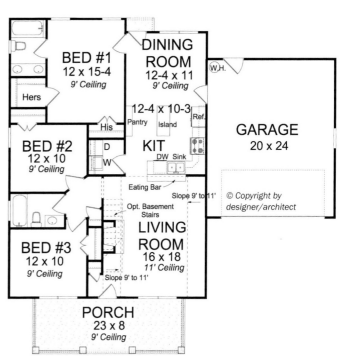

© Copyright by designer/architect

Plan #F09-130D-0367

Dimensions: 51' W x 50' D
Heated Sq. Ft.: 1,277
Bedrooms: 3   **Bathrooms:** 2
Foundation: Slab standard; crawl space or basement for an additional

See index for more information

Images provided by designer/architect

Plan #F09-032D-1135

Dimensions:	65' W x 50' D
Heated Sq. Ft.:	1,788
Bonus Sq. Ft.:	1,788
Bedrooms: 2	Bathrooms: 2
Exterior Walls:	2" x 6"

Foundation: Basement standard; crawl space, floating slab or monolithic slab for an additional fee

See index for more information

Images provided by designer/architect

Features

- Stylish one-level living offering an open modern feel that is easy to come home to
- Directly off the foyer is the office/den, perfect for easy access with business associates
- The master suite enjoys his and hers walk-in closets that lead to a posh private bath
- The kitchen has an open feel to the nearby dining room and beyond to the living room featuring a cozy fireplace
- A handy mud room connects the garage to the rest of the home
- The optional lower level has an additional 1,788 square feet of living area
- 2-car front entry garage

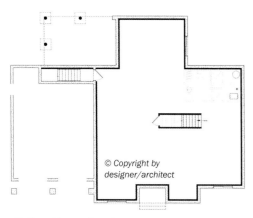

© Copyright by designer/architect

Optional Lower Level
1,788 sq. ft.

First Floor
1,788 sq. ft.

Plan #F09-011D-0627

Dimensions:	52' W x 61' D
Heated Sq. Ft.:	1,878
Bedrooms: 3	Bathrooms: 2
Exterior Walls:	2" x 6"

Foundation: Joisted crawl space standard; slab for an additional fee

See index for more information

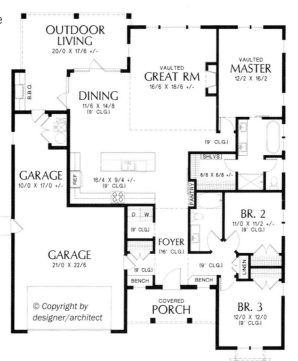

Features

- Upon entering the foyer that is flanked by benches, there is a soaring 16' ceiling allowing for plenty of natural light to enter the space
- Beautiful family-friendly design with a centrally located great room, dining room and kitchen combination and the sleeping quarters in a private wing
- The master suite is complete with the amenities of a walk-in closet, a double-bowl vanity and separate tub and shower units in the private bath
- Enjoy outdoor living on the covered rear patio that has a built-in barbecue grill and cabinets for ease when cooking outdoors
- 2-car front entry garage

Images provided by designer/architect

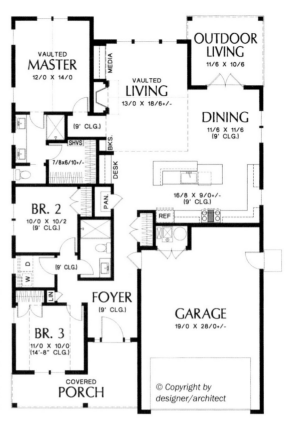

Plan #F09-011D-0674

Dimensions:	40' W x 60'6" D
Heated Sq. Ft.:	1,552
Bedrooms: 3	Bathrooms: 2
Exterior Walls:	2" x 6"

Foundation: Crawl space standard; slab or basement for an additional fee

See index for more information

Images provided by designer/architect

Plan #F09-169D-0001

Dimensions:	50' W x 30' D
Heated Sq. Ft.:	1,400
Bedrooms: 3	Bathrooms: 2
Foundation:	Crawl space

See index for more information

Images provided by designer/architect

© Copyright by designer/architect

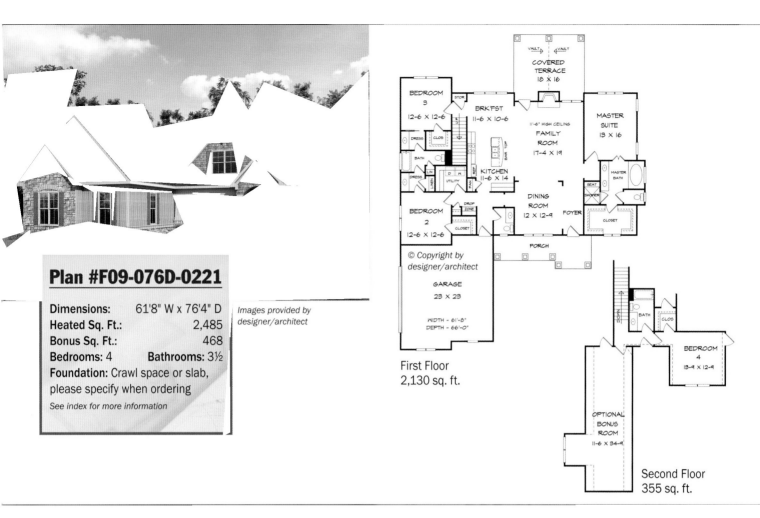

Plan #F09-076D-0221

Dimensions:	61'8" W x 76'4" D
Heated Sq. Ft.:	2,485
Bonus Sq. Ft.:	468
Bedrooms: 4	Bathrooms: 3½

Foundation: Crawl space or slab, please specify when ordering

See index for more information

Images provided by designer/architect

First Floor
2,130 sq. ft.

Second Floor
355 sq. ft.

© Copyright by designer/architect

Plan #F09-156D-0014

Dimensions:	25' W x 28' D
Heated Sq. Ft.:	551
Bedrooms: 1	Bathrooms: 1
Foundation:	Slab

See index for more information

Images provided by designer/architect

© Copyright by designer/architect

Plan #F09-101D-0056

Dimensions:	72' W x 77' D
Heated Sq. Ft.:	2,593
Bonus Sq. Ft.:	1,892
Bedrooms: 2	Bathrooms: 2½
Exterior Walls:	2" x 6"
Foundation:	Walk-out basement

See index for more information

Features

- This stunning home has the look and feel homeowners love with its sleek interior and open floor plan
- The great room, kitchen and dining area combine maximizing the square footage and making these spaces functional and comfortable
- The master bedroom enjoys a first floor location adding convenience for the homeowners
- The optional lower level has an additional 1,892 square feet of living area and adds extra amenities like a media area, billiards space, recreation and exercise rooms
- 3-car front entry garage

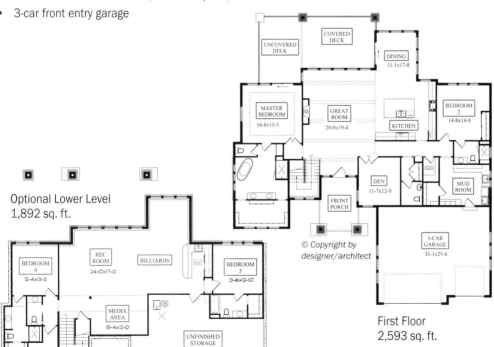

Optional Lower Level
1,892 sq. ft.

BEDROOM 4
12-4x13-3

REC ROOM
24-0x17-0

BILLIARDS

BEDROOM 3
13-6x12-10

MEDIA AREA
15-4x12-0

UNFINISHED STORAGE

EXERCISE ROOM
13-8x12-0

UNCOVERED DECK

COVERED DECK

DINING
11-1x17-8

MASTER BEDROOM
16-8x15-5

GREAT ROOM
20-0x19-0

KITCHEN

BEDROOM 2
14-8x14-8

DEN
11-7x12-9

MUD ROOM

FRONT PORCH

3-CAR GARAGE
31-1x25-6

© Copyright by designer/architect

First Floor
2,593 sq. ft.

Images provided by designer/architect

Plan #F09-150D-0007

Dimensions:	88'6" W x 58'3" D
Heated Sq. Ft.:	2,901
Bedrooms: 3	Bathrooms: 2½
Exterior Walls:	SIP
Foundation:	Basement

See index for more information

Images provided by designer/architect

Features

- This Craftsman house plan combines elegance with rustic charm and features a magnificent wrap-around timbered porch that opens into the spacious entry area
- The two-story great room is cathedral-like and features a timber-framed area with two balconies, a fireplace, and Palladian windows that fill the room with light
- The formal dining room adjoins the kitchen, which opens to the great room and the sunny breakfast nook
- The secluded master suite features a sloped ceiling and luxurious private bath, with twin walk-in closets and a whirlpool tub
- 2-car side entry garage

© Copyright by designer/architect

First Floor
2,078 sq. ft.

Second Floor
823 sq. ft.

Plan #F09-016D-0105

Dimensions: 81'3" W x 63'8" D
Heated Sq. Ft.: 2,065
Bedrooms: 3   **Bathrooms:** 2½
Foundation: Crawl space or slab
standard; basement for an additional fee

See index for more information

Images provided by designer/architect

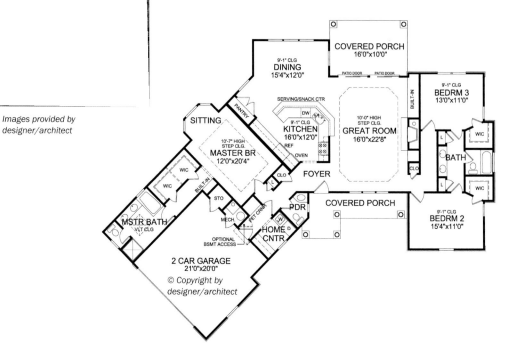

© Copyright by designer/architect

Plan #F09-143D-0003

Dimensions: 70'6" W x 27'4" D
Heated Sq. Ft.: 1,324
Bedrooms: 3   **Bathrooms:** 2
Exterior Walls: 2" x 6"
Foundation: Basement, crawl
space or slab, please specify when
ordering

See index for more information

Images provided by designer/architect

© Copyright by designer/architect

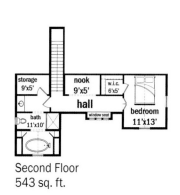

Plan #F09-167D-0002

Dimensions: 74' W x 49'5" D
Heated Sq. Ft.: 2,063
Bedrooms: 3   Bathrooms: 2½
Exterior Walls: 2" x 6"
Foundation: Slab standard; crawl space for an additional fee

See index for more information

Images provided by designer/architect

© Copyright by designer/architect

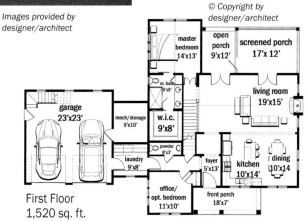

First Floor
1,520 sq. ft.

Second Floor
543 sq. ft.

Plan #F09-091D-0522

Dimensions: 64' W x 60'4" D
Heated Sq. Ft.: 2,148
Bonus Sq. Ft.: 387
Bedrooms: 3   Bathrooms: 2½
Exterior Walls: 2" x 6"
Foundation: Basement or crawl space standard; slab or walk-out basement for an additional fee

See index for more information

Images provided by designer/architect

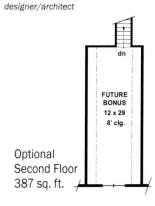

Optional
Second Floor
387 sq. ft.

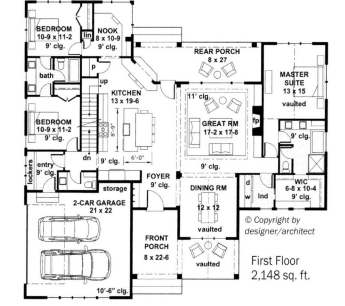

© Copyright by designer/architect

First Floor
2,148 sq. ft.

Plan #F09-101D-0125

Dimensions:	118'3" W x 70' D
Heated Sq. Ft.:	2,970
Bonus Sq. Ft.:	2,014
Bedrooms: 2	Bathrooms: 2½
Exterior Walls:	2" x 6"
Foundation:	Basement

See index for more information

Features

- This rustic modern masterpiece offers an open concept floor plan with the utmost style and distinction
- Step into the foyer and be greeted by an open and expansive great room topped with a stunning ceiling
- The bright and stylish kitchen has a huge island, rustic beams above and plenty of cabinetspace for maintaining a sleek appearance free of clutter
- The first floor master bedroom enjoys a beamed ceiling, covered deck access, a luxury bath and a huge walk-in closet
- A guest room with its own private bath can be found on the opposite side of the first floor from the master bedroom for extra privacy
- The optional lower level has an additional 2,014 square feet of living area including a wet bar with island, a rec room, a game nook, three additional bedrooms, one full bath and a half bath
- 2-car front entry garage, and a 1-car side entry garage

Images provided by designer/architect

Optional Lower Level
2,014 sq. ft.

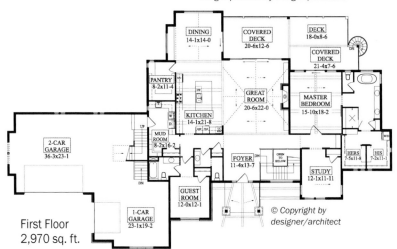

First Floor
2,970 sq. ft.

© Copyright by designer/architect

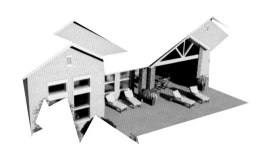

Plan #F09-019S-0008

Dimensions: 104'3" W x 80'8" D
Heated Sq. Ft.: 4,420
Bedrooms: 4
Bathrooms: 4 full, 2 half
Foundation: Slab standard; crawl space or basement for an additional fee

See index for more information

Images provided by designer/architect

© Copyright by designer/architect

Plan #F09-122D-0001

Dimensions: 33' W x 35' D
Heated Sq. Ft.: 1,105
Bedrooms: 2   **Bathrooms:** 1½
Foundation: Slab

See index for more information

Images provided by designer/architect

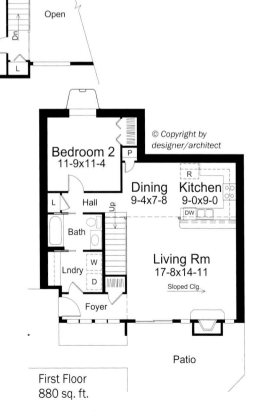

Second Floor
225 sq. ft.

© Copyright by designer/architect

First Floor
880 sq. ft.

Plan #F09-020D-0397

Dimensions:	59' W x 50' D
Heated Sq. Ft.:	1,608
Bedrooms: 3	**Bathrooms:** 2
Exterior Walls:	2" x 6"

Foundation: Crawl space standard; slab for an additional fee

See index for more information

Images provided by designer/architect

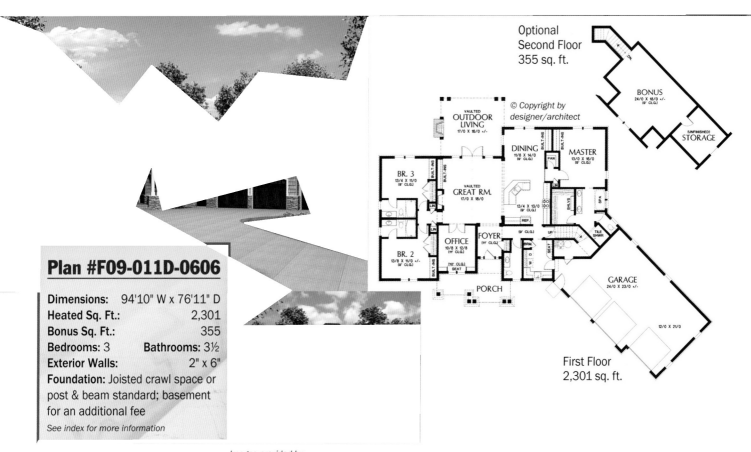

Plan #F09-011D-0606

Dimensions:	94'10" W x 76'11" D
Heated Sq. Ft.:	2,301
Bonus Sq. Ft.:	355
Bedrooms: 3	**Bathrooms:** 3½
Exterior Walls:	2" x 6"

Foundation: Joisted crawl space or post & beam standard; basement for an additional fee

See index for more information

Images provided by designer/architect

Optional Second Floor 355 sq. ft.

First Floor 2,301 sq. ft.

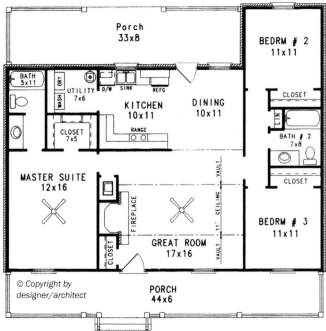

Plan #F09-069D-0006

Dimensions: 44' W x 41' D
Heated Sq. Ft.: 1,277
Bedrooms: 3   **Bathrooms:** 2
Foundation: Crawl space or slab, please specify when ordering

See index for more information

Images provided by designer/architect

Plan #F09-143D-0007

Dimensions: 49'2" W x 47' D
Heated Sq. Ft.: 1,380
Bedrooms: 3   **Bathrooms:** 2
Exterior Walls: 2" x 6"
Foundation: Basement, crawl space or slab, please specify when ordering

See index for more information

Images provided by designer/architect

Plan #F09-152D-0079

Dimensions:	19' W x 27' D
Heated Sq. Ft.:	361
Bedrooms: 1	Bathrooms: 1
Exterior Walls:	2" x 6"
Foundation:	Slab

See index for more information

Images provided by designer/architect

living
18' x 10'

sliding doors

© Copyright by designer/architect

porch
19' x 8'

down

Plan #F09-007D-0159

Dimensions:	27' W x 26' D
Heated Sq. Ft.:	615
Bedrooms: 1	Bathrooms: 1
Foundation:	Slab

See index for more information

Images provided by designer/architect

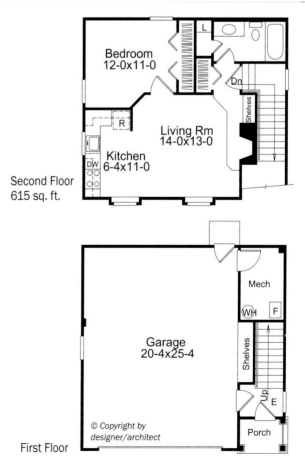

Second Floor
615 sq. ft.

Bedroom
12-0x11-0

Living Rm
14-0x13-0

Kitchen
6-4x11-0

Mech

Garage
20-4x25-4

Shelves

Porch

© Copyright by designer/architect

First Floor

Plan #F09-051D-0970

Dimensions:	37' W x 68' D
Heated Sq. Ft.:	1,354
Bedrooms: 2	**Bathrooms:** 2
Exterior Walls:	2" x 6"

Foundation: Basement standard; crawl space or slab for an additional fee

See index for more information

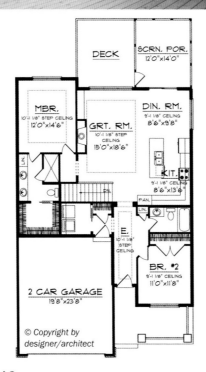

Features

- Small and stylish, this home offers the layout everyone loves in an easy-to-maintain size
- The covered front porch is large enough for relaxing, while the rear has a screened porch with access onto an open deck, perfect when grilling
- The private master bedroom has a private bath with an oversized walk-in shower, a double-bowl vanity, and a spacious walk-in closet
- Bedroom 2 is just steps away from a full bath
- 2-car front entry garage

Images provided by designer/architect

DECK

SCRN. POR.
12'0"x14'0"

MBR.
10'-1 1/8" STEP CEILING
12'0"x14'6"

GRT. RM.
10'-1 1/8" STEP CEILING
15'0"x18'6"

DIN. RM.
9'-1 1/8" CEILING
8'6"x9'8"

KIT.
9'-1 1/8" CEILING
8'6"x13'6"

PAN.

E.
10'-1 1/8" STEP CEILING

BR. #2
9'-1 1/8" CEILING
11'0"x11'8"

2 CAR GARAGE
19'8"x23'8"

© Copyright by designer/architect

Plan #F09-011D-0013

Dimensions:	60' W x 50' D
Heated Sq. Ft.:	2,001
Bedrooms: 3	Bathrooms: 2
Exterior Walls:	2" x 6"

Foundation: Joisted crawl space, post & beam, or TrusJoist floor system standard; slab or basement for an additional fee

Features

- A large wrap-around counter with breakfast bar in the kitchen is accessible from the dining area and the great room
- Double-doors keep the den secluded from the other living areas maintaining privacy
- Decorative columns adorn the entry leading into the vaulted great room with fireplace and optional corner media center
- The vaulted master bedroom has a walk-in closet and a private bath with a spa style tub
- 3-car front entry tandem garage

Images provided by designer/architect

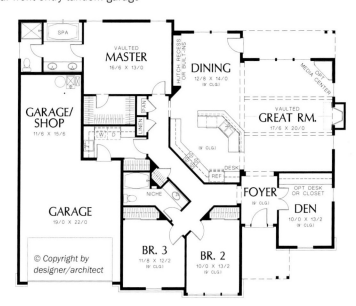

© Copyright by designer/architect

Second Floor
546 sq. ft.

Images provided by designer/architect

Plan #F09-141D-0233

Dimensions: 38'2" W x 38'6" D
Heated Sq. Ft.: 1,835
Bonus Sq. Ft.: 600
Bedrooms: 3   **Bathrooms:** 2½
Foundation: Basement standard; crawl space, slab or walk-out basement for an additional fee

See index for more information

Optional Lower Level
600 sq. ft.

First Floor
1,289 sq. ft.

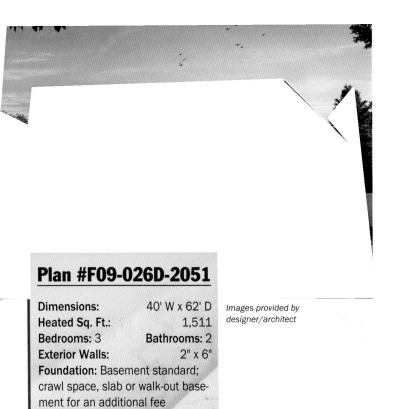

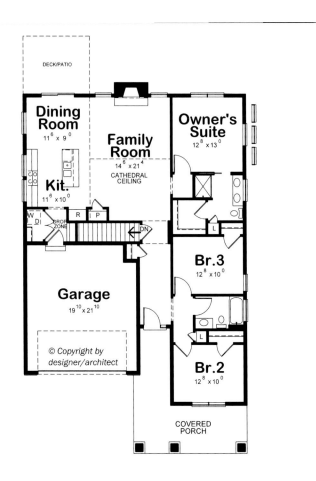

Plan #F09-026D-2051

Dimensions: 40' W x 62' D
Heated Sq. Ft.: 1,511
Bedrooms: 3   **Bathrooms:** 2
Exterior Walls: 2" x 6"
Foundation: Basement standard; crawl space, slab or walk-out basement for an additional fee

See index for more information

Images provided by designer/architect

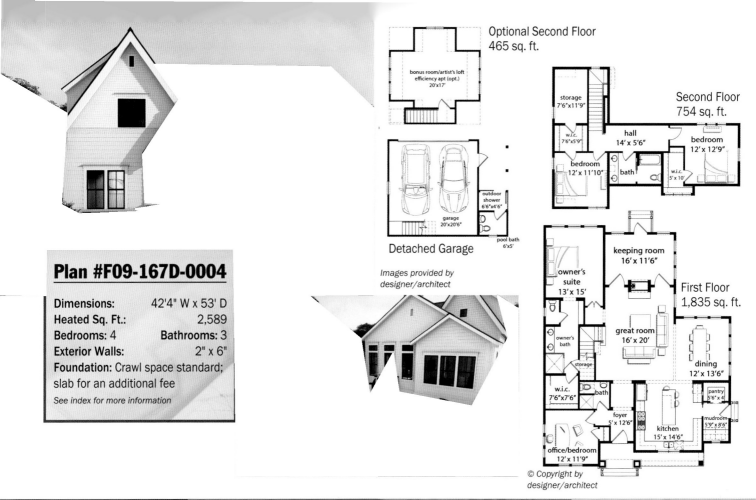

Optional Second Floor
465 sq. ft.

bonus room/artist's loft
efficiency apt (opt.)
20'x17'

Detached Garage

outdoor shower
6'6"x4'6"

garage
20'x20'6"

pool bath
6'x5'

Second Floor
754 sq. ft.

storage
7'6"x11'9"

w.i.c.
7'6"x5'9"

hall
14' x 5'6"

bedroom
12' x 12'9"

bedroom
12' x 11'10"

bath

w.i.c.
5'x10'

Images provided by designer/architect

First Floor
1,835 sq. ft.

owner's suite
13' x 15'

keeping room
16' x 11'6"

owner's bath

great room
16' x 20'

storage

dining
12' x 13'6"

w.i.c.
7'6"x7'6"

bath

pantry
5'6" x 4'

foyer
5' x 12'6"

kitchen
15' x 14'6"

mudroom
5'9" x 8'6"

office/bedroom
12' x 11'9"

© Copyright by designer/architect

Plan #F09-167D-0004

Dimensions: 42'4" W x 53' D
Heated Sq. Ft.: 2,589
Bedrooms: 4   Bathrooms: 3
Exterior Walls: 2" x 6"
Foundation: Crawl space standard; slab for an additional fee

See index for more information

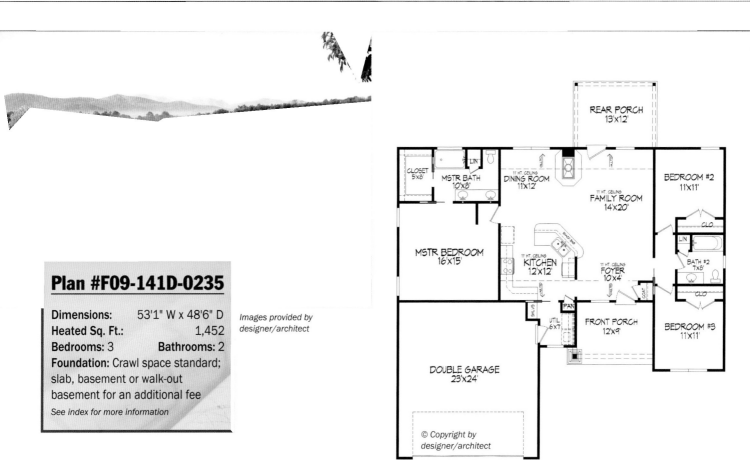

REAR PORCH
13'x12'

CLOSET
5'x8'

MSTR BATH
10'x8'

DINING ROOM
11'x12'

FAMILY ROOM
14'x20'

BEDROOM #2
11'x11'

CLO

MSTR BEDROOM
16'x15'

KITCHEN
12'x12'

FOYER
10'x4'

LIN

BATH #2
7'x8'

UTIL
6'x7'

FRONT PORCH
12'x9'

BEDROOM #3
11'x11'

DOUBLE GARAGE
23'x24'

© Copyright by designer/architect

Plan #F09-141D-0235

Dimensions: 53'1" W x 48'6" D
Heated Sq. Ft.: 1,452
Bedrooms: 3   Bathrooms: 2
Foundation: Crawl space standard; slab, basement or walk-out basement for an additional fee

See index for more information

Images provided by designer/architect

Plan #F09-163D-0003

Dimensions:	56' W x 40' D
Heated Sq. Ft.:	1,416
Bedrooms: 3	Bathrooms: 2
Exterior Walls:	2" x 6"
Foundation:	Crawl space

See index for more information

Images provided by designer/architect

Features

- Covered front and back porches are large enough to enjoy the outdoors in comfort
- The great room is open to both the kitchen and dining area on the left side of the house for an open, airy feel
- All three bedrooms are located on the right side of the house with the master suite having a private sitting porch
- The laundry room is conveniently located just off of the kitchen

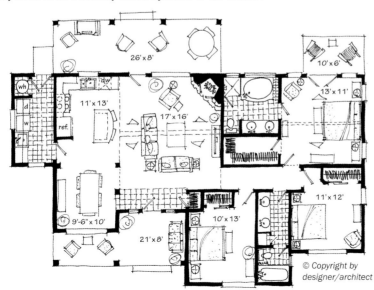

© Copyright by designer/architect

Plan #F09-024S-0021

Dimensions:	80' W x 66' D
Heated Sq. Ft.:	5,862
Bedrooms: 6	**Bathrooms:** 5

Foundation: Basement or pier, please specify when ordering

See index for more information

Features

- Decorative columns line the perimeter of the formal dining room for an elegant, open feel
- The family room enjoys a vaulted ceiling for a spacious atmosphere
- The master bedroom features a private sitting area that leads to the covered porch
- One of the second floor bedrooms has direct access to a private balcony
- This plan features an above ground basement option
- 3-car drive under side entry garage

Second Floor
901 sq. ft.

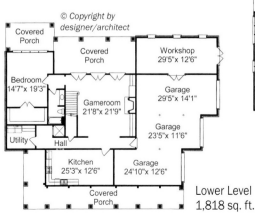

© Copyright by designer/architect

Lower Level
1,818 sq. ft.

First Floor
3,143 sq. ft.

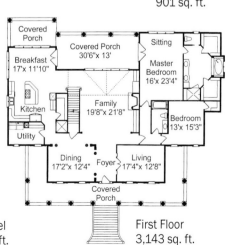

Images provided by designer/architect

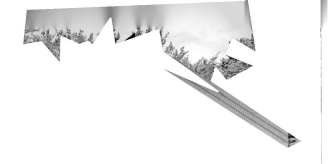

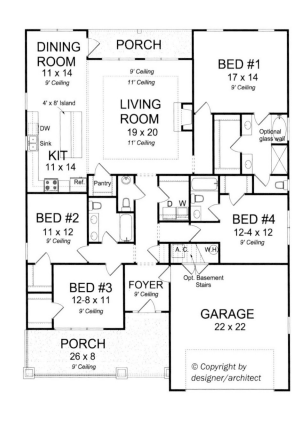

8'-6"x12'-0"
2,59x3,66

12'-6"x12'-0"
3,81x3,66

16'-0"x12'-0"
4,88x3,66

© Copyright by
designer/architect

Plan #F09-126D-1012

Dimensions:	30' W x 30' D
Heated Sq. Ft.:	815
Bedrooms: 1	Bathrooms: 1
Exterior Walls:	2" x 6"
Foundation:	Basement

See index for more information

*Images provided by
designer/architect*

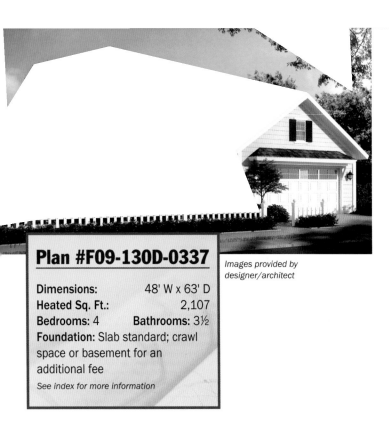

Plan #F09-130D-0337

*Images provided by
designer/architect*

Dimensions:	48' W x 63' D
Heated Sq. Ft.:	2,107
Bedrooms: 4	Bathrooms: 3½
Foundation:	Slab standard; crawl space or basement for an additional fee

See index for more information

DINING ROOM
11 x 14
9' Ceiling

PORCH
9' Ceiling

11' Ceiling

BED #1
17 x 14
9' Ceiling

4' x 8' Island

DW

Sink

KIT
11 x 14

LIVING ROOM
19 x 20
11' Ceiling

Optional glass wall

Ref. Pantry

BED #2
11 x 12
9' Ceiling

D W

BED #4
12-4 x 12
9' Ceiling

A. C. W.H.

BED #3
12-8 x 11
9' Ceiling

FOYER
9' Ceiling

Opt. Basement Stairs

GARAGE
22 x 22

PORCH
26 x 8
9' Ceiling

© Copyright by
designer/architect

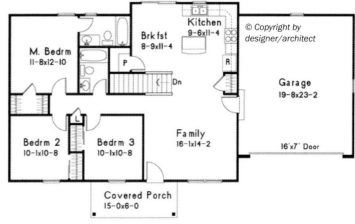

© Copyright by designer/architect

Kitchen 9-6x11-4

Brk fst 8-9x11-4

M. Bedrm 11-8x12-10

P

Dn

Garage 19-8x23-2

Bedrm 2 10-1x10-8

L

Bedrm 3 10-1x10-8

Family 16-1x14-2

16'x7' Door

Covered Porch 15-0x6-0

Plan #F09-058D-0231

Dimensions:	60' W x 36' D
Heated Sq. Ft.:	1,158
Bedrooms: 3	**Bathrooms:** 2
Foundation:	Basement

See index for more information

Images provided by designer/architect

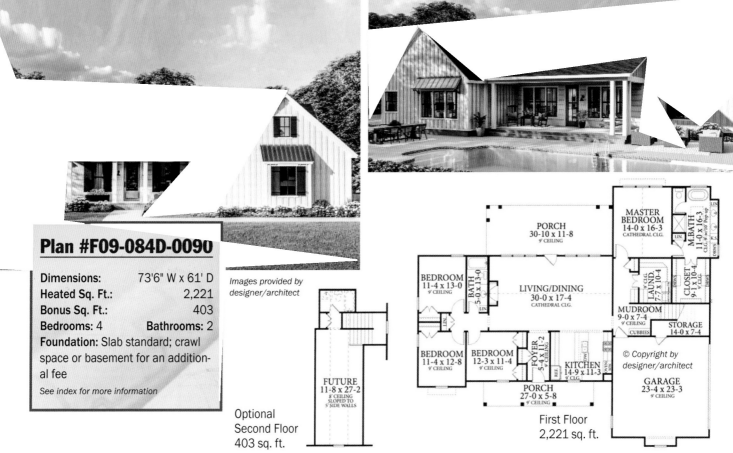

Plan #F09-084D-0090

Dimensions:	73'6" W x 61' D
Heated Sq. Ft.:	2,221
Bonus Sq. Ft.:	403
Bedrooms: 4	**Bathrooms:** 2
Foundation:	Slab standard; crawl space or basement for an additional fee

See index for more information

Images provided by designer/architect

FUTURE 11-8 x 27-2
8' CEILING SLOPED TO 5' SIDE WALLS

Optional Second Floor 403 sq. ft.

MASTER BEDROOM 14-0 x 16-3 CATHEDRAL CLG.

M.BATH 11-0 x 16-3

PORCH 30-10 x 11-8 9' CEILING

BEDROOM 11-4 x 13-0 9' CEILING

BATH 5-0 x 13-0

LIVING/DINING 30-0 x 17-4 CATHEDRAL CLG.

LAUND. 7-7 x 10-4

CLOSET 9-1 x 10-4

BEDROOM 11-4 x 12-8 9' CEILING

BEDROOM 12-3 x 11-4 9' CEILING

FOYER 5-4 x 11-2 9' CEILING

KITCHEN 14-9 x 11-3

MUDROOM 9-0 x 7-4 9' CEILING

STORAGE 14-0 x 7-4

© Copyright by designer/architect

PORCH 27-0 x 5-8 9' CEILING

GARAGE 23-4 x 23-3 9' CEILING

First Floor 2,221 sq. ft.

Plan #F09-077D-0058

Dimensions: 64'6" W x 61'4" D
Heated Sq. Ft.: 2,002
Bedrooms: 3   **Bathrooms:** 2
Exterior Walls: 2" x 6"
Foundation: Slab, crawl space or basement, please specify when ordering

See index for more information

Images provided by designer/architect

© Copyright by designer/architect

Plan #F09-032D-1124

Dimensions: 66' W x 50' D
Heated Sq. Ft.: 2,117
Bonus Sq. Ft.: 360
Bedrooms: 3   **Bathrooms:** 2
Exterior Walls: 2" x 6"
Foundation: Crawl space standard; basement, floating slab or monolithic slab for an additional fee

See index for more information

Images provided by designer/architect

Optional
Second Floor
360 sq. ft.

First Floor
2,117 sq. ft.

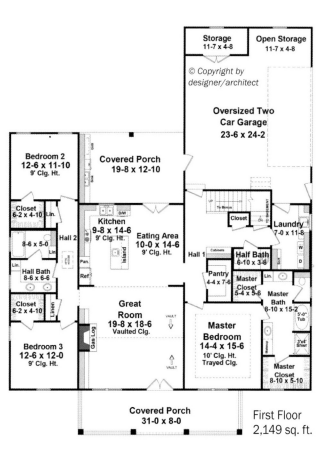

Plan #F09-077D-0291

Dimensions: 57' W x 74' D
Heated Sq. Ft.: 2,149
Bonus Sq. Ft.: 429
Bedrooms: 3 **Bathrooms:** 2½
Foundation: Slab, crawl or basement, please specify when ordering
See index for more information

Images provided by designer/architect

Storage 11-7 x 4-8

Open Storage 11-7 x 4-8

© Copyright by designer/architect

Oversized Two Car Garage 23-6 x 24-2

Bedroom 2 12-6 x 11-10 9' Clg. Ht.

Covered Porch 19-8 x 12-10

Closet 6-2 x 4-10

Kitchen 9-8 x 14-6 9' Clg. Ht.

Eating Area 10-0 x 14-6 9' Clg. Ht.

Laundry 7-0 x 11-8

Hall Bath 8-6 x 5-0

Half Bath 6-10 x 3-6

Master Closet 5-4 x 5-6

Master Bath 8-10 x 15-2

Hall Bath 8-6 x 6-6

Pantry 4-4 x 7-6

Closet 6-2 x 4-10

Great Room 19-8 x 18-6 Vaulted Clg.

Master Bedroom 14-4 x 15-6 10' Clg. Ht. Trayed Clg.

Bedroom 3 12-6 x 12-0 9' Clg. Ht.

Master Closet 8-10 x 5-10

Bonus Room 13-0 x 22-6 8' Clg. Ht.

Bonus Bath 7-2 x 8-10

Optional Second Floor 429 sq. ft.

Covered Porch 31-0 x 8-0

First Floor 2,149 sq. ft.

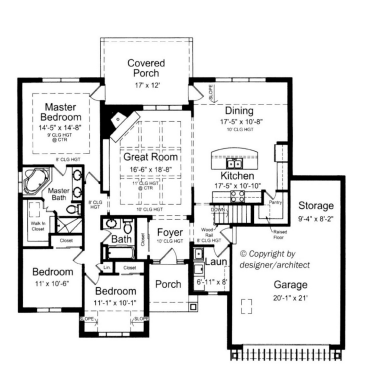

Plan #F09-065D-0355

Dimensions: 60' W x 55'1" D
Heated Sq. Ft.: 1,791
Bedrooms: 3 **Bathrooms:** 2
Foundation: Basement
See index for more information

Images provided by designer/architect

Covered Porch 17' x 12'

Master Bedroom 14'-5" x 14'-8" 9' CLG HGT @ CTR 8' CLG HGT

Dining 17'-5" x 10'-8" 10' CLG HGT

Great Room 16'-6" x 18'-8" 11' CLG HGT @ CTR 10' CLG HGT

Kitchen 17'-5" x 10'-10"

Master Bath

Walk In Closet

Storage 9'-4" x 8'-2"

Bath

Foyer 10' CLG HGT

© Copyright by designer/architect

Bedroom 11' x 10'-6"

Bedroom 11'-1" x 10'-1"

Porch

Laun 6'-11" x 8'

Garage 20'-1" x 21'

Plan #F09-121D-0028

Dimensions: 36' W x 54' D
Heated Sq. Ft.: 1,433
Bedrooms: 2 **Bathrooms:** 2
Foundation: Basement standard; crawl space or slab for an additional fee

See index for more information

Images provided by designer/architect

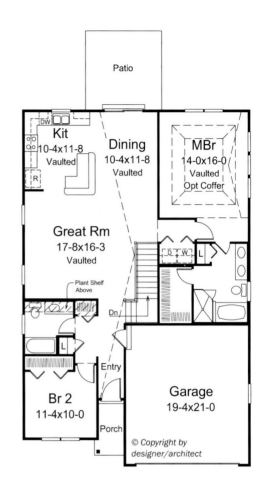

Patio

Kit 10-4x11-8 Vaulted

Dining 10-4x11-8 Vaulted

MBr 14-0x16-0 Vaulted Opt Coffer

Great Rm 17-8x16-3 Vaulted

Plant Shelf Above

Dn

Br 2 11-4x10-0

Entry

Porch

Garage 19-4x21-0

Plan #F09-011D-0307

Dimensions: 40' W x 57' D
Heated Sq. Ft.: 1,529
Bedrooms: 3 **Bathrooms:** 2
Exterior Walls: 2" x 6"
Foundation: Joisted crawl space or post & beam standard; slab or basement for an additional fee

See index for more information

Images provided by designer/architect

VAULTED **MASTER** 12/0 X 14/6

MEDIA
TV OVER

VAULTED **OUTDOOR LIVING** 11/6 X 10/0

LIVING 13/0 X 18/0 (11' CLG.)

DINING 11/6 X 11/6 (9' CLG.)

BKS
BUILT-IN

(9' CLG.)

SHLVS

PAN

16/8 X 9/0 + (9' CLG.)

O. REF

BR. 2 10/0 X 10/2 (9' CLG.)

FOYER (9' CLG.)

GARAGE 19/0 X 22/0 +/-

BR. 3 11/0 X 10/0 (9' CLG.)

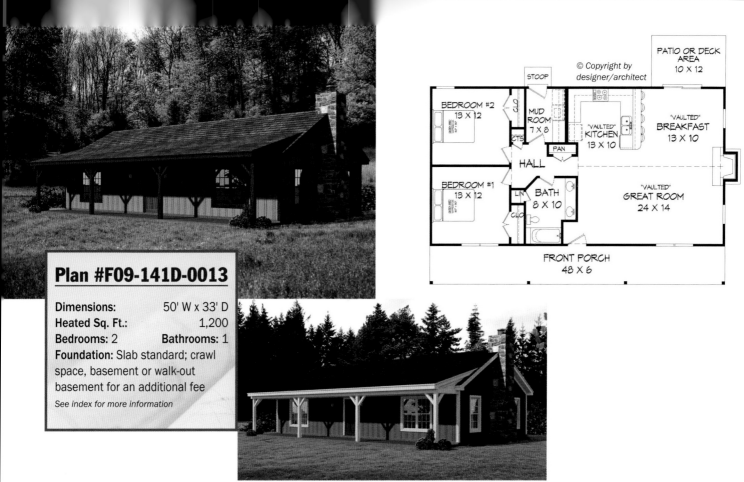

Plan #F09-141D-0013

Dimensions: 50' W x 33' D
Heated Sq. Ft.: 1,200
Bedrooms: 2 **Bathrooms:** 1
Foundation: Slab standard; crawl space, basement or walk-out basement for an additional fee
See index for more information

Images provided by designer/architect

Plan #F09-051D-0859

Dimensions: 60' W x 56' D
Heated Sq. Ft.: 1,850
Bedrooms: 2 **Bathrooms:** 2½
Exterior Walls: 2" x 6"
Foundation: Basement standard; crawl space or slab for an additional fee
See index for more information

Images provided by designer/architect

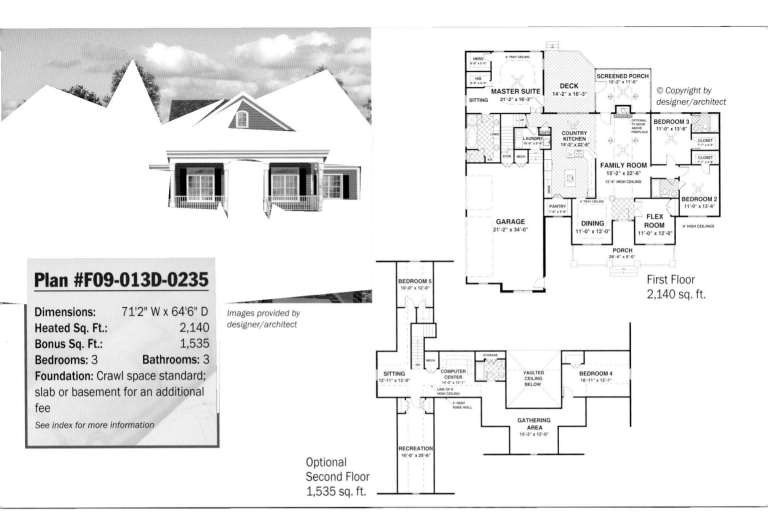

Plan #F09-013D-0235

Dimensions:	71'2" W x 64'6" D
Heated Sq. Ft.:	2,140
Bonus Sq. Ft.:	1,535
Bedrooms: 3	Bathrooms: 3

Foundation: Crawl space standard; slab or basement for an additional fee

See index for more information

Images provided by designer/architect

First Floor
2,140 sq. ft.

Optional
Second Floor
1,535 sq. ft.

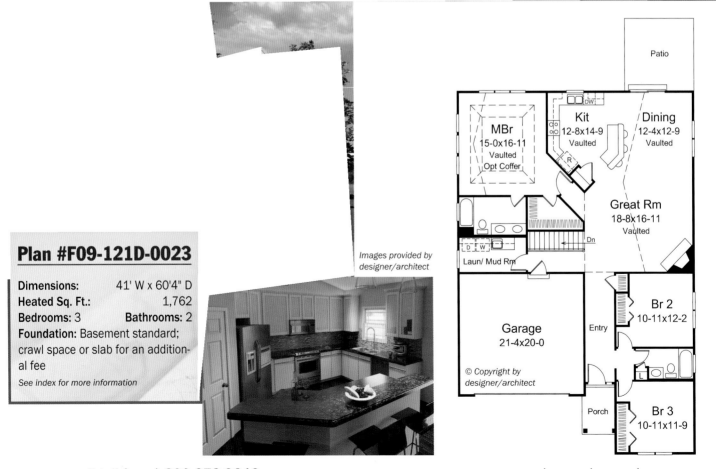

Plan #F09-121D-0023

Dimensions:	41' W x 60'4" D
Heated Sq. Ft.:	1,762
Bedrooms: 3	Bathrooms: 2

Foundation: Basement standard; crawl space or slab for an additional fee

See index for more information

Images provided by designer/architect

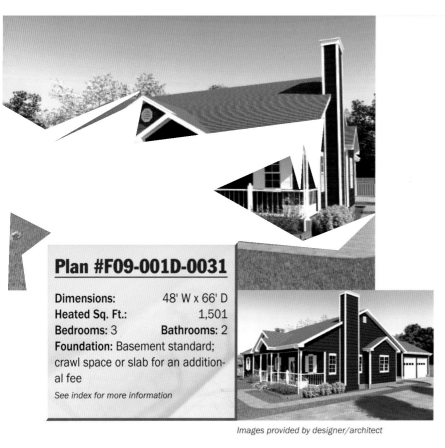

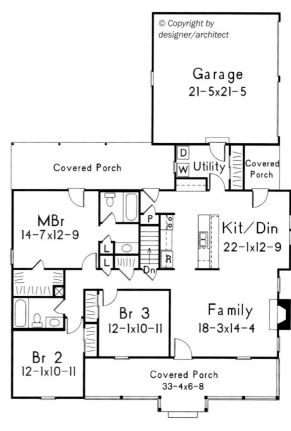

© Copyright by designer/architect

Garage
21-5x21-5

Covered Porch

Utility

Covered Porch

MBr
14-7x12-9

Kit/Din
22-1x12-9

Br 3
12-1x10-11

Family
18-3x14-4

Br 2
12-1x10-11

Covered Porch
33-4x6-8

Plan #F09-001D-0031

Dimensions:	48' W x 66' D
Heated Sq. Ft.:	1,501
Bedrooms: 3	**Bathrooms:** 2

Foundation: Basement standard; crawl space or slab for an additional fee

See index for more information

Images provided by designer/architect

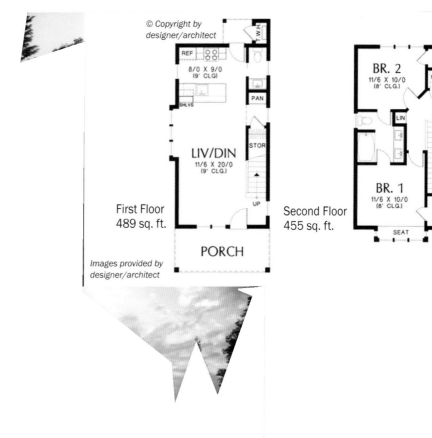

© Copyright by designer/architect

REF
8/0 X 9/0
(9' CLG.)

PAN

SHLVS

LIV/DIN
11/6 X 20/0
(9' CLG.)

STOR

UP

First Floor
489 sq. ft.

PORCH

BR. 2
11/6 X 10/0
(8' CLG.)

W/D

LIN

DN.

BR. 1
11/6 X 10/0
(8' CLG.)

SEAT

Second Floor
455 sq. ft.

Images provided by designer/architect

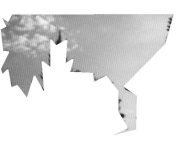

Plan #F09-011D-0683

Dimensions:	17' W x 41' D
Heated Sq. Ft.:	944
Bedrooms: 2	**Bathrooms:** 1½
Exterior Walls:	2" x 6"

Foundation: Crawl space standard; slab or basement for an additional fee

See index for more information

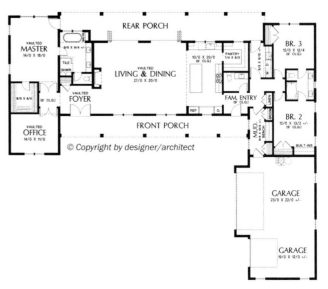

Images provided by designer/architect

REAR PORCH

VAULTED
MASTER
14/0 X 18/0

VAULTED
LIVING & DINING
27/0 X 20/0

10/0 X 20/0
(9' CLG.)

PANTRY
7/4 X 8/0

BR. 3
12/0 X 12/4
(9' CLG.)

VAULTED
FOYER

FAM. ENTRY
(9' CLG.)

BR. 2
12/0 X 13/2 +/-
(9' CLG.)

VAULTED
OFFICE
14/0 X 11/0

FRONT PORCH

MUD.

BUILT-INS

© Copyright by designer/architect

GARAGE
23/0 X 22/0 +/-

GARAGE
19/0 X 12/0 +/-

Plan #F09-141D-0031

Dimensions: 65' W x 64'6" D
Heated Sq. Ft.: 2,100
Bedrooms: 3   Bathrooms: 2½
Foundation: Slab standard; crawl space, basement or walk-out basement for an additional fee
See index for more information

Images provided by designer/architect

'VAULTED'
REAR PORCH
16 x 7

BREAKFAST
10 x 12

BEDROOM #2
12 x 11

'TRAY CEILING'
MASTER BEDROOM
14 x 15

'VAULTED'
FAMILY ROOM
16 x 19

KITCHEN
13 x 16

CLOSET
6 x 4

HALL

BATH #2
6 x 8

SINGLE GARAGE
11 x 22

'VAULTED'
MASTER
BATH
7 x 16

1/2
BATH

HALL

BUTLER'S
PANTRY

SHOWER
7 x 5

FOYER
5 x 13

WALK-IN
PANTRY
6 x 5

CLOSET
6 x 4

LOCKERS
/ BENCH

HALL

BEDROOM #3
12 x 12

'TRAY CEILING'
DINING
11 x 13

UTILITY
6 x 8

13 x 7
CLOSET

'VAULTED'

'VAULTED'
FRONT PORCH
17 x 8

© Copyright by
designer/architect

DOUBLE GARAGE
21 x 20

STORAGE
10 x 2

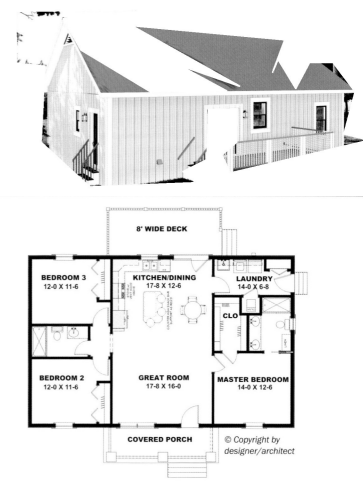

Plan #F09-028D-0100

Dimensions:	46' W x 42'6" D
Heated Sq. Ft.:	1,311
Bedrooms: 3	Bathrooms: 2
Exterior Walls:	2" x 6"

Foundation: Crawl space or slab, please specify when ordering

See index for more information

Images provided by designer/architect

8' WIDE DECK

BEDROOM 3
12-0 X 11-6

KITCHEN/DINING
17-8 X 12-6

LAUNDRY
14-0 X 6-8

CLO

BEDROOM 2
12-0 X 11-6

GREAT ROOM
17-8 X 16-0

MASTER BEDROOM
14-0 X 12-6

COVERED PORCH

© Copyright by designer/architect

Plan #F09-130D-0366

Dimensions:	38' W x 52' D
Heated Sq. Ft.:	1,720
Bedrooms: 3	Bathrooms: 2½

Foundation: Slab standard; crawl space or basement for an additional fee

Please see the index for more information

Images provided by designer/architect

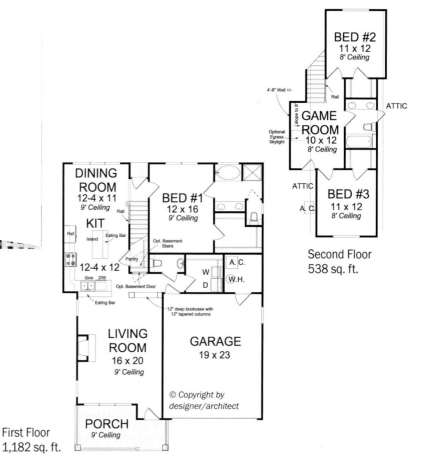

BED #2
11 x 12
8' Ceiling

4'-8" Wall +/-

Rail

ATTIC

Optional Egress Skylight

GAME ROOM
10 x 12
8' Ceiling

slope to 8'

ATTIC

A.C.

BED #3
11 x 12
8' Ceiling

Second Floor
538 sq. ft.

DINING ROOM
12-4 x 11
9' Ceiling

KIT

Ref.

Island Eating Bar

12-4 x 12

Sink DW

Eating Bar

Pantry

Rail

BED #1
12 x 16
9' Ceiling

Opt. Basement Stairs

Opt. Basement Door

W D

A. C.

W.H.

12" deep bookcase with 12" tapered columns

LIVING ROOM
16 x 20
9' Ceiling

GARAGE
19 x 23

© Copyright by designer/architect

PORCH
9' Ceiling

First Floor
1,182 sq. ft.

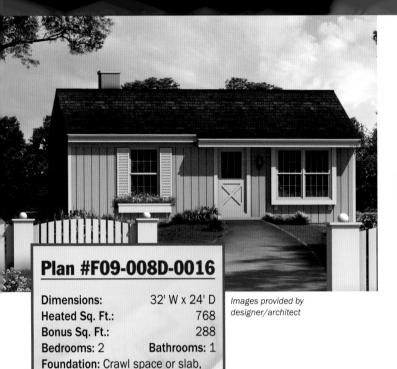

Plan #F09-008D-0016

Dimensions:	32' W x 24' D
Heated Sq. Ft.:	768
Bonus Sq. Ft.:	288
Bedrooms: 2	**Bathrooms: 1**

Foundation: Crawl space or slab, please specify when ordering

See index for more information

Images provided by designer/architect

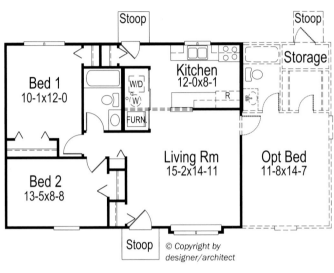

© Copyright by designer/architect

Plan #F09-167D-0001

Dimensions:	59'6" W x 60' D
Heated Sq. Ft.:	2,017
Bedrooms: 3	**Bathrooms: 3**
Exterior Walls:	2" x 6"

Foundation: Crawl space standard; slab for an additional fee

See index for more information

Images provided by designer/architect

© Copyright by designer/architect

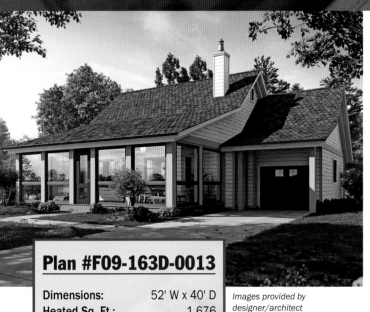

Plan #F09-163D-0013

Dimensions:	52' W x 40' D
Heated Sq. Ft.:	1,676
Bedrooms: 3	Bathrooms: 3
Exterior Walls:	2" x 6"

Foundation: Crawl space or slab, please specify when ordering

See index for more information

Images provided by designer/architect

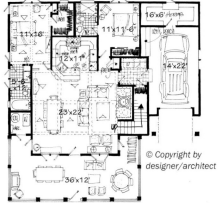

Second Floor
257 sq. ft.

First Floor
1,419 sq. ft.

© Copyright by designer/architect

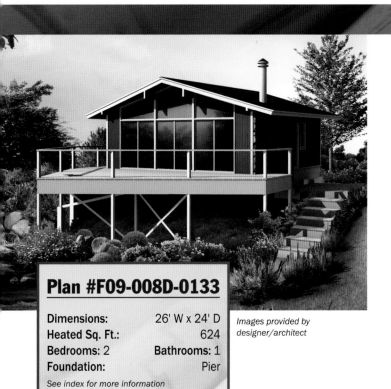

Plan #F09-008D-0133

Dimensions:	26' W x 24' D
Heated Sq. Ft.:	624
Bedrooms: 2	Bathrooms: 1
Foundation:	Pier

See index for more information

Images provided by designer/architect

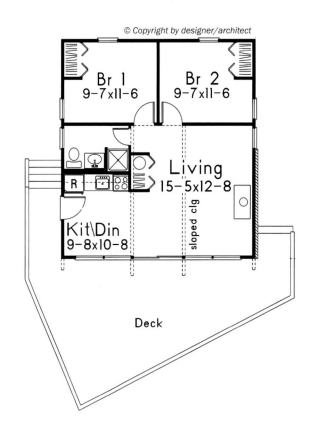

© Copyright by designer/architect

Br 1
9-7x11-6

Br 2
9-7x11-6

Living
15-5x12-8

sloped clg

Kit\Din
9-8x10-8

Deck

Plan #F09-172D-0050

Dimensions:	50'6" W x 52' D
Heated Sq. Ft.:	1,709
Bonus Sq. Ft.:	2,245
Bedrooms: 3	**Bathrooms:** 2
Exterior Walls:	2" x 6"

Foundation: Basement standard; crawl space, monolithic slab, stem wall slab, daylight basement or walk-out basement for an additional fee

See index for more information

Features

- This one-story home has wonderful curb appeal and would fit into any neighborhood
- Step inside and find a large open family room extending off the kitchen and dining area
- The kitchen includes a breakfast bar with dining space
- The laundry room is right around the corner for convenience
- The sunny bayed dining area has access to the backyard
- There's an optional lower level with an additional 2,245 square feet of living area that includes a separate apartment with direct access to the outdoors as well as two additional bedrooms and a family room
- 2-car front entry garage

Images provided by designer/architect

Optional Lower Level
2,245 sq. ft.

First Floor
1,709 sq. ft.

© Copyright by designer/architect

Plan #F09-056D-0125

Dimensions:	82' W x 74'6" D
Heated Sq. Ft.:	2,243
Bonus Sq. Ft.:	1,986
Bedrooms: 3	**Bathrooms:** 2½

Foundation: Basement standard; crawl space or slab for an additional fee

See index for more information

Features

- This European cottage has the ever-popular split bedroom layout
- The vaulted lodge room is completely open to the kitchen and breakfast area making it the focal point of the interior
- The office/dining room is flexible and adapts to your needs
- The optional lower level has an additional 1,499 square feet of living area, while the optional second floor has an additional 487 square feet of living area
- 2-car front entry garage

Optional Second Floor
487 sq. ft.

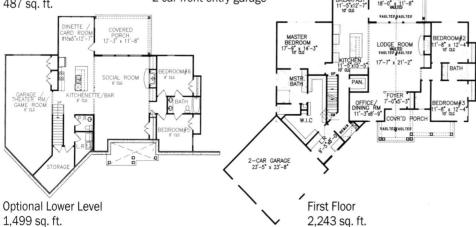

Optional Lower Level
1,499 sq. ft.

First Floor
2,243 sq. ft.

Images provided by designer/architect

Plan #F09-121D-0017

Dimensions: 40' W x 52' D
Heated Sq. Ft.: 1,379
Bedrooms: 2   **Bathrooms:** 1
Foundation: Basement standard; crawl space or slab for an additional fee

Please see the index for more information

Images provided by designer/architect

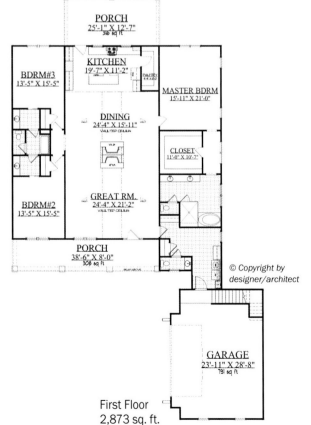

Patio

Opt Invert Vault

MBr
13-4x14-6
Vaulted

Brkfst
11-5x11-11
Vaulted

Plant Shelf

Great Rm
14-0x20-5
Vaulted

DW

Kit
11-5x11-0
Vaulted

R

Dine

Dn

Laun/ Mud Rm

W D

Br 2
13-4x12-10

Entry

Porch

Garage
20-4x21-8

© Copyright by designer/architect

Plan #F09-157D-0023

Images provided by designer/architect

Dimensions: 65'11" W x 107' D
Heated Sq. Ft.: 2,873
Bonus Sq. Ft.: 552
Bedrooms: 3   **Bathrooms:** 2½
Foundation: Crawl space standard; slab for an additional fee

See index for more information

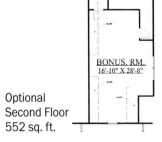

PORCH
25'-1" X 12'-7"
316 sq ft

KITCHEN
19'-7" X 11'-2"

BDRM#3
13'-5" X 15'-5"

PANTRY

MASTER BDRM
15'-11" X 21'-0"

DINING
24'-4" X 15'-11"
VAULTED CEILING

CLOSET
11'-0" X 10'-7"

BDRM#2
13'-5" X 15'-5"

GREAT RM.
24'-4" X 21'-2"
VAULTED CEILING

PORCH
38'-6" X 8'-0"
308 sq ft

BONUS. RM.
16'-10" X 28'-8"

Optional Second Floor
552 sq. ft.

GARAGE
23'-11" X 28'-8"
791 sq ft

© Copyright by designer/architect

First Floor
2,873 sq. ft.

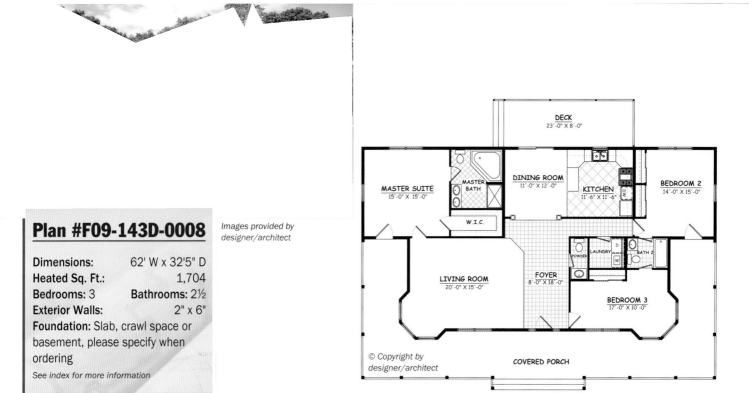

Plan #F09-143D-0008

Images provided by designer/architect

Dimensions:	62' W x 32'5" D
Heated Sq. Ft.:	1,704
Bedrooms: 3	Bathrooms: 2½
Exterior Walls:	2" x 6"

Foundation: Slab, crawl space or basement, please specify when ordering

See index for more information

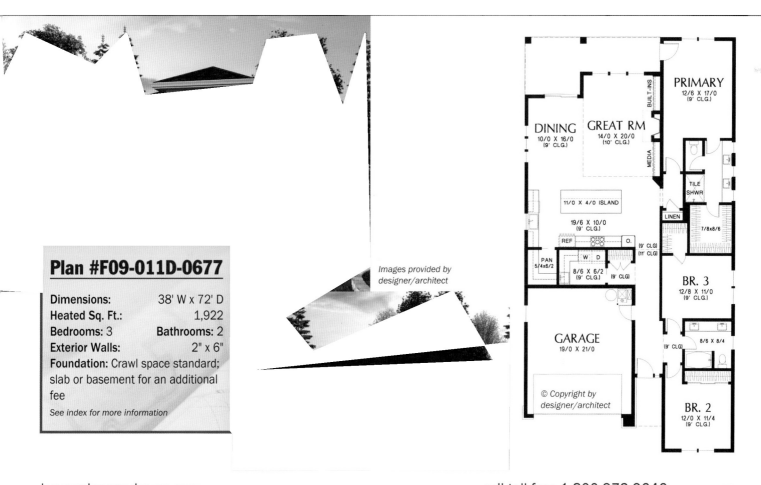

Plan #F09-011D-0677

Images provided by designer/architect

Dimensions:	38' W x 72' D
Heated Sq. Ft.:	1,922
Bedrooms: 3	Bathrooms: 2
Exterior Walls:	2" x 6"

Foundation: Crawl space standard; slab or basement for an additional fee

See index for more information

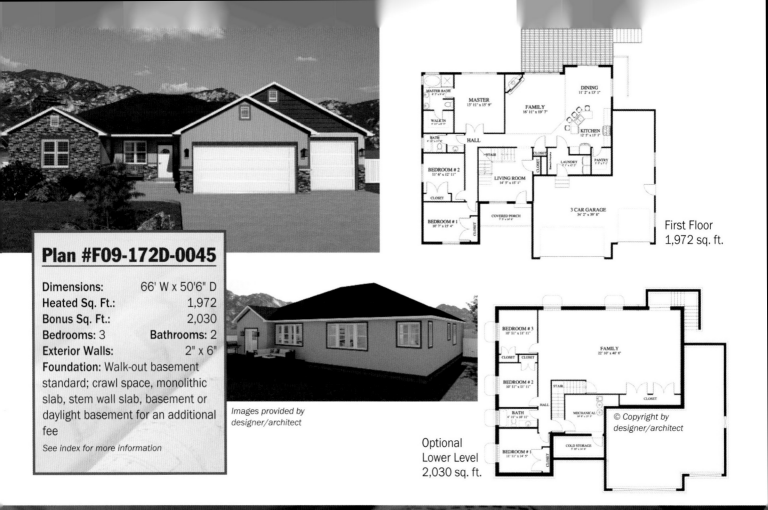

First Floor
1,972 sq. ft.

Optional
Lower Level
2,030 sq. ft.

© Copyright by
designer/architect

Plan #F09-172D-0045

Dimensions:	66' W x 50'6" D
Heated Sq. Ft.:	1,972
Bonus Sq. Ft.:	2,030
Bedrooms: 3	Bathrooms: 2
Exterior Walls:	2" x 6"

Foundation: Walk-out basement standard; crawl space, monolithic slab, stem wall slab, basement or daylight basement for an additional fee

See index for more information

Images provided by designer/architect

Plan #F09-111D-0048

Dimensions:	56'6" W x 51'2" D
Heated Sq. Ft.:	1,972
Bedrooms: 3	Bathrooms: 2

Foundation: Slab standard; crawl space or basement for an additional fee

See index for more information

Images provided by designer/architect

© Copyright by
designer/architect

Plan #F09-155D-0136

Dimensions:	48'2" W x 52'6" D
Heated Sq. Ft.:	1,438
Bedrooms: 3	Bathrooms: 2

Foundation: Crawl space or slab standard; basement or daylight basement for an additional fee

See index for more information

Images provided by designer/architect

© Copyright by designer/architect

Plan #F09-166D-0004

Images provided by designer/architect

Dimensions:	63'10" W x 71'5" D
Heated Sq. Ft.:	2,512
Bedrooms: 4	Bathrooms: 3
Exterior Walls:	2" x 6"
Foundation:	Slab

See index for more information

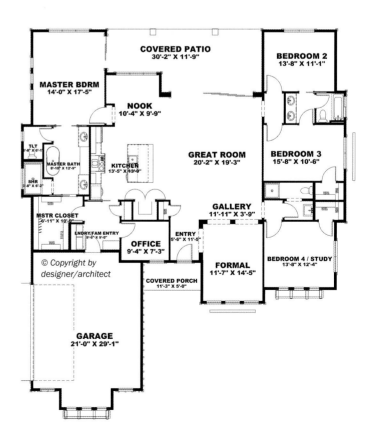

© Copyright by designer/architect

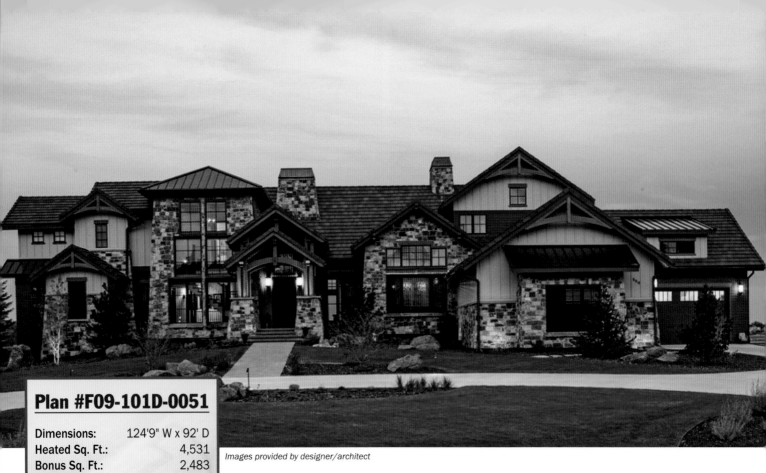

Plan #F09-101D-0051

Dimensions:	124'9" W x 92' D
Heated Sq. Ft.:	4,531
Bonus Sq. Ft.:	2,483
Bedrooms:	3
Bathrooms:	2 full, 2 half
Exterior Walls:	2" x 6"
Foundation:	Walk-out basement

See index for more information

Images provided by designer/architect

Features

- A large open interior gives this rustic luxury home an open feel
- The first floor consists of a great room, a huge kitchen with island, casual and formal dining spaces, a mud room, and a private luxury master bedroom and bath
- The second floor has two bedrooms with walk-in closets that share a Jack and Jill bath
- The optional lower level has an additional 2,483 square feet of living area and features a guest room and a guest suite, a game area, an exercise room, and a media area
- Above the garage you'll discover a craft room and a vaulted playroom
- 2-car side entry garage, and a 2-car front entry garage

Second Floor
1,420 sq. ft.

© Copyright by
designer/architect

First Floor
3,111 sq. ft.

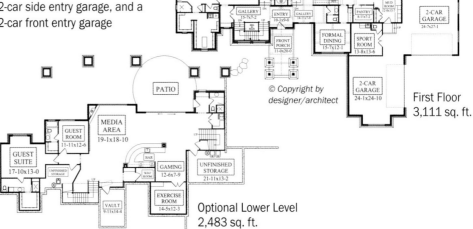

Optional Lower Level
2,483 sq. ft.

looking inside today's best
smart homes

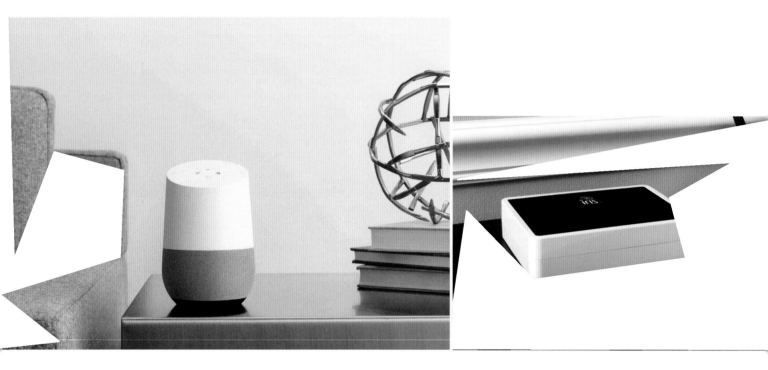

Since the beginning of time, interest in making life easier has always brought curiosity to inventors as well as architects. Even as far back as the Victorian era homebuilders included "dumbwaiters" in homes. Similar to an elevator but on a smaller scale that often used pulleys, a dumbwaiter was an easy method to help homeowners move things from one floor to another. So, it comes as no surprise that homeowners are still constantly searching for ways to make life easier. Whether the gadget or appliance is small such as the crockpot in the 60s and 70s, or the Keurig® of today, we are always yearning for the latest technology to tackle life's everyday hassles with better ease.

Today's gadgets and smart home features are more seamless than ever. Most are now powered by an app that can be downloaded onto your tablet or smart phone allowing your home to be managed even while you're away. Often these added conveniences are time-saving, but they also provide better safety and health benefits. If you're interested in incorporating smart features into your new home, there are many innovative options available to homeowners and the market is continuing to grow.

Page 134, left: Google Home Smart Assistant 2, store.google.com, photo from gadgetflow.com; right: Iris Hub, irisbylowes.com, photo from techive.com; Page 135, clockwise from top right: Ecobee4 is more than a thermostat, shop.ecobee.com; GE Z-Wave Wireless Smart Lighting Control Appliance Module works with Amazon Alexa, amazon.com; Quirky + GE Aros Smart Window Air Conditioner, amazon.com; The Smart Bridge and Lutron App for Caséta Wireless are the perfect foundations for creating a connected home system, casetawireless.com; Nest Learning Thermostat, store.nest.com.

command attention

From automated lock systems to apps that manage the temperature on your thermostat, tech companies have responded to the homeowner's need for a central command hub. A hub device is designed to allow you to control all of the various apps managing functions throughout your home in one master application. Some of the top hubs on the market today include: Google Echo, Samsung SmartThings *(smartthings.com)*, Iris Smart Hub® *(lowes. com)*, Staples Connect™ *(staples.com)*, and Wink *(homedepot.com)*. If you're a homeowner that's also a tech junkie, then seamlessly managing all of your apps and home functions in one central hub really cuts down on the app clutter and confusion.

Other wireless options include Wi-Fi plug modules. GE's appliance module plugs into the wall, then plug any small appliance into the module and it instantly goes wireless and can be managed from your smart phone. There are also in-wall outlets that make the outlets themselves app-adjustable. Don't ever fear again that you left the curling iron on, and you won't be home for hours. Yes, there's now an app for that!

home basics 101

Digital thermostats, such as the ones from Nest®, sync with an app on your smart phone and even learn your habits. Then, they program themselves to turn up the temperature, or turn it down based on your routine. The Ecobee4 has a responsive display, a remote sensor and tons of smart integrations, including a built-in Amazon Alexa speaker, making it unmatched on the market.

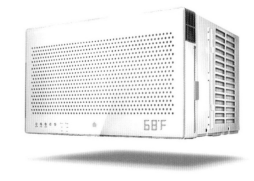

Or, install Quirky + GE Aros Smart Air Conditioner that responds to commands from your smart phone and also uses GPS to turn itself on and off depending on where you are, resulting in money and energy savings.

Ceiling fans have also gone high tech. The Vizia RF +® Fan Speed Control *(leviton. com)* can adjust a fan to any speed, turn it off, set it to start at a certain time, and can also coordinate with light dimmers all while using Wi-Fi.

Control the amount of light throughout your home and the intensity with app controlled light dimmers. Some great options on the market include: Lutron Caseta® Wireless In-Wall Dimmer, left *(homedepot.com)*, Aspire RF with Z-Wave® Dimmer *(staples.com)*, and Leviton DZMX Z-Wave Dimmer *(leviton.com)*. If you're interested in other smart lighting options, then the Philips Hue Wireless Dimming Kit is a simple and affordable way to get started.

Tech is even moving outdoors and getting in on the smart stuff with the Skydrop™ sprinkler system that reviews the local weather forecasts to determine watering needs and adjusts its settings accordingly. It includes both automatic and manual modes, and now works with Nest®.

interior decor

Windows, Blinds & Shades

Control the amount of light that enters your home even remotely with shades from Bali or Serena. Or, automate your shades so that as the sun shifts in the sky, the shades adjust for better efficiency and privacy.

Flooring

From cutting edge carpets to floor textiles, some new flooring options are able to track your every move and even show you the way. Lauzon Pure Genius® Smart Floor breaks down airborne contaminants. Activated by light, Pure Genius® flooring works on its own and acts as if having 3 trees inside your home. Natural or artificial light activates the titanium dioxide in Pure Genius®, setting the air-purifying agent in motion. The flooring is triggered by movement, whether from movement through a room, or a fan. The active nanoparticles in Pure Genius® decompose toxic contaminants in the air (formaldehyde and other pollutants) and convert them into harmless water and carbon dioxide molecules. Toto's Hydrotect Tile has a special coating that's antimicrobial and repels oil and dirt. So, cleaning the floor just got a whole lot faster and easier. A house coated in HydroTect purifies the same amount of air as a forest the size of four tennis courts, or decomposes the same amount of pollution produced by 30 cars driving a little over 18 miles a day.

Home Accessories

You spend more time in bed than anywhere else in your home. So why not invest in a smart bed? Sensors in the Sleep Number Mattress using their SleepIQ® Technology *(sleepnumber.com)* communicate with a corresponding app that calculates your breathing, heart rate, and frequency of movement. Then, outfit your smart bed with the Outlast® Temperature Regulating Sheets System that absorbs and releases excess body heat and moisture, so no need to steal, or kick the blankets off all night long anymore.

engage your senses

Today's homeowners are interested in living cleaner lifestyles free of chemicals and allergens trapped within their home. Becoming less popular are unnatural chemical laden room freshening sprays and deodorizers and taking their place are aromatherapy diffusers. These diffusers can be adjusted to run for any period of time and they use natural essential oils to eliminate odors, relieve stress, or discourage germs.

A method for monitoring home air quality is placing smoke and carbon monoxide detectors around your home. Now, these devices send your phone alerts and communicate with other units. Some distinguish between smoke and carbon dioxide and even tell you where the problem lies in a human voice. If you're concerned with water leaks and mold, then a Wally Sensor *(wallyhome.com)* can send you alerts about leaks and mold. a WallyHome Multi-Sensor detects and alerts you of water leaks, temperature and humidity changes, and when doors and windows open.

If you love having live plants and flowers around your home, but hate not knowing how to keep them thriving, then the Click and Grow Smartpot *(clickandgrow.com)* was created just for you. It dispenses the correct amount of water and nutrients for up to a month making it also great for those who travel frequently. Or, use a Parrot® Flower Power *(global.parrot.com)* and place the sensor into the soil and it will tell you exactly how to tend to the plant via your smart phone.

Page 136, top: Skydrop™ Smart Watering Sprinkler Controller has 8 built-in zones using the most advanced technology that accesses local weather data, calculates water, and adjusts watering schedules helping you spend less money, skydrop.com; Lauzon Pure Genius® flooring, lauzon.com; Page 137, top: i10 with FlexFit 3 and Sleep IQ®, sleepnumber.com; top, middle: Your WallyHome Sensor connects your home and keeps you informed through text message, email, push notifications or phone calls, wallyhome. com; right: The Click and Grow Smartpot enables you to grow fresh herbs, fruits and flowers with zero effort, clickandgrow.com.

Let yourself wake up in a more peaceful state thanks to the Yantouch Diamond+ Speaker and Alarm *(yantouch.com)*. This unique device washes the wall in soft light in millions of colors and wakes you up with sunrise hues all while playing accompanying music. Or, if drifting off to sleep tends to be more of a problem for you, then use a Drift™ Light by Saffron *(drift-light.com)*, which functions as a normal bulb until you flip the switch twice, then it softly fades in 37 minutes, which is the average time of a sunset. The bulb's warm light also induces melatonin production, which naturally controls your body's sleep and wake cycles.

Even your bathroom can be outfitted with amazing smart features such as the Sunstruck® Bathtub with Bask® *(us.kohler.com)*. This tub acts as a Bluetooth speaker when empty, but when it's filled the music waves ripple through the water and creates a hydrotherapy spa. It will even play your music library, or select one of their programmed mixes for total relaxation. Shower controls can also be set and regulated so the water is the optimal temperature or, sing along with your favorite playlist right inside your shower with Kohler's Moxie™ showerhead with removable speaker by Harman Kardon.

Page 138 top: Yantouch Diamond+ world's first Music+Light LED Lifestyle Bluetooth Speaker, yantouch.com/diamond; bottom: Kohler's Sunstruck® Oval Freestanding bathtub with Bask® heated surface, us.kohler.com; left: Moxie™ showerhead with built-in Harman Kardon speaker, us.kohler.com; Page 139, top, left and right: Crock-Pot® 6-Quart Smart Slow Cooker with WeMo® App, Item #SCCPWM600-V2, crock-pot.com; middle, right: Samsung French Door Refrigerator with Family Hub™, samsung.com; Bottom: Dacor Discovery™ iQ Wall Oven is controllable from an app, Item# DYO230, dacor.com; middle, left: 782 Taylor TemPerfect™ Floating Thermometers, taylor-enviro.com.

no excuse for the perfect meal

Kitchen gadgets and appliances have come a long way and almost make it impossible to ruin a meal. For instance, there's no longer a need to hang by the oven or stove when cooking thanks to a kitchen thermometer that will ping you via an app when the meat you're cooking in the oven reaches the correct temperature. So, you can finally enjoy spending time with family and friends on the patio before dinner is served thanks to this handy device.

Or, upgrade your crockpot to the Crock-Pot® 6-Quart. Smart Slow Cooker with WeMo® *(crock-pot.com)*. It monitors and adjusts the time and temperature remotely and will send you a notification to your smart phone when the set time has finished.

Taylor's TEMPerfect™ Floating Rings indicate a liquid's ideal temperature for poaching, simmering or boiling. Or, try their butter dish that changes color when the butter reaches room temperature.

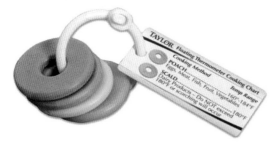

innovative home appliances

Refridgerators

Sub-Zero's® IT-36CIID Refrigerator and Freezer *(subzero-wolf.com)* uses NASA technology and includes an air purifier that rids the inside of mold and bacteria every 20 minutes. Another popular option great for busy families is the Samsung® Smart Hub Refrigerator that has a large touchscreen that lets you leave notes, view other family members' schedules, order groceries, play music, and even watch TV. It also has three cameras on the inside that can take a picture and email it to you every time you close the door. Now you can stop guessing if you need milk when grocery shopping.

Ovens

Dacor's Discovery™ iQ Wall Oven *(dacor.com)* not only screams fun since it's available in a variety of colors, but it can be controlled via Wi-Fi and features an LCD screen where you can access recipes.

Stoves

The Alno Kitchen Display, left *(alno-usa.com)* allows the chef of the family to look up recipes on-line, watch cooking shows, or even take a video call, while sautéing tonight's dinner.

Washers & Dryers

The Whirlpool® Smart Front-Load Washer and Dryer sends alerts making you aware of peak energy-using hours and connects to your Amazon account so you can order laundry supplies easily.

other top-notch smart home electronics

Televisions

The Roku™ TV comes with fully integrated streaming and works with gaming consoles and other devices to provide hundreds of channels and platforms like Netflix™.

Sound Systems

BeoLab18 speaker towers, left *(bang-olufsen.com)* operate on a frequency that's not affected by other wireless networks. So, gone are the days of having a song stop right in the middle, or showing other signs of interference with static. You will be able to enjoy crystal clear uninterrupted sound.

Monitoring Systems

Fido feeling lonely? Then, Petcube *(petcube.com)* may be the answer. Place the cube where your pet stays when you aren't home and it streams video to your tablet or smart phone. Or, monitor your pet with PetChatz HD®, left *(petchatz.com)*, or Petzi Treat Cam® *(petzi.com)*, which is similar to the Petcube, but instead of a laser that plays with your pet, it dispenses treats.

If outdoor security is your interest, then SkyBell's® video doorbell quality is terrific, and integrations with Alexa, Nest®, and If This Then That (IFTTT) help it stand out in an increasingly competitive market. It also includes free online video storage and a resolution of 1080p, which are also major pluses.

Page 140 top: Alno kitchen displays allow you to look up recipes online while cooking, alno-usa.com; middle: Bang Olufsen's BeoLab 18 delivers exceptional wireless sound, and placement flexibility, bang-olufsen.com; bottom: PetChatz HD® Pet Camera Two-Way Audio/Video System dispenses treats and provides motion/noise sensing, petchatz.com.

Voice Activated Assistance

Amazon's Echo and Alexa retrieve on-line information, play music, set reminders and more all by using voice commands. Jibo *(myjibo.com)* recognizes faces, learns your tastes, gives you reminders and communicates with you using sound effects and graphics.

Robots

Robot vacuums are one of the most popular gadgets that make cleaning less of a chore. These machines are only getting better with some that now even mop.

And, don't protect these fancy gadgets and electronics the old-fashioned way with a standard surge protector, use the Wink Pivot Surge Protector, which of course is Wi-Fi enabled.

With homeowners constantly being bombarded by alerts, messages, notifications, texts and emails, it's easy to see why gadgets and devices that reduce the amount of clutter electronically are the latest rage in home design. Incorporating these smart products into your new home will take it into the future and generally make life easier from the minute you move in. Stop wasting time and let these savvy tech items run your household like a champ; giving you more time to relax and enjoy life.

quirky finds

- Porkfolio *(wink.com)* is a piggy bank that tracks your savings and deposits, and helps you set goals. And, you can actually drop in coins and its snout lights up!

- Nokia's Body+ Health Mate Body Composition Wi-Fi Scale (health. nokia.com) monitors your weight, BMI, body fat percentage and heart rate.

- GlowCap® *(nanthealth.com/vitality)* is a pill bottle lid that reminds you to take your medicine by lighting up. It shares information with your doctor and submits prescription refills.

- Petnet iO Smartfeeder schedules pet feeding times, manages portions, and sends notifications right to your phone.

Page 141 clockwise from top: Amazon Echo uses Alexa to play music, make calls, send messages, and get information instantly, amazon. com; Porkfolio Piggy bank uses the Wink app to monitor the amount of change you've put into its belly and track your savings goals, wink. com; Nokia's Body+ Health Mate Body Composition Wi-Fi Scale centralizes your health information to help you achieve your health goals, health.nokia.com; Vitality Glowcap® syncs with an app and reminds you to take your medicine by lighting up the cap, nanthealth.com/vitality; The Petnet iO SmartFeeder is an automatic pet feeder that dispenses food on a schedule, petnet.io.

DESIGNAMERICA

SEE YOUR HOME ON YOUR LOT BEFORE IT'S BUILT.

Selecting the right home design for your needs and lifestyle requires a lot of thought as your new home is an investment in both the present and the future. The site for your new home will have a definite impact on the home plan you select. It's a good idea to select a home design that will complement your site. And you've come to the right place to make this happen! With the Design America Innovative 3D App you can see your home on your lot before it's built. Simply follow the instructions on page 143 and look for the Design America 3D logo on the pages of plans that you can view in 3D.

Let your Dream Home come to life in 3D!

Install the Design America 3D app

Instructions:
How to use the 3D App:

Finding your dream home just got a little easier. We, at Design America, have been bringing the best in residential design to homeowners for over 30 years. To help you in your search for that perfect home, we're introducing 3D technology to 2D home plans. Now, even before you purchase any blueprints, you can actually view your dream home on your lot, from any direction. Just follow the easy steps below. It's a great tool...and it's fun!

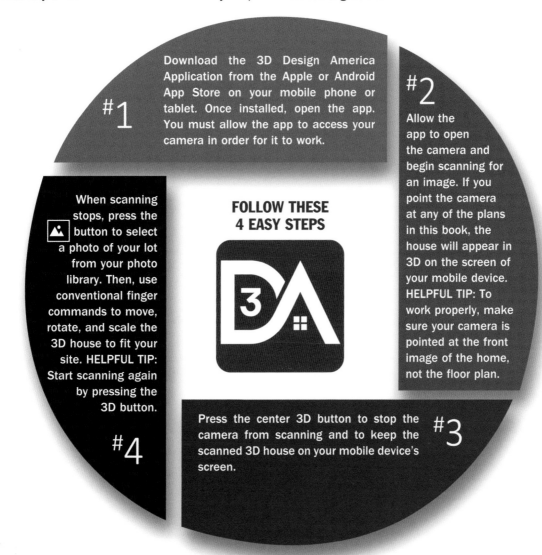

#1 Download the 3D Design America Application from the Apple or Android App Store on your mobile phone or tablet. Once installed, open the app. You must allow the app to access your camera in order for it to work.

#2 Allow the app to open the camera and begin scanning for an image. If you point the camera at any of the plans in this book, the house will appear in 3D on the screen of your mobile device. HELPFUL TIP: To work properly, make sure your camera is pointed at the front image of the home, not the floor plan.

FOLLOW THESE 4 EASY STEPS

#3 Press the center 3D button to stop the camera from scanning and to keep the scanned 3D house on your mobile device's screen.

#4 When scanning stops, press the button to select a photo of your lot from your photo library. Then, use conventional finger commands to move, rotate, and scale the 3D house to fit your site. HELPFUL TIP: Start scanning again by pressing the 3D button.

THE SMALL ICONS ON THE BOTTOM BAR OF THE 3D APP PERFORM DIFFERENT FUNCTIONS:

Turn shadows on and off, and rotate the sun's position.

View the 3D house with the live camera in the background, or with a gray flat background.

Start, stop, or resume scanning the front image of the homes in this book.

Select a photo from your photo library, such as a photo of your lot, and use it as the background for the 3D house.

Take a screenshot of the 3D house and save it in your photo library on your mobile device.

Plan #F09-007D-0060

Dimensions:	38'8" W x 48'4" D
Heated Sq. Ft.:	1,268
Bedrooms: 3	**Bathrooms:** 2

Foundation: Basement standard; crawl space or slab for an additional fee

See index for more information

Features

- Multiple gables, a large porch, and arched windows create a classy exterior
- Innovative design provides openness in the great room, kitchen and breakfast room
- The separated vaulted master bedroom is spacious and features a bath with a separate shower, spa tub and a walk-in closet
- The secondary bedrooms have a private hall with bath
- 2-car front entry garage

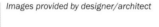

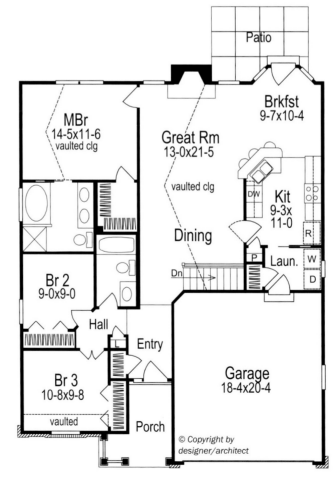

Patio

MBr
14-5x11-6
vaulted clg

Great Rm
13-0x21-5

vaulted clg

Brkfst
9-7x10-4

Dining

Kit
9-3x
11-0

DW

R

P

Laun.

W

D

Dn

Br 2
9-0x9-0

Hall

Entry

Garage
18-4x20-4

Br 3
10-8x9-8

vaulted

Porch

© Copyright by designer/architect

Plan #F09-011D-0007

Dimensions:	50' W x 48' D
Heated Sq. Ft.:	1,580
Bedrooms: 3	Bathrooms: 2½
Exterior Walls:	2" x 6"

Foundation: Joisted crawl space, TrusJoist floor system or post & beam standard; slab or basement for an additional fee

See index for more information

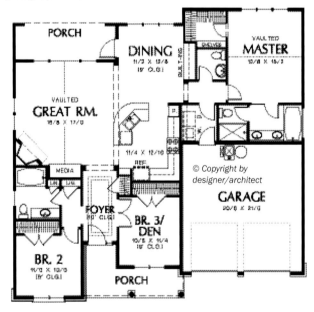

© Copyright by designer/architect

Features

- A large fireplace and a built-in media center create a cozy feel in the vaulted great room while the covered porch extends the living space outdoors

- An angled serving bar opens the kitchen to the great room and dining space for easy entertaining

- Built-in bookshelves flank one wall of the dining room providing the perfect spot for collectibles or cookbooks

- The secluded master bedroom enjoys a vaulted ceiling, a private bath with a double vanity and a large walk-in closet

- 2-car front entry garage

Plan #F09-005D-0001

Dimensions: 72' W x 34'4" D
Heated Sq. Ft.: 1,400
Bedrooms: 3   **Bathrooms:** 2
Foundation: Basement standard; crawl space or slab for an additional fee

See index for more information

Features

- Triple roof dormers and an inviting covered front porch add great curb appeal
- The vaulted living room creates a spacious feel
- A raised snack bar creates a smooth transition from the kitchen to the dining room
- A split bedroom design offers privacy
- The oversized two-car garage has additional storage space
- 2-car front entry garage

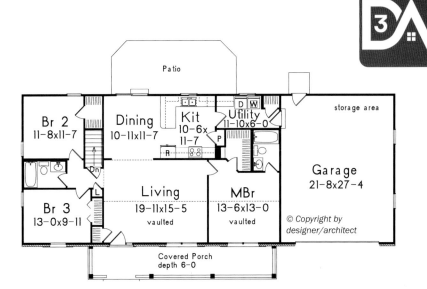

Patio

Br 2
11-8x11-7

Dining
10-11x11-7

Kit
10-6x
11-7

Utility
11-10x6-0

storage area

Garage
21-8x27-4

Br 3
13-0x9-11

Living
19-11x15-5
vaulted

MBr
13-6x13-0
vaulted

© Copyright by designer/architect

Covered Porch
depth 6-0

Plan #F09-007D-0124

Dimensions:	65' W x 51' D
Heated Sq. Ft.:	1,944
Bedrooms: 3	**Bathrooms:** 2

Foundation: Basement standard; crawl space or slab for an additional fee

See index for more information

Features

- The spacious surrounding porch, a covered patio, and a stone fireplace create an expansive appearance

- The large entry leads to a grand-sized great room featuring a vaulted ceiling, fireplace, wet bar and access to a porch through three patio doors

- The U-shaped kitchen is open to the hearth room and enjoys a snack bar, fireplace and patio access

- A luxury bath, walk-in closet and doors to porch are a few of the amenities of the master bedroom

- Optional 3-car detached garage

Detached Garage
34-4x23-4

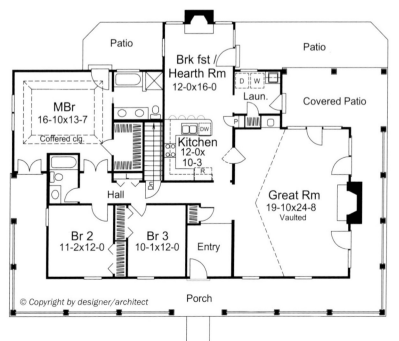

Patio

Brk fst / Hearth Rm
12-0x16-0

Patio

MBr
16-10x13-7

Coffered clg.

Laun.

Covered Patio

Kitchen
12-0x 10-3

Hall

Great Rm
19-10x24-8
Vaulted

Br 2
11-2x12-0

Br 3
10-1x12-0

Entry

© Copyright by designer/architect

Porch

Images provided by designer/architect

Plan #F09-007D-0136

Dimensions:	71'8" W x 38' D
Heated Sq. Ft.:	1,532
Bonus Sq. Ft.:	740
Bedrooms: 3	Bathrooms: 2
Foundation:	Walk-out basement

See index for more information

Features

- Multiple gables and stonework deliver a warm and inviting exterior to this wonderful home

- The vaulted great room has a stylish fireplace and spectacular views accomplished with a two-story atrium window wall

- A covered rear porch is easily accessed from the charming breakfast room or garage

- The optional lower level has an additional 740 square feet of living area

- 2-car front entry garage

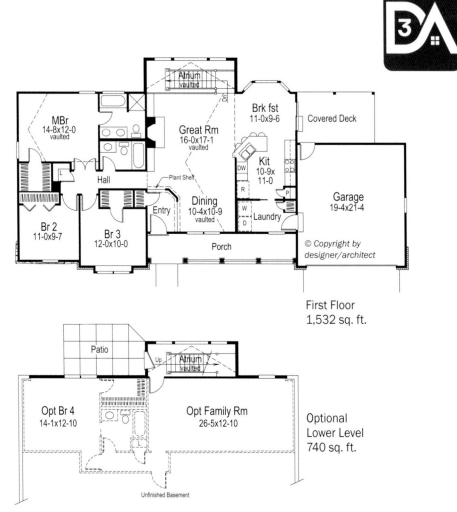

First Floor
1,532 sq. ft.

Optional
Lower Level
740 sq. ft.

Images provided by designer/architect

Plan #F09-077D-0019

Dimensions: 54' W x 47' D
Heated Sq. Ft.: 1,400
Bedrooms: 3   Bathrooms: 2
Foundation: Slab, basement or crawl space, please specify when ordering
See index for more information

Features

- The efficiently shaped kitchen has plenty of counterspace for preparing meals
- Beautiful French doors lead from the appealing dining room to the large rear patio
- The comfortable master bedroom is set apart from the rest of the house for additional privacy and boasts a large walk-in closet and private bath with two separate vanities and a relaxing garden tub
- 2-car front entry garage

PATIO
19-8 x 11-6

Garden Tub

Bath

Bath

Stor.

Clos.

Master Bedroom
15-8 x 14-8
8-0 Ceiling

Kitchen
9-10 x 12-0

Dining
9-10 x 12-0
8-0 Ceiling

W/D Utility

Entry

Great Room
19-8 x 15-6
8-0 Ceiling

Bedroom 2
12-2 x 11-0
8-0 Ceiling

Clos.

Hall

Hall Bath

Clos.

Bedroom 3
12-2 x 11-0
8-0 Ceiling

Covered Porch
19-8 x 5

OPTIONAL STAIRS TO BASEMENT

© Copyright by designer/architect

Two Car Garage
22-2 x 25-0

NOTE: ALL DASHED WALLS INDICATE OPTIONAL WALL LOCATIONS IF BASEMENT OPTION IS CHOSEN.

Plan #F09-007D-0040

Dimensions:	28' W x 26' D
Heated Sq. Ft.:	632
Bedrooms: 1	Bathrooms: 1
Foundation:	Slab

See index for more information

Features

- A porch leads to a vaulted entry and stairs with feature window, coat closet and access to the garage/laundry

- The cozy living room offers a vaulted ceiling, a fireplace, a large Palladian window and a pass-through to the kitchen

- The kitchen features an eating bar for two perfect for casual meals

- The bedroom has a sizable closet and is close to a roomy bath with a garden tub that has an arched window above

- 2-car front entry garage

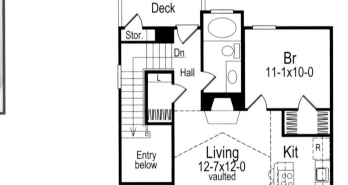

Second Floor
512 sq. ft.

© Copyright by designer/architect

First Floor
120 sq. ft.

Plan #F09-007D-0010

Dimensions:	83' W x 42'4" D
Heated Sq. Ft.:	1,845
Bonus Sq. Ft.:	889
Bedrooms: 3	**Bathrooms: 2**

Foundation: Walk-out basement standard; crawl space or slab for an additional fee

See index for more information

Images provided by designer/architect

Features

- Vaulted dining and great rooms are immersed in sunlight from an atrium window wall
- The bayed breakfast room opens onto the covered porch
- The kitchen has a wrap-around casual counter with seating for four and a large corner pantry
- The optional lower level has an additional 889 square feet of living area
- 3-car front entry garage

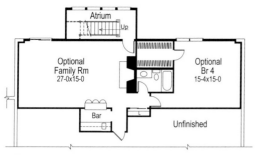

Optional
Lower Level
889 sq. ft.

First Floor
1,845 sq. ft.

Plan #F09-007D-0140

Dimensions: 62' W x 45' D
Heated Sq. Ft.: 1,591
Bedrooms: 3   **Bathrooms:** 2
Foundation: Basement standard; crawl space or slab for an additional fee

See index for more information

Images provided by designer/architect

Features

- The spacious porch and patio provide lots of outdoor enjoyment
- The large entry foyer leads to a cheerful kitchen and breakfast room which welcomes the sun through a wide array of windows
- The great room features a vaulted ceiling, a corner fireplace, a wet bar and a door that accesses the rear patio
- Double walk-in closets, a private porch and a luxury bath are a few special highlights of the vaulted master bedroom suite
- 2-car side entry garage

Plan #F09-007D-0114

Dimensions:	32' W x 39'4" D
Heated Sq. Ft.:	1,671
Bedrooms: 3	**Bathrooms:** 2½

Foundation: Basement standard; crawl space or slab for an additional fee

See index for more information

Features

- Triple gables and a stone facade create great curb appeal on the exterior of this home
- The two-story entry with hallway leads to a spacious family room, a dining area with a bay window and a U-shaped kitchen
- The second floor features a large master bedroom with a luxury bath, a huge walk-in closet, an overlook to the entry and two secondary bedrooms with a hall bath
- 2-car front entry garage

Second Floor
991 sq. ft.

© Copyright by
designer/architect

First Floor
680 sq. ft.

Images provided by designer/architect

Plan #F09-055D-0193

Dimensions: 63'10" W x 72'2" D
Heated Sq. Ft.: 2,131
Bedrooms: 3   **Bathrooms:** 2½
Foundation: Slab or crawl space standard; basement or daylight basement for an additional fee

See index for more information

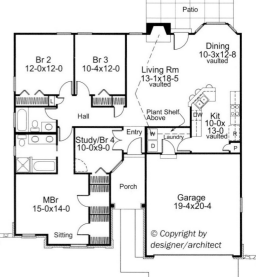

Images provided by designer/architect

Plan #F09-007D-0162

Dimensions: 47'8" W x 47'4" D
Heated Sq. Ft.: 1,519
Bedrooms: 4   **Bathrooms:** 2
Foundation: Crawl space standard; basement or slab for an additional fee

See index for more information

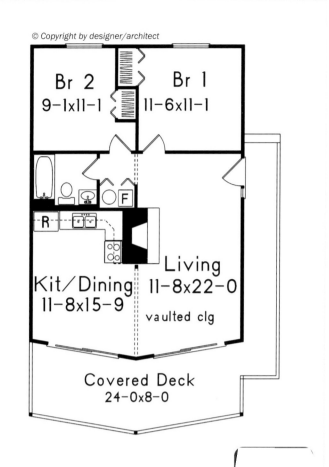

Br 2
9-1x11-1

Br 1
11-6x11-1

F

R

Kit/Dining
11-8x15-9

Living
11-8x22-0
vaulted clg

Covered Deck
24-0x8-0

Plan #F09-008D-0153

Images provided by designer/architect

Dimensions: 24' W x 42' D
Heated Sq. Ft.: 792
Bedrooms: 2   **Bathrooms:** 1
Foundation: Crawl space standard; slab for an additional fee

See index for more information

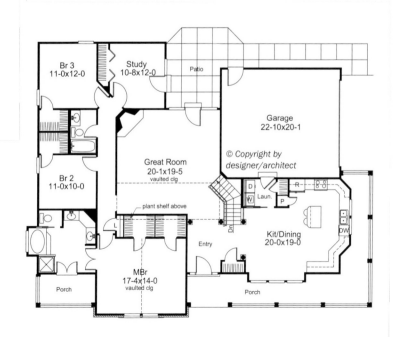

Br 3
11-0x12-0

Study
10-8x12-0

Patio

Garage
22-10x20-1

Great Room
20-1x19-5
vaulted clg

Br 2
11-0x10-0

D
W
Laun.
P
R

plant shelf above

Kit/Dining
20-0x19-0

DW

Entry

MBr
17-4x14-0
vaulted clg

Porch

Porch

Plan #F09-007D-0055

Images provided by designer/architect

Dimensions: 67' W x 51'4" D
Heated Sq. Ft.: 2,029
Bedrooms: 3   **Bathrooms:** 2
Foundation: Basement standard; crawl space or slab for an additional fee

See index for more information

Images provided by
designer/architect

Plan #F09-016D-0062

Dimensions: 48' W x 43'4" D
Heated Sq. Ft.: 1,380
Bonus Sq. Ft.: 385
Bedrooms: 3   Bathrooms: 2
Foundation: Slab or crawl space
standard; walk-out basement or
basement for an additional fee
See index for more information

DECK

COV. PORCH

BEDRM #3
11'-4" x
10'-0"

BATH
#2

GREAT RM
20'-0" x 15'-4"
10' CLG

FIREPLACE

BEDRM #2
11'-4" x
12'-4"

COV. PORCH

DINING RM
11'-0" x
15'-4"
9' CLG

KITCHEN
9'-0" x
10'-0"

LAUN
RM

UTIL

WICL

MSTR
BATH

OPTIONAL TWO CAR GARAGE
20'-0" x 20'-0"

© Copyright by
designer/architect

TRAY CEIL
MSTR BEDRM
12'-0" x
16'-4"

Images provided by
designer/architect

Plan #F09-121D-0010

Dimensions: 37'6" W x 52' D
Heated Sq. Ft.: 1,281
Bedrooms: 3   Bathrooms: 2
Foundation: Basement standard;
crawl space or slab for an
additional fee
Please see the index for more information

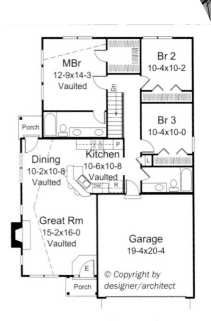

MBr
12-9x14-3
Vaulted

Br 2
10-4x10-2

Porch

Dining
10-2x10-8
Vaulted

Kitchen
10-6x10-8
Vaulted

Br 3
10-4x10-0

Great Rm
15-2x16-0
Vaulted

Garage
19-4x20-4

Porch

© Copyright by
designer/architect

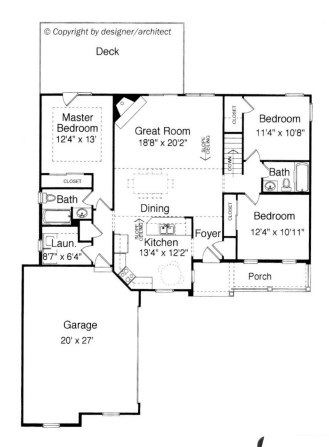

Deck

Master Bedroom
12'4" x 13'

Great Room
18'8" x 20'2"

Bedroom
11'4" x 10'8"

CLOSET

SLOPE CEILING

DOWN

Bath

Bath

CLOSET

Dining

Bedroom
12'4" x 10'11"

SLOPE CEILING

Laun.
8'7" x 6'4"

Kitchen
13'4" x 12'2"

Foyer

CLOSET

Porch

Garage
20' x 27'

Images provided by designer/architect

Plan #F09-065D-0062

Dimensions: 50' W x 55'8" D
Heated Sq. Ft.: 1,390
Bedrooms: 3   **Bathrooms:** 2
Foundation: Walk-out basement standard; slab for an additional fee

See index for more information

4' WALL

6'8" LINE

8' LINE

ATTIC STORAGE

BATH

GAME ROOM
37'-4" X 18'-8"

8' LINE

6'8" LINE

VAULTED

4' WALL

Optional
Second Floor
812 sq. ft.

DECK

GRILLING PORCH
18'-0" X 12'-0"

BEDROOM 2
12'-2" X 12'-2"

DINING / HEARTH ROOM
13'-0" X 18'-0"

ATRIUM DOORS

LAU.
13'-8" X 6'-8"

GARAGE
23'-8" X 21'-4"

BATH

KITCHEN
14'-6" X 18'-6"

M. BATH
13'-8" X 7'-4"

CLAWFOOT TUB

PAN

REF

BEDROOM 3
12'-2" X 12'-2"

LIVING RM.
21'-0" X 18'-0"

MASTER SUITE
13'-8" X 13'-10"

MEDIA CENTER

8' COVERED PORCH

First Floor
1,921 sq. ft.

Images provided by designer/architect

Plan #F09-055D-0162

Dimensions: 84' W x 55'6" D
Heated Sq. Ft.: 1,921
Bonus Sq. Ft.: 812
Bedrooms: 3   **Bathrooms:** 2
Foundation: Crawl space or slab standard; basement or daylight basement for an additional fee

See index for more information

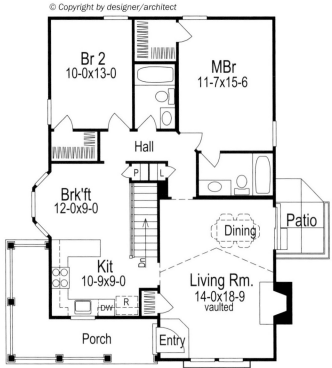

Images provided by designer/architect

Plan #F09-007D-0105

Dimensions: 35' W x 40'8" D
Heated Sq. Ft.: 1,084
Bedrooms: 2 **Bathrooms:** 2
Foundation: Basement standard; crawl space or slab for an additional fee

See index for more information

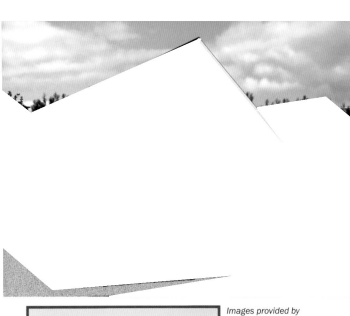

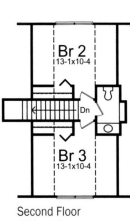

Second Floor
434 sq. ft.

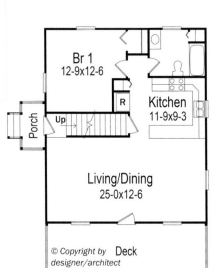

Images provided by designer/architect

Plan #F09-001D-0086

Dimensions: 28' W x 30' D
Heated Sq. Ft.: 1,154
Bedrooms: 3 **Bathrooms:** 1½
Foundation: Crawl space standard; slab or basement for an additional fee

See index for more information

First Floor
720 sq. ft.

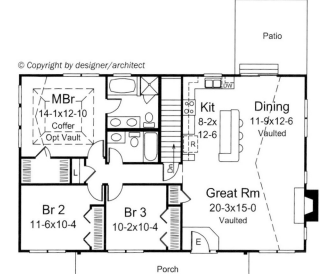

Garage
23-4x23-4

© Copyright by
designer/architect

Patio

© Copyright by designer/architect

MBr
14-1x12-10
Coffer
Opt Vault

Kit
8-2x
12-6

Dining
11-9x12-6
Vaulted

Br 2
11-6x10-4

Br 3
10-2x10-4

Great Rm
20-3x15-0
Vaulted

Dn

L

E

DW

R

Porch

Plan #F09-121D-0025

Dimensions:	50' W x 34'6" D
Heated Sq. Ft.:	1,368
Bedrooms: 3	Bathrooms: 2

Foundation: Basement standard; crawl space or slab for an additional fee

See index for more information

Images provided by designer/architect

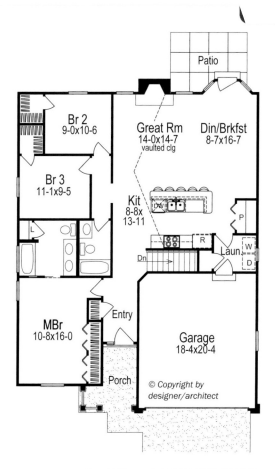

Patio

Br 2
9-0x10-6

Great Rm
14-0x14-7
vaulted clg

Din/Brkfst
8-7x16-7

Br 3
11-1x9-5

Kit
8-8x
13-11

L

Dn

R

Laun

W
D

P

DW

MBr
10-8x16-0

Entry

Garage
18-4x20-4

Porch

© Copyright by
designer/architect

Plan #F09-007D-5060

Dimensions:	38' W x 48'4" D
Heated Sq. Ft.:	1,344
Bedrooms: 3	Bathrooms: 2

Foundation: Basement standard; crawl space or slab for an additional fee

See index for more information

Images provided by designer/architect

© Copyright by designer/architect

Plan #F09-051D-0757

Dimensions:	55' W x 51'8" D
Heated Sq. Ft.:	1,501
Bedrooms: 3	Bathrooms: 2
Exterior Walls:	2" x 6"

Foundation: Basement standard; crawl space or slab for an additional fee

See index for more information

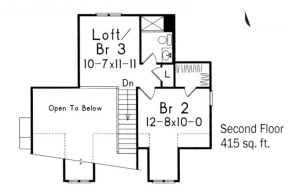

Second Floor
415 sq. ft.

Plan #F09-058D-0020

Dimensions:	46' W x 42'6" D
Heated Sq. Ft.:	1,428
Bedrooms: 3	Bathrooms: 2
Foundation:	Basement

See index for more information

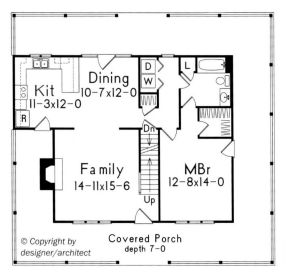

© Copyright by designer/architect

First Floor
1,013 sq. ft.

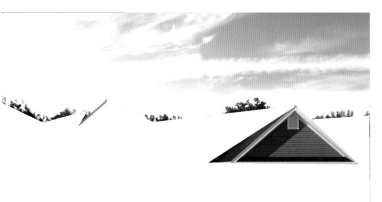

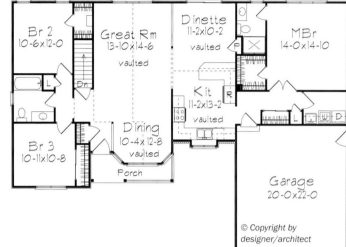

Plan #F09-033D-0012

Dimensions:	60' W x 43' D
Heated Sq. Ft.:	1,546
Bedrooms: 3	Bathrooms: 2
Foundation:	Basement

See index for more information

Images provided by designer/architect

© Copyright by designer/architect

Plan #F09-001D-0085

Dimensions:	28' W x 38' D
Heated Sq. Ft.:	720
Bedrooms: 2	Bathrooms: 1
Foundation: Crawl space standard; slab for an additional fee	

See index for more information

Images provided by designer/architect

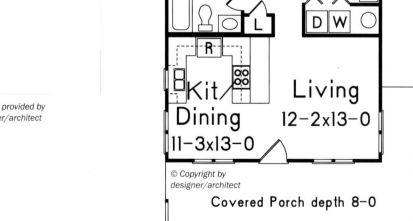

© Copyright by designer/architect

Covered Porch depth 8-0

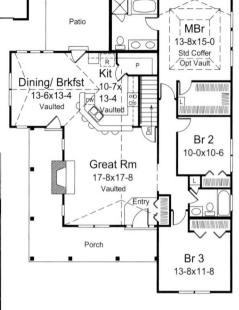

Detached Garage
23-4x23-4

© Copyright by
designer/architect

Plan #F09-121D-0016

Dimensions: 42'4" W x 54' D
Heated Sq. Ft.: 1,582
Bedrooms: 3   Bathrooms: 2
Foundation: Basement standard;
crawl space or slab for an
additional fee

See index for more information

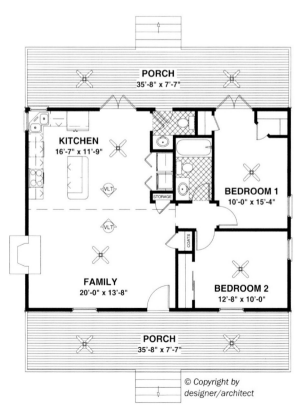

Plan #F09-013D-0133

Dimensions: 36' W x 42'4" D
Heated Sq. Ft.: 953
Bedrooms: 2   Bathrooms: 1½
Foundation: Crawl space standard;
basement or slab for an additional
fee

See index for more information

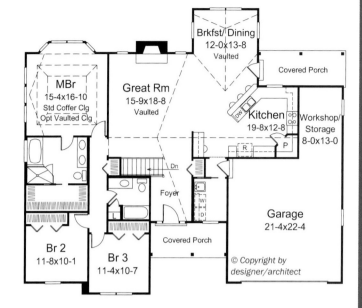

Images provided by designer/architect

Plan #F09-121D-0036

Dimensions: 60'4" W x 52' D
Heated Sq. Ft.: 1,820
Bedrooms: 3   **Bathrooms:** 2
Foundation: Basement standard; crawl space or slab for an additional fee

See index for more information

Images provided by designer/architect

Plan #F09-007D-0108

Dimensions: 25' W x 60' D
Heated Sq. Ft.: 983
Bedrooms: 3   **Bathrooms:** 2
Foundation: Crawl space standard; slab for an additional fee

See index for more information

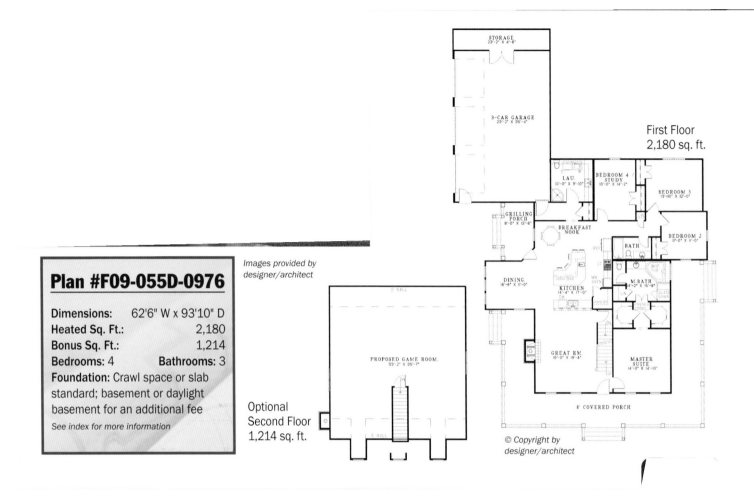

First Floor
2,180 sq. ft.

© Copyright by
designer/architect

Images provided by
designer/architect

Optional
Second Floor
1,214 sq. ft.

PROPOSED GAME ROOM.
33'-2" X 35'-7"

Plan #F09-055D-0976

Dimensions:	62'6" W x 93'10" D
Heated Sq. Ft.:	2,180
Bonus Sq. Ft.:	1,214
Bedrooms: 4	Bathrooms: 3

Foundation: Crawl space or slab standard; basement or daylight basement for an additional fee

See index for more information

Layout for
Slab and
Crawl Space
Foundation

Images provided by
designer/architect

© Copyright by designer/architect

Plan #F09-001D-0024

Dimensions:	68' W x 38' D
Heated Sq. Ft.:	1,360
Bedrooms: 3	Bathrooms: 2

Foundation: Basement standard; crawl space or slab for an additional fee

See index for more information

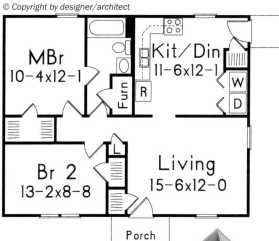

MBr
10-4x12-1

Kit/Din
11-6x12-1

Furn

R

W

D

Br 2
13-2x8-8

Living
15-6x12-0

Porch

Images provided by designer/architect

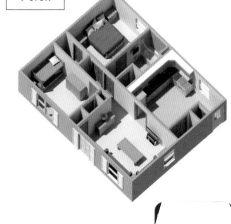

Plan #F09-001D-0088

Dimensions: 32' W x 25' D
Heated Sq. Ft.: 800
Bedrooms: 2 **Bathrooms:** 1
Foundation: Crawl space standard;
slab for an additional fee

See index for more information

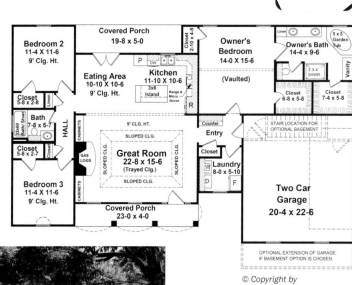

Covered Porch
19-8 x 5-0

Bedroom 2
11-4 X 11-6
9' Clg. Ht.

Closet
5-8 x 2-8

Linen

Eating Area
10-10 X 10-6
9' Clg. Ht.

Kitchen
11-10 X 10-6

Island

3x6

Range & Micro. Above

P

DW

Closet
2-10 x 4-8

Owner's
Bedroom
14-0 X 15-6

(Vaulted)

Linen

Owner's Bath
14-4 x 9-6

5 x 5
Garden
Tub

3 x 4
SHWR

Vanity

Closet
6-8 x 5-8

Closet
7-4 x 5-8

Bath
7-8 x 5-7

HALL

CABINETS

Closet
5-8 x 2-7

9' CLG. HT.

SLOPED CLG.

SLOPED CLG.

SLOPED CLG.

Great Room
22-8 x 15-6
(Trayed Clg.)

SLOPED CLG.

GAS
LOGS

Counter

Entry

Closet

STAIR LOCATION FOR
OPTIONAL BASEMENT

Bedroom 3
11-4 X 11-6
9' Clg. Ht.

Covered Porch
23-0 x 4-0

W

D

F

Laundry
8-0 x 5-10

Two Car
Garage
20-4 x 22-6

OPTIONAL EXTENSION OF GARAGE
IF BASEMENT OPTION IS CHOSEN.

Plan #F09-077D-0039

Dimensions: 64' W x 39' D
Heated Sq. Ft.: 1,654
Bedrooms: 3 **Bathrooms:** 2
Foundation: Basement, crawl
space or slab, please specify when
ordering

See index for more information

Images provided by designer/architect

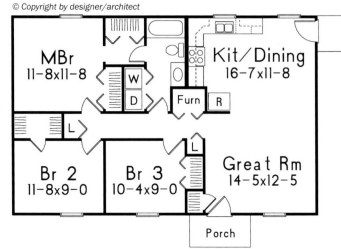

© Copyright by designer/architect

MBr
11-8x11-8

Kit/Dining
16-7x11-8

W

D

Furn

R

L

Br 2
11-8x9-0

Br 3
10-4x9-0

L

Great Rm
14-5x12-5

Porch

Plan #F09-001D-0041

Dimensions:	40' W x 25' D
Heated Sq. Ft.:	1,000
Bedrooms: 3	Bathrooms: 1

Foundation: Crawl space standard;
basement or slab for an additional
fee

See index for more information

Patio

© Copyright by
designer/architect

R

Kit
7-10x
9-8
vaulted

DW

Living
15-6x12-0
vaulted

skylights
above

plant
shelf
above

Bedroom
11-1x11-0
vaulted

Hall

L

Entry

Porch

*Images provided by
designer/architect*

Plan #F09-007D-0029

Dimensions:	24' W x 30' D
Heated Sq. Ft.:	576
Bedrooms: 1	Bathrooms: 1

Foundation: Crawl space standard;
slab for an additional fee

See index for more information

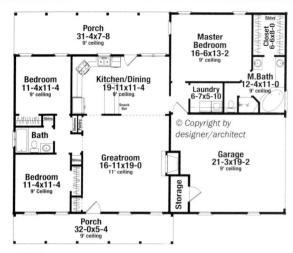

Porch
31-4x7-8
9' ceiling

Master
Bedroom
16-6x13-2
9' ceiling

Closet
6-6x8-0

Bedroom
11-4x11-4
9' ceiling

Kitchen/Dining
19-11x11-4
9' ceiling

M.Bath
12-4x11-0
9' ceiling

Snack Bar

Laundry
6-7x5-10

Bath

© Copyright by
designer/architect

Bedroom
11-4x11-4
9' Ceiling

Greatroom
16-11x19-0
11' ceiling

Garage
21-3x19-2
9' ceiling

Storage

Porch
32-0x5-4
9' ceiling

*Images provided by
designer/architect*

Plan #F09-084D-0016

Dimensions: 56' W x 45'8" D
Heated Sq. Ft.: 1,492
Bedrooms: 3 **Bathrooms:** 2
Foundation: Slab standard; crawl
space or basement for an additional fee

See index for more information

© Copyright by designer/architect

BATH
12-4" x 7'-10"

SCREENED PORCH
17'-2" x 10'-9"

DECK
12'-5" x 10'-8"

BEDROOM 3
11'-4" x 11'-0"

SITTING

FAMILY ROOM
17'-6" X 16'-3"
10' HIGH CEILING

MASTER BDRM
15'-0" x 15'-4"

KITCHEN
9'-6" X 10'-2"

DW

BEDROOM 2
11'-4" x 11'-0"

CLOSET
5'-8" x 7'-0"

PANTRY

LAUNDRY
5'-4" x 6'-6"

BREAKFAST
10'-4" X 8'-10"

DINING
12'-0" x 11'-0"

ENTRY
6'-8" x 3'-6"

WORK SHOP

TO OPTIONAL BONUS ROOM
UP

PORCH
18'-7" x 12'-8"

LINE OF 5' HIGH
KNEE WALL OF
BONUS ROOM

BONUS ROOM
11'-8" x 21'-2"

GARAGE
23'-4" x 26'-8"

*Images provided by
designer/architect*

Plan #F09-013D-0134

Dimensions: 55' W x 58' D
Heated Sq. Ft.: 1,496
Bonus Sq. Ft.: 301
Bedrooms: 3 **Bathrooms:** 2
Foundation: Slab standard; crawl
space or basement for an extra fee

See index for more information

Images provided by designer/architect

Plan #F09-007D-0113

Dimensions:	66' W x 66' D
Heated Sq. Ft.:	2,547
Bedrooms: 4	Bathrooms: 2½
Foundation:	Basement

See index for more information

Features

- A grand-sized great room features a 12' volume ceiling, fireplace with built-in wrap-around shelving and patio doors with sidelights and stylish transom windows
- The walk-in pantry, computer desk, large breakfast island for seven and bayed breakfast area are the many features of this outstanding kitchen
- The master bedroom enjoys a luxurious bath, large walk-in closets and patio access
- 3-car side entry garage

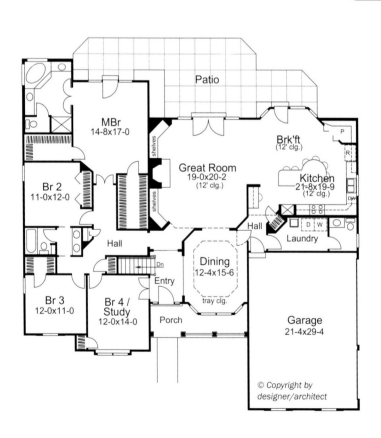

First Floor
1,217 sq. ft.

WALK-IN
4'-0" X 5'-8"

WALK-IN
7'-10" X 5'-8"

BEDROOM #2
10'-0" X 11'-0"

LINEN

MASTER BEDROOM
14'-0" X 12'-0"

SHOWER

BATHROOM
8'-10" X 5'-10"

DOWN

REF

KITCHEN
14'-0" X 12'-8"

BALCONY
12'-0" X 30'-0"

CATHEDRAL CEILING

LIVING ROOM
15'-0" X 13'-6"

DINING ROOM
14'-0" X 13'-8"

Plan #F09-148D-0048

Dimensions:	44' W x 30' D
Heated Sq. Ft.:	1,217
Bonus Sq. Ft.:	1,217
Bedrooms: 2	**Bathrooms:** 1
Exterior Walls:	2" x 6"
Foundation:	Walk-out basement

See index for more information

Images provided by designer/architect

Optional Lower Level
1,217 sq. ft.

STORAGE
14'-2" X 6'-0"

SHOWER

BATHROOM
10'-0" X 8'-2"

BEDROOM #4
10'-6" X 10'-4"

STORAGE

PLAYING ROOM
14'-2" X 17'-8"

UP

FAMILY ROOM
13'-4" X 13'-2"

BEDROOM #3
14'-2" X 11'-0"

© Copyright by designer/architect

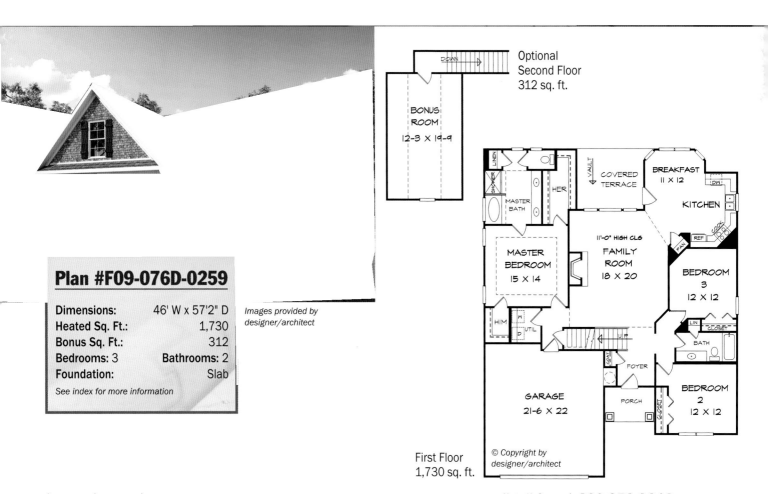

Optional Second Floor
312 sq. ft.

DOWN

BONUS ROOM
12-3 X 14-9

LINEN

SHOWER

MASTER BATH

HER

VAULT

COVERED TERRACE

BREAKFAST
11 X 12

DW

KITCHEN

REF

11'-0" HIGH CLG

FAMILY ROOM
18 X 20

BEDROOM 3
12 X 12

MASTER BEDROOM
15 X 14

HIM

UTIL

UP

FOYER

LIN

CLOSET

BATH

GARAGE
21-6 X 22

PORCH

BEDROOM 2
12 X 12

Plan #F09-076D-0259

Dimensions:	46' W x 57'2" D
Heated Sq. Ft.:	1,730
Bonus Sq. Ft.:	312
Bedrooms: 3	**Bathrooms:** 2
Foundation:	Slab

See index for more information

Images provided by designer/architect

First Floor
1,730 sq. ft.

© Copyright by designer/architect

Plan #F09-161D-0001

Dimensions:	145'9" W x 93' D
Heated Sq. Ft.:	4,036
Bedrooms: 3	Bathrooms: 3½
Exterior Walls:	2" x 8"

Foundation: Crawl space or slab, please specify when ordering

See index for more information

Images provided by designer/architect

Features

- Craftsman and modern style collide with this stunning rustic one-story home
- The open floor plan is ideal for maximizing square footage
- The master suite can be found in its own wing and it features a huge bath and two walk-in closets
- Built-ins and a walk-in pantry keep the kitchen sleek and clutter-free
- There is a flex space perfect as a kid's playroom
- 3-car side entry garage

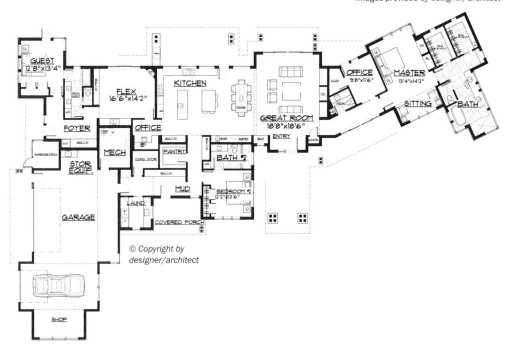

© Copyright by designer/architect

First Floor
1,787 sq. ft.

Optional Lower Level
415 sq. ft.

Images provided by designer/architect

© Copyright by designer/architect

Plan #F09-007D-0085

Dimensions:	59'8" W x 40' D
Heated Sq. Ft.:	1,787
Bonus Sq. Ft.:	415
Bedrooms: 3	Bathrooms: 2
Foundation:	Walk-out basement

See index for more information

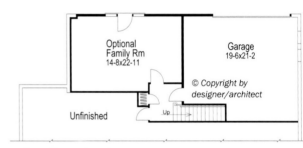

Optional Second Floor
420 sq. ft.

Images provided by designer/architect

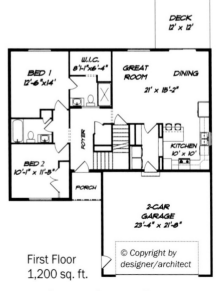

Optional Lower Level
864 sq. ft.

First Floor
1,200 sq. ft.

© Copyright by designer/architect

Plan #F09-159D-0017

Dimensions:	44' W x 48' D
Heated Sq. Ft.:	1,200
Bonus Sq. Ft.:	1,284
Bedrooms: 2	Bathrooms: 2
Exterior Walls:	2" x 6"
Foundation:	Basement or walk-out basement, please specify when ordering

See index for more information

Plan #F09-011D-0679

Dimensions: 53' W x 58' D
Heated Sq. Ft.: 1,821
Bedrooms: 3   **Bathrooms:** 2
Exterior Walls: 2" x 6"
Foundation: Crawl space standard; slab or basement for an additional fee

See index for more information

Images provided by designer/architect

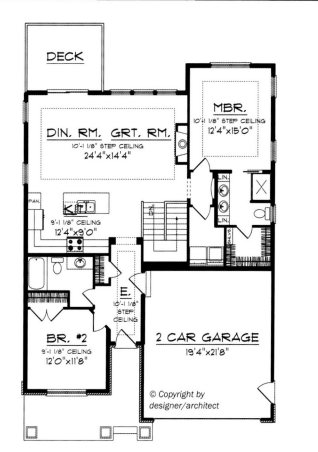

Plan #F09-051D-0850

Dimensions: 38' W x 52' D
Heated Sq. Ft.: 1,334
Bedrooms: 2   **Bathrooms:** 2
Exterior Walls: 2" x 6"
Foundation: Basement standard; crawl space or slab for an additional fee

See index for more information

Images provided by designer/architect

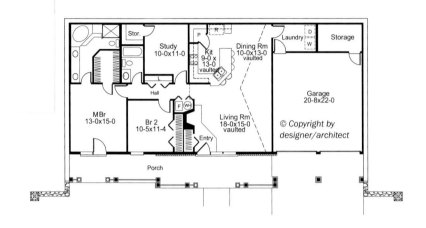

Plan #F09-007D-0161

Dimensions:	70' W x 36' D
Heated Sq. Ft.:	1,480
Bedrooms: 2	Bathrooms: 2
Exterior Walls:	2" x 6"
Foundation:	Slab

See index for more information

Images provided by designer/architect

© Copyright by designer/architect

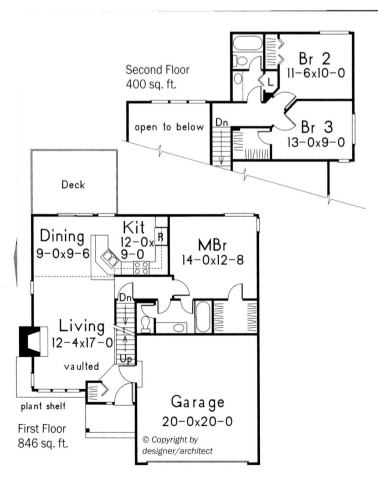

Plan #F09-022D-0002

Dimensions:	36'8" W x 38'8" D
Heated Sq. Ft.:	1,246
Bedrooms: 3	Bathrooms: 2
Foundation:	Basement

See index for more information

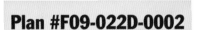

Images provided by designer/architect

© Copyright by designer/architect

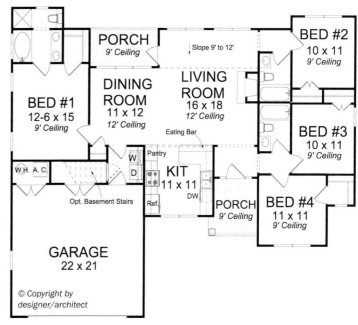

Plan #F09-130D-0364

Dimensions:	56'4" W x 48'10" D
Heated Sq. Ft.:	1,492
Bedrooms: 4	**Bathrooms:** 3
Foundation: Slab standard; crawl space or basement for an additional fee	

Please see the index for more information

Images provided by designer/architect

PORCH
9' Ceiling

Slope 9' to 12'

BED #2
10 x 11
9' Ceiling

BED #1
12-6 x 15
9' Ceiling

DINING ROOM
11 x 12
12' Ceiling

LIVING ROOM
16 x 18
12' Ceiling

Eating Bar

BED #3
10 x 11
9' Ceiling

W.H. A.C.

W
D

Pantry

KIT
11 x 11

DW

Ref.

PORCH
9' Ceiling

BED #4
11 x 11
9' Ceiling

Opt. Basement Stairs

GARAGE
22 x 21

© Copyright by designer/architect

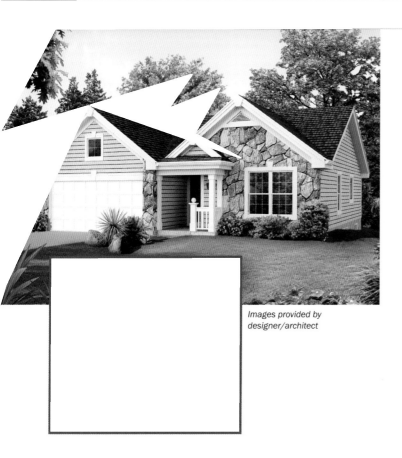

Images provided by designer/architect

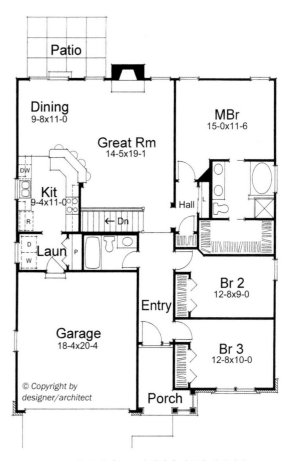

Patio

Dining
9-8x11-0

Great Rm
14-5x19-1

MBr
15-0x11-6

DW

Kit
9-4x11-0

Hall

L

Dn

R

D
W

Laun

P

Entry

Br 2
12-8x9-0

Garage
18-4x20-4

Br 3
12-8x10-0

© Copyright by designer/architect

Porch

Plan #F09-071S-0006

Dimensions:	90' W x 66'6" D
Heated Sq. Ft.:	4,100
Bedrooms: 4	Bathrooms: 3½
Exterior Walls:	2" x 6"
Foundation:	Crawl space

See index for more information

Images provided by designer/architect

Features

- The family room connects to this home's other casual living areas for convenience
- Double-doors keep the cozy den private from the rest of the first floor allowing it to easily convert to a home office space
- A beautiful sitting area extends the master bedroom
- The bonus room on the second floor is included in the square footage and is perfect as a children's play room
- 3-car side entry garage

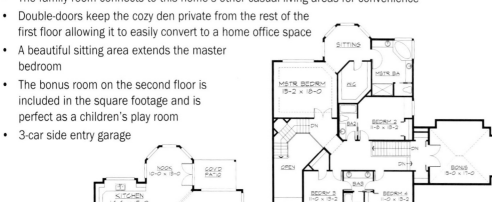

Second Floor
2,090 sq. ft.

© Copyright by
designer/architect

First Floor
2,010 sq. ft.

Plan #F09-032D-0932

Dimensions:	38' W x 30'4" D
Heated Sq. Ft.:	1,102
Bonus Sq. Ft.:	1,102
Bedrooms: 2	Bathrooms: 1
Exterior Walls:	2" x 6"

Foundation: Basement standard; crawl space, floating slab or monolithic slab for an additional fee

See index for more information

Features

- Step into the entry hall from the charming covered porch and discover a walk-in closet for keeping the entry clutter-free

- The open-concept floor plan has the kitchen and dining space blending perfectly with the main living area

- The kitchen has an L-shape and features an island with dining space and a walk-in pantry with a barn door for a rustic modern farmhouse feel

- The bedroom enjoys close proximity to the pampering bath that features a shower as well as a free-standing tub in one corner

- A vaulted beamed ceiling tops the great room, dining and kitchen for a spacious, open feel you will love

- Two bedrooms share the full bath between that features both a tub and a walk-in shower

- The optional lower level has an additional 1,102 square feet of living area

First Floor
1,102 sq. ft.

Optional Lower Level
1,102 sq. ft

© Copyright by designer/architect

Images provided by designer/architect

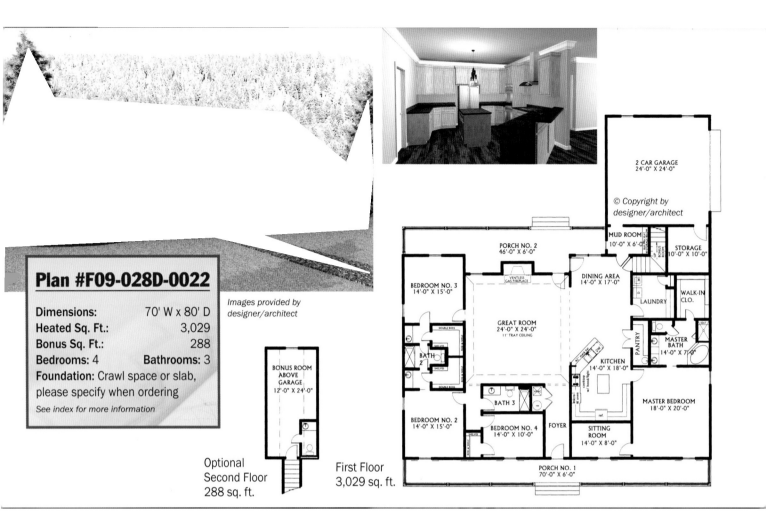

Plan #F09-028D-0022

Dimensions:	70' W x 80' D
Heated Sq. Ft.:	3,029
Bonus Sq. Ft.:	288
Bedrooms: 4	Bathrooms: 3

Foundation: Crawl space or slab, please specify when ordering

See index for more information

Images provided by designer/architect

Optional Second Floor 288 sq. ft.

First Floor 3,029 sq. ft.

BONUS ROOM ABOVE GARAGE 12'-0" X 24'-0"

2 CAR GARAGE 24'-0" X 24'-0"

© Copyright by designer/architect

MUD ROOM 10'-0" X 6'-0"

STORAGE 10'-0" X 10'-0"

PORCH NO. 2 46'-0" X 6'-0"

DINING AREA 14'-0" X 17'-0"

LAUNDRY

WALK-IN CLO.

BEDROOM NO. 3 14'-0" X 15'-0"

VENTLESS GAS FIREPLACE

GREAT ROOM 24'-0" X 24'-0" 11' TRAY CEILING

BATH

PANTRY

MASTER BATH 14'-0" X 7'-0"

BATH 3

KITCHEN 14'-0" X 18'-0"

BEDROOM NO. 2 14'-0" X 15'-0"

BEDROOM NO. 4 14'-0" X 10'-0"

FOYER

SITTING ROOM 14'-0" X 8'-0"

MASTER BEDROOM 18'-0" X 20'-0"

PORCH NO. 1 70'-0" X 6'-0"

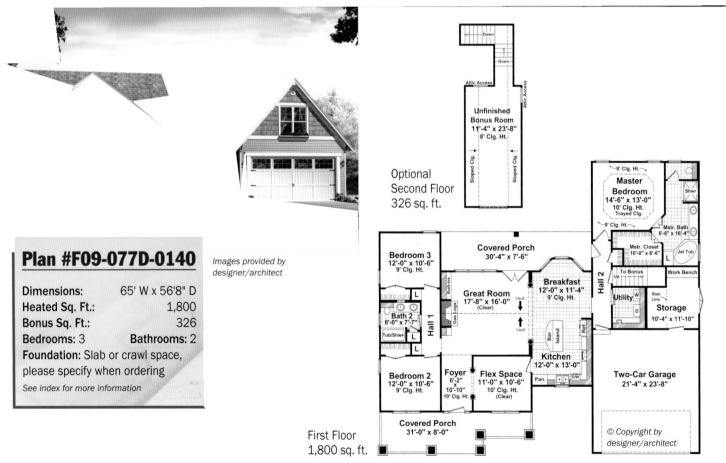

Plan #F09-077D-0140

Dimensions:	65' W x 56'8" D
Heated Sq. Ft.:	1,800
Bonus Sq. Ft.:	326
Bedrooms: 3	Bathrooms: 2

Foundation: Slab or crawl space, please specify when ordering

See index for more information

Images provided by designer/architect

Optional Second Floor 326 sq. ft.

Unfinished Bonus Room 11'-4" x 23'-8" 8' Clg. Ht.

Attic Access

Sloped Clg.

Down

First Floor 1,800 sq. ft.

Master Bedroom 14'-6" x 13'-0" 10' Clg. Ht. Trayed Clg.

Mstr. Bath 6'-6" x 16'-4"

Mstr. Closet 10'-0" x 6'-6"

Jet Tub

Bedroom 3 12'-0" x 10'-6" 9' Clg. Ht.

Covered Porch 30'-4" x 7'-6"

Breakfast 12'-0" x 11'-4" 9' Clg. Ht.

Hall 2

Utility

Work Bench

Bath 2 8'-0" x 7'-7"

Hall 1

Great Room 17'-8" x 16'-0" (Clear)

Storage 10'-4" x 11'-10"

Tub/Shwr

Bar Island

To Bonus

Kitchen 12'-0" x 13'-0"

Bedroom 2 12'-0" x 10'-6" 9' Clg. Ht.

Foyer 6'-2" x 10'-10" 10' Clg. Ht.

Flex Space 11'-0" x 10'-6" 10' Clg. Ht. (Clear)

Two-Car Garage 21'-4" x 23'-8"

Covered Porch 31'-0" x 8'-0"

© Copyright by designer/architect

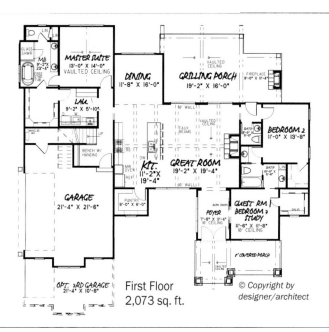

Plan #F09-155D-0147

Images provided by designer/architect

Dimensions: 70'6" W x 58'2" D
Heated Sq. Ft.: 2,073
Bonus Sq. Ft.: 316
Bedrooms: 3   Bathrooms: 2½
Foundation: Crawl space or slab standard; basement or daylight basement for an additional fee

See index for more information

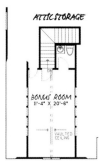

ATTIC STORAGE

BONUS ROOM
11'-4" X 20'-6"

Optional
Second Floor
316 sq. ft.

First Floor
2,073 sq. ft.

© Copyright by designer/architect

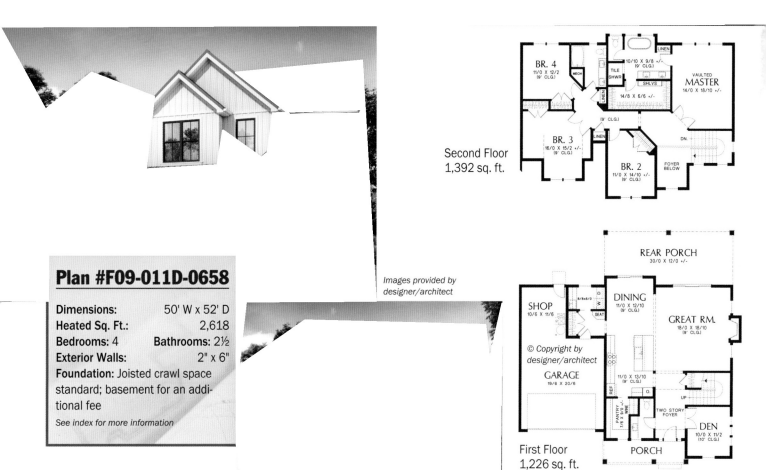

Second Floor
1,392 sq. ft.

Plan #F09-011D-0658

Images provided by designer/architect

Dimensions: 50' W x 52' D
Heated Sq. Ft.: 2,618
Bedrooms: 4   Bathrooms: 2½
Exterior Walls: 2" x 6"
Foundation: Joisted crawl space standard; basement for an additional fee

See index for more information

© Copyright by designer/architect

First Floor
1,226 sq. ft.

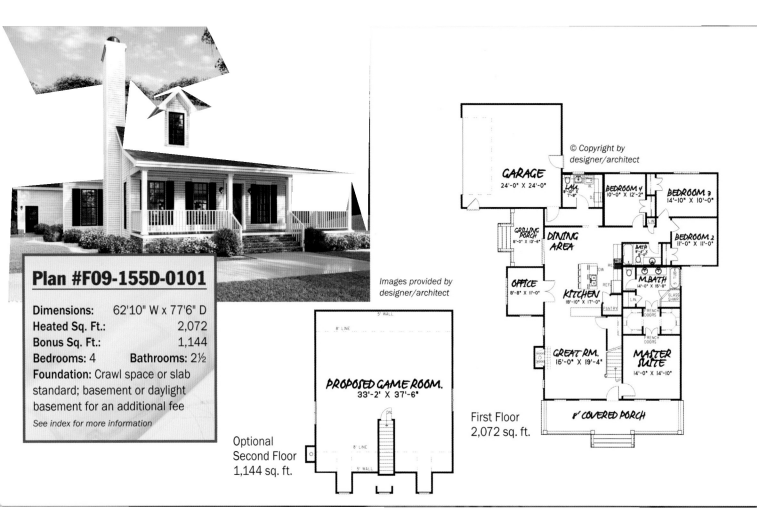

Plan #F09-155D-0101

Dimensions: 62'10" W x 77'6" D
Heated Sq. Ft.: 2,072
Bonus Sq. Ft.: 1,144
Bedrooms: 4   **Bathrooms:** 2½
Foundation: Crawl space or slab standard; basement or daylight basement for an additional fee
See index for more information

Images provided by designer/architect

© Copyright by designer/architect

PROPOSED GAME ROOM.
33'-2" X 37'-6"

Optional
Second Floor
1,144 sq. ft.

First Floor
2,072 sq. ft.

GARAGE 24'-0" X 24'-0"
BEDROOM 4 10'-0" X 12'-2"
BEDROOM 3 14'-10" X 10'-0"
BEDROOM 2 11'-0" X 11'-0"
GRILLING PORCH 8'-0" X 13'-6"
DINING AREA
BATH
M.BATH 14'-0" X 15'-8"
OFFICE 8'-8" X 11'-0"
KITCHEN 18'-10" X 17'-0"
GREAT RM. 15'-0" X 19'-4"
MASTER SUITE 14'-0" X 14'-10"
8' COVERED PORCH

Plan #F09-126D-1167

Dimensions: 34' W x 32' D
Heated Sq. Ft.: 1,022
Bedrooms: 2   **Bathrooms:** 1
Exterior Walls: 2" x 6"
Foundation: Basement
See index for more information

Images provided by designer/architect

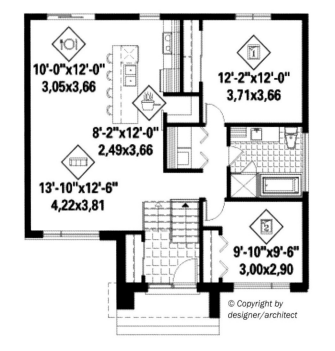

10'-0"x12'-0"
3,05x3,66

12'-2"x12'-0"
3,71x3,66

8'-2"x12'-0"
2,49x3,66

13'-10"x12'-6"
4,22x3,81

9'-10"x9'-6"
3,00x2,90

© Copyright by designer/architect

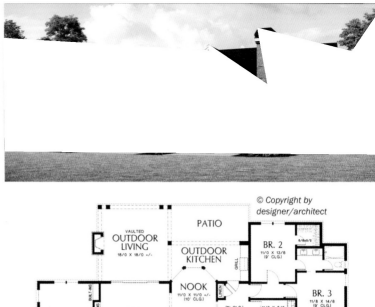

Images provided by designer/architect

Plan #F09-011D-0661

Dimensions:	76' W x 62' D
Heated Sq. Ft.:	2,508
Bedrooms: 3	Bathrooms: 2½
Exterior Walls:	2" x 6"

Foundation: Joisted continuous footings standard; basement for an additional fee

See index for more information

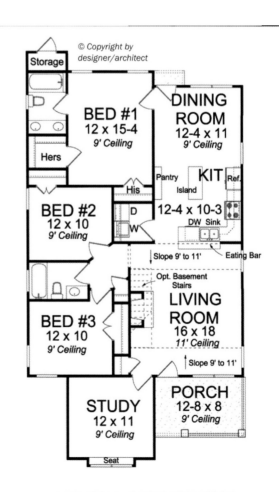

Plan #F09-130D-0396

Dimensions:	31' W x 57' D
Heated Sq. Ft.:	1,420
Bedrooms: 3	Bathrooms: 2
Exterior Walls:	2" x 6"

Foundation: Slab standard; basement or crawl space for an additional fee

See index for more information

Images provided by designer/architect

housing solutions for
TODAY'S FAMILIES

Families are changing from generation to generation and so are their needs and requirements in living arrangements. The main demographic groups that currently make up the majority of the individuals living in the United States include: Millennials (born 1980-1994), Generation X'ers (born 1961-1981), Baby Boomers (born 1943-1964); with a portion of this segment also known as the Sandwich Generation (born 1940s-1970s), and Seniors (born 1945 or earlier). Millennials and Baby Boomers are the two groups home designers are primarily trying to cater to today primarily because they make up the majority of the population. Architects are scrambling to include the features these two groups want into today's new home designs.

what features do most buyers consider essential?

what features do buyers think are desirable in a new home?

Across the board, there are similarities from generation to generation. Regardless of age, all new homeowners are looking for a home design that would help them save energy and keep the home organized. ENERGY STAR® appliances and windows, more insulation than what's required by code, a conveniently located laundry room, extra garage storage, and a walk-in pantry are the top features home buyers want regardless of their age. Also, high on a homebuyers' most wanted list are exterior lighting, a patio, a full bath on the main level, and hardwood floors.

People across all generations are typically looking for a new home that is a different size than what they currently have. But, it's the open floor plan that's most popular for the average single-family home layout right now. Single level homes are also slightly edging out two-story designs by a narrow margin, while the once popular split level drops to last place.

Energy efficient home designs are the most desired type of homes being built right now. Following closely are smart home designs, which may include anything from a thermostat controlled by your smart phone to a Wi-Fi video doorbell.

millenials

Millennials have a no-nonsense attitude toward home design. They are moving away from homes with excess and challenging architects to design practical homes that are open, have a natural flow from room to room, and maximize every square foot for a spacious feel in a smaller footprint, all while using building materials that favor the environment.

The homes they are drawn toward are sleeker, less cluttered visually, and blend seamlessly with the outdoor areas creating a feeling of a larger home overall. They are foregoing large backyards and the extra bells and whistles like a media room, and want to build a functional home they can truly afford. They want less maintenance both inside and out. Millennials want a home that features a deck, a patio, and a front porch. Extending living space to the outdoors is a concept fully embraced by younger generations.

Like the older segments of the population, Millennials appreciate builders who design homes with flex spaces that can adapt to future needs. This group may need a home office now since many people work from home, but in a few years, this space may need to be adapted to a nursery, or a guest room. When a Millennial builds a new home, flexibility is key because chances are, they're not just purchasing for today, but 20 to 30 years down the road.

Unless noted, copyright by designer/architect; Page 183: top: Millennial couple looking at home plans, istockphoto.com; middle: Seamless outdoor living, Plan #056S-0015, Raef Grohne, photographer; bottom, left to right: Front porch initiates socializing, Plan #026D-1891, Regan Morton, Crown Photography, LLC; Flex space converted to an office, with ClosetMaid® shelving, closetmaid.com; Mid-Century Modern home with open floor plan, Plan #011D-0343; See additional photos and purchase plans at houseplansandmore.com.

Because Millennials are shopping and communicating primarily from their smart phones, Wi-Fi access and community websites are important ways for them to feel connected.

Millennials are known for their fascination with technology, so their preference in the kitchen would be to have a TV over a second oven. Home automation is most important to this group of homeowners. Most believe the technological capabilities of a house are more important than its "curb appeal." This generation is extremely comfortable with technology since they are the first generation to become homeowners who were raised using a smart phone.

The homes of Millennials will use technology to the fullest and literally the entire home will be managed through smart phone apps or voice activated automation. Home technology hubs will make their entertainment choices, monitor the arrival of their packages, schedule repairmen, juggle their children's schedules, and improve their health and well-being. When it comes to their product choices, they're savvy readers of online ratings, comments and reviews, and they know what's worth it, and what isn't.

This generation knows how to easily search out ideas online by creating Pinterest boards, reading and curating blogs, and by joining online communities to gain more knowledge about their preferences and hobbies. Most have already found every element they could ever want for their dream home online, and now they're ready to recreate it in real life.

the sandwich generation

Are you a part of the Sandwich Generation? Members of the Sandwich Generation are typically 45 to 64 years old, and are a part of all cultures and ethnicities. This demographic group was created in recent years and has been steadily increasing. Lifespans are much longer than in the past, so there's a need for ongoing and sometimes long-term elderly care. Additionally, college graduates now tend to return home until they find employment. These situations can cause quite an emotional and financial strain on the family members that are "sandwiched" between these two generations, especially since the Sandwich Generation are also trying to save for their own retirement not too far in the distance.

It can be a hard struggle to handle costs for aging parents, while simultaneously supporting young, and adult children most likely still attending college. Reports show that there are about 10 million Americans finding themselves in this situation. Nursing homes and in-home care are often too expensive for many families. Similarly, managing multiple property costs can weigh heavily on the bank account. These financial hardships cause many families to explore the option of a multiple generational household.

Several generations living under the same roof can have its benefits as well as some downfalls. The older family members enjoy the companionship and personal care they receive when they move in with their younger family members. Additionally, it is a more effective option financially. It cuts costs dramatically for the family overall with the absence of another home payment, nursing home, or in-home care. Furthermore, the adult children that move back home can help with the caring of their grandparents, while the Sandwich Generation focuses on providing the majority of the financial support. Younger children willing to help their grandparents should be encouraged to do so, too. And, live-in grandparents can be incredibly helpful watching the younger children, while the parents are at work; therefore, saving on childcare expenses. In multi-generational households, personal space is a huge issue. Since the home is accommodating more family members, it is very important that individuals feel they have their own dedicated space.

trend spotting

Today's homebuilders are noticing this trend and are integrating these family shift demands into their floor plans when designing new homes. The main change in home design once again is the need for flexible spaces. Architects are eliminating formal rooms such as the living and dining rooms and are opting for a space that can be used for a variety of purposes including a home office, or even an in-law suite. Floor plans are being designed with additional bedrooms and baths for more comfort with multiple adult family members. This trend is likely to continue since many families during the pandemic couldn't see each other due to social distancing. Having all family members under one roof will reduce the risk of a family member being inaccessible or isolated.

The most popular requests from home buyers in this group today are floor plans that include two master suites, each with its own luxury bath and walk-in closet. And, as homeowners age, they want a first floor master suite, and sometimes that means two master suites on the main floor if there's also an aging elderly parent living there, too.

multiple masters

Home designers are also redesigning two-car garages, or a three-car garage to include a guest room, or an in-law suite. Other popular floor plan arrangements include a guest or in-law suite that features a kitchenette, living room, a full bath, and a bedroom that is separate from the rest of the home, but often attached via a breezeway. These living areas, referred to as in-law suites, are an apartment within a larger house. Some homeowners that have two large living areas choose to install a kitchenette in a living room near an extra bedroom.

privacy, please

Another popular choice for homeowners that have plenty of land is to build an apartment garage, or a "granny pod" near their existing home. An apartment garage provides privacy for the live-in relative as well as additional parking and storage space for everyone.

get in the zone

With so many adults sharing a space, the need for organization and storage is very important. So, it comes as no surprise that a drop zone with a charging station and a mail organization place is a very helpful feature for maintaining an organized home not laden with clutter and personal belongings. Homeowners are enjoying the idea of having a designated tech center at the garage entrance right alongside the laundry room and drop zone, so architects and designers are taking notice. Homeowners no longer want their washer and dryer located in a basement, either. They're looking for ease in all aspects of managing their home and stowing these frequently used appliances out of sight makes this chore more of a chore. And, if all bedrooms are on the second floor, then home designers are moving the laundry room to that level for even more convenience. Why drag all of your dirty laundry to the first floor just to have to carry it all back upstairs when clean again?

Unless noted, copyright by designer/architect; Page 186, top: Plan #F09-101D-0125 on page 102; bottom: Bonus room converted to home theater, Plan #101D-0091, Rebecca of Sunnybrook Photo, photographer; This floor plan has a studio apartment included, Plan #013D-0204; Page 187, top: Apartment garage Plan #142D-7519; Home organization spot is a great drop zone, ClosetMaid®, closetmaid.com. See additional photos and purchase plans at houseplansandmore.com.

two is better than one

Another terrific and creative home design option is to build a duplex, or multi-family design. The major benefit of a duplex is having two separate homes that share a common wall. This provides privacy for grown children, or elderly parents who need daily assistance, but still want to maintain some amount of independence. This is also excellent for empty nesters that have children who visit often, or return home from college. Residing in close proximity to family can truly be a wonderful and fun experience as long as everyone has some personal space of their own that they can retreat to.

The advantages of living as well as owning a duplex are numerous. You can save money with home maintenance, tax breaks, and easier family care. It is more private than living in an apartment and usually has larger room sizes. There is also the benefit of having multiple garages and a yard. Additionally, by renting the other half of the multi-family home, a duplex owner can make money and cut their cost of living expenses.

Over 25% of American families partake in a multi-generational living arrangement. Economic factors, housing costs, and the need for personal care have forced many people to consider sharing home space. Although multiple generations living under one roof can be challenging, many families discover that they become happier individuals by enjoying the company of their elders as well as the younger generation of their family at the same time. This arrangement offers less stress trying to manage multiple households and provides the opportunity to make memories with their family on a daily basis.

baby boomers

Baby boomers were born between 1946 and 1964. Around 80 million people fit into this group with around a third over the age of 50, which also means that some baby boomers are also a part of the "Sandwich Generation." Not surprisingly, Baby Boomers and seniors typically want to downsize to a home that is less than 1,900 square feet. Baby boomers often change homes due to their health or increased physical limitations. But, what if you aren't providing additional assistance to older parents, or older children? Are the lifestyle demands of this large segment of the population different, then? The answer is definitely YES! Home design needs will be different for this aging segment of individuals, who have money to spend, maintain a very active lifestyle, but will need a home that can adapt to future changes in their health, and mobility.

flex your dollars

Besides luxury master suites and amenity-filled kitchens ideal for entertaining, baby boomers are looking for a couple of other types of spaces in new homes. This group, like Millennials, is also demanding more flex spaces. A flex space is an area that can be adapted to suit the homeowner's needs. For some homeowners, it may become a guest suite, a craft room, or a home office. And, if it's located in a convenient area of the home, it may include an extra bath as well.

too old for tech?

Baby boomers also are loving the idea of a tech center. This area is not the stuffy book-filled study of days gone-by, but it's an open space with computer hookups, charging stations and a work area. This type of space often works perfectly in a loft space. As boomers age, they are not slowing down, so having the ability to work from home in a comfortable environment is key. Many homeowners in this group will continue to work late in their 60s and 70s often as consultants and advisors, so having a dedicated home work space that's efficient and comfortable is key as they transition into retirement.

Overall, baby boomers choose one-story living options. They want everything they need on a daily basis on one floor and highly accessible to them. However, adding a finished lower level for guests and grandchildren, is the preferred floor plan layout. Then, boomers have their own space on the first floor, while providing a private adequate space for guests at the same time. Think bright, open staircases and walk-outs; these are not the dark cavern-like basements of the 70s. Once again, these lower level spaces offer flexibility families need, and provide a great space for an older parent, or an adult child. Or, these spaces can also include areas for hobbies like a wine cellar, or billiards. They are limitless and will make a home feel like it was designed specifically for its owner in every way.

Baby boomers are educated, active, tech savvy, and not afraid to make decisions. With their active lifestyle, they are also looking for neighborhoods that are walkable. They are willing to live in smaller spaces than their previous homes and that sacrifice is worth it if where they are moving allows them to walk to restaurants and stores rather than driving. They are sophisticated buyers who know what they want, and are financially able to get it. They want to live well, and they want to live in comfort.

The biggest consensus between generations is the need for a home that is energy efficient and organized. Baby boomers listed Energy Star® appliances as their top most wanted feature in a home. For all buyers, the most wanted feature was a laundry room.

good design practices

When designing and building a new home, no matter what your age, it is wise to consider incorporating features of universal design into it. That is, homes designed for people of all ages for all abilities. Whether you are a young mother with a stroller, or an older person confined to a wheelchair, both homeowners want ease of movement and convenience in their everyday life. Some minor changes to a floor plan can make it more compatible for everyone.

Today's home products and design elements are very aesthetically pleasing, even those designed for universally minded homes. The home design features and ideas below add convenience for all ages without compromising style, and many times these features enhance the aesthetics, desirability, and value of a home:

general layout

- Choose an open floor plan with little or no walls - anything more narrow, or with bends makes travel difficult.

- Widen exterior doors – they should be a minimum of 32" wide, or incorporate 5' x 5' clear entrance space and 36" wide doors for uninhibited movement.

- Widen interior hallways - these are the hallways needed to reach the bedrooms and baths; widen them to 4' wide and straighten.

- Make exterior doors level at the entrances.

- Select a floor plan with first floor or main floor bathrooms and bedrooms.

- Create good acoustics.

- Integrate home automation to make it easy to change the temperature, lighting, or security with the tap of a finger on your smart phone. If not all family members are tech savvy, use remote controls for lights, shades, and other items.

- Fire alarms/smoke detectors that flash, as well as make sound ensure awareness regardless of sight or hearing impairments.

- Consider a residential elevator if you choose a multi-story dwelling.

fixtures & finishes

- Select lever-style door handles. Or, choose swing away hinges, which increase the door width by 2".

- Use less furniture for greater ease of movement.

- Choose non-skid flooring options like hardwood, luxury vinyl laminate, or tile. If you decide to change flooring types between rooms, it is imperative that the sub-floor is laid properly so that the transition between rooms is seamless. If there's a bump or rise in the flooring level between rooms, it's more difficult for a wheelchair user to move freely. And, large tile flooring is easiest to keep clean. Wheelchairs track in considerable dirt and moisture from the outdoors, so the less grout, the better. Be careful when considering carpet and steer away from plush varieties, which would make movement impossible. Opt for Berber or other low-pile carpet options, if desired.

- Add extra lighting, both inside and out especially near halls and walkways for increased visibility.

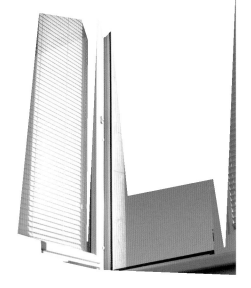

- Install casement windows that use cranks and easily open with just one hand instead of cumbersome double-hung windows. Remember to place carefully, if you want someone seated in a wheelchair to be able to reach. For most wheelchair heights, the windowsills should be lower than the standard placement height. Often a fixed window or transom window can be placed below, or above the operable casement window to make a window appear larger.

- Choose low-maintenance finishes, or even better select sustainable products.

Unless noted, copyright by designer/architect; Page 190, top: Luxury laundry space is a must-have for homeowners of all ages, Plan #011S-0189; A floor plan with many features people are looking for today, Plan #020D-0348; An open floor plan is a must, Plan #020D-0348, J Shannon Williams, photographer; Page 191 top, right: Ideal open floor plan, Plan #011D-0343; Stick with hardwood or laminate flooring for an open feel and universal design, Plan #051D-0852; See additional photos and purchase plans at houseplansandmore.com.

kitchens & baths

To keep the kitchen open for a family member using a wheelchair, here are a few important necessities to consider:

- A 5' diameter clearance is needed for a wheelchair to turn.

- Countertops should be lowered to 30" and offer knee clearance. This is 6" lower than the standard 36". Offering knee clearance provides a workstation.

- Select a single lever sink faucet, or a no-touch motion sensor design.

- A side-by-side refrigerator is the perfect choice.

- Add adjustable storage shelving.

- Choose an oven that has the buttons and dials across the front.

- For storage, add "Lazy Susans" to the lower cabinets, so it will be easy to access pot and pans. This is also a great idea in the food pantry.

- If items are hard to reach, keep "reachers" in convenient areas throughout the kitchen that can grab items from high shelves or overhead cabinets.

- Install top loading washers, dryers, and pull out dishwashers.

- Choose multiple counter heights.

- Select taller toilets.

- Choose curb-less showers, or walk-in shower designs in one or all bathrooms. It is recommended that the concrete sub-floor in the bathroom be lowered by an inch to make transitioning from the hallway to the bathroom smooth.

- Apply bath safety treads to the floor of the shower to avoid slipping.

Page 192, left, top: This universally designed kitchen is completely accessible by all family members, including teenagers, a mother who uses an electric wheelchair, and a grandmother, Mikiten Architecture, Berkeley, CA, mikitenarch.com; top, right: Stunning curb-less shower, Trending Accessibility™, trendingaccessibility.com; bottom, left: ADA Compliant Dishwasher is sleek and modern, GE Profile™ Series 18" Built-In Dishwasher, Item #PDW1860KSS, products.geappliances. com; bottom, right: Merillat Standard Base Tray offers stylish universal storage, merillat.com.

- Select accessible sinks, which allow a wheelchair user's knees to slide underneath the sink basin since the drain is placed at the very back. These basins extend out from the front of the counter for even more ease. Then, consider a faucet that can be turned on with one hand or with movement and offers anti-scald temperature controls.

- Add balance bars in the bathroom near the shower, bathtub and toilet.

Adding some or all of these features into an existing home, or when building a new home will ensure that whatever physical challenges you, or another family member encounters in the future, all will be able to live independently for longer.

As more home designers and architects are seeing the need for flexible living spaces and open floor plans, Universal Design practices are basically becoming mainstream. With expected life spans increasing and the strong desire and determination of people wanting to remain in their homes as long as they can, both young and old alike want similar things; greater convenience, time efficiency, flexibility, and features that integrate comfort and security. Remember that technologies are always evolving and your family's lifestyle is similarly inclined to change at a moment's notice. Universal Design allows your home to transition with you as life happens rather than forcing you to work around frustrating and avoidable obstacles and barriers.

Page 193, top, left: Universal sink design can be very stylish with today's home design trends; Kohler Ronde Sink, us.kohler.com; top, right: Stunning curb-less shower by Trending Accessibility™, trendingaccessibility.com; People-centered design is what Toto® calls this bathroom, totousa.com.

**Optional
Second Floor
472 sq. ft.**

OPTIONAL
BONUS RM /
BEDROOM
5

**First Floor
2,435 sq. ft.**

PATIO

BEDROOM
3
12 X 12

BREAKFAST
11 X 13

MASTER
SUITE
14 X 16

MASTER
BATH

11'-0" HIGH CEILING

FAMILY
ROOM
21 X 18-6

CLOSET

KITCHEN
10 X 16-6

PANTRY

BEDROOM
2
12 X 12

STUDY /
OPT. BR. RM
12 X 12

FOYER

DINING
ROOM
12 X 13

UTILITY

PORCH

GARAGE
23-6 X 22-6

© Copyright by
designer/architect

Plan #F09-076D-0255

*Images provided by
designer/architect*

Dimensions: 68'4" W x 63'7" D
Heated Sq. Ft.: 2,435
Bonus Sq. Ft.: 472
Bedrooms: 4   Bathrooms: 2½
Foundation: Basement, crawl
space or slab, please specify when
ordering

See index for more information

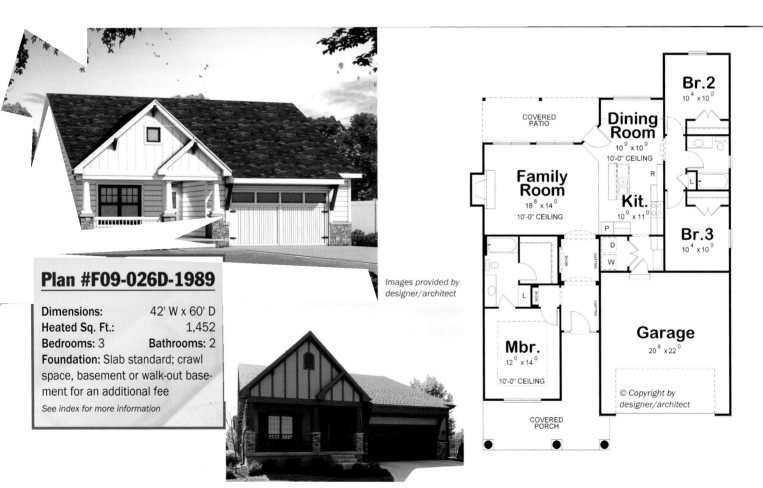

Plan #F09-026D-1989

Dimensions: 42' W x 60' D
Heated Sq. Ft.: 1,452
Bedrooms: 3   Bathrooms: 2
Foundation: Slab standard; crawl
space, basement or walk-out base-
ment for an additional fee

See index for more information

*Images provided by
designer/architect*

COVERED
PATIO

Br.2
10⁴ x 10⁰

**Dining
Room**
10⁰ x 10⁰
10'-0" CEILING

**Family
Room**
18⁸ x 14⁰
10'-0" CEILING

Kit.
10⁰ x 11⁰

Br.3
10⁴ x 10⁰

GALLERY

Mbr.
12⁰ x 14⁰
10'-0" CEILING

Garage
20⁸ x 22⁰

COVERED
PORCH

© Copyright by
designer/architect

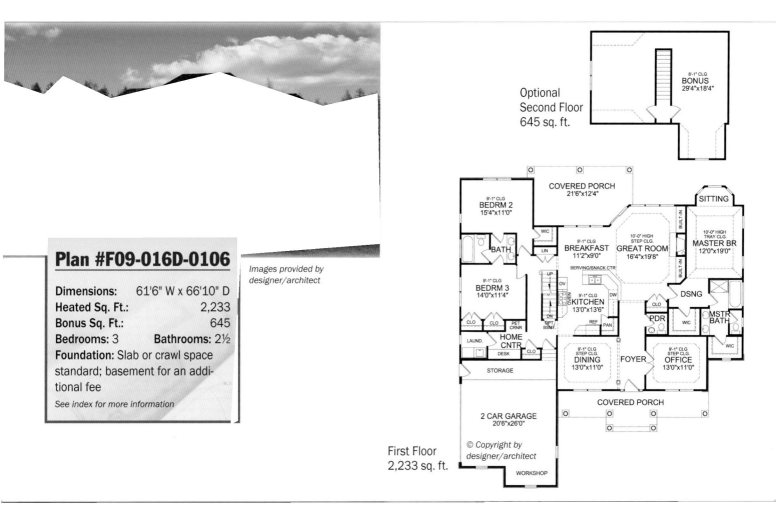

Optional Second Floor
645 sq. ft.

BONUS
29'4"x18'4"
8'-1" CLG

Plan #F09-016D-0106

Images provided by designer/architect

Dimensions: 61'6" W x 66'10" D
Heated Sq. Ft.: 2,233
Bonus Sq. Ft.: 645
Bedrooms: 3   **Bathrooms:** 2½
Foundation: Slab or crawl space standard; basement for an additional fee

See index for more information

COVERED PORCH 21'6"x12'4"

BEDRM 2 15'4"x11'0" — 9'-1" CLG

SITTING

BATH — WIC — LIN

BREAKFAST 11'2"x9'0" — 9'-1" CLG

GREAT ROOM 16'4"x19'8" — 10'-0" HIGH STEP CLG.

MASTER BR 12'0"x19'0" — 10'-0" HIGH TRAY CLG.

BUILT-IN

BEDRM 3 14'0"x11'4" — 9'-1" CLG

SERVING/SNACK CTR

UP — DN — OPT. BSMT. — OV — OVEN

KITCHEN 13'0"x13'6" — 9'-1" CLG

DW — DSNG

CLO — PDR — WIC — MSTR BATH

CLO — CLO — PET CRNR — REF — PAN — CLO

LAUND. — HOME CNTR — DESK — CLO

DINING 13'0"x11'0" — 9'-1" CLG STEP CLG.

FOYER

OFFICE 13'0"x11'0" — 9'-1" CLG STEP CLG.

WIC

STORAGE

2 CAR GARAGE 20'6"x26'0"

COVERED PORCH

First Floor
2,233 sq. ft.

© Copyright by designer/architect

WORKSHOP

Plan #F09-045D-0018

Images provided by designer/architect

Dimensions: 20' W x 21' D
Heated Sq. Ft.: 858
Bedrooms: 2   **Bathrooms:** 1
Foundation: Crawl space

See index for more information

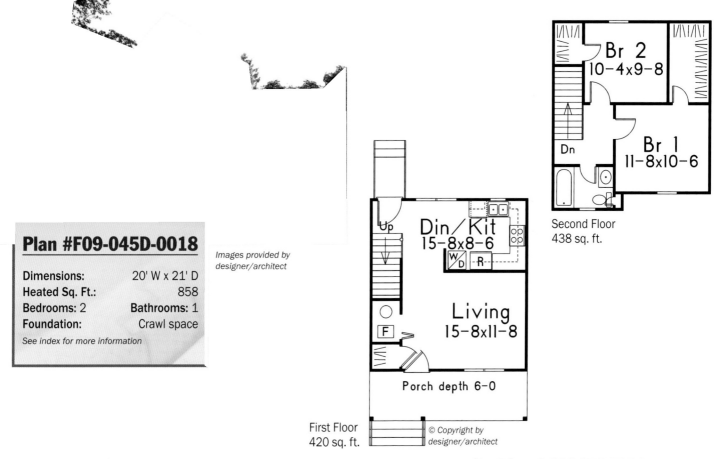

Br 2 10-4x9-8

Br 1 11-8x10-6

Dn

Second Floor
438 sq. ft.

Up

Din/Kit 15-8x8-6

W/D — R

Living 15-8x11-8

F

Porch depth 6-0

First Floor
420 sq. ft.

© Copyright by designer/architect

Plan #F09-161D-0013

Dimensions:	99'4" W x 87'10" D
Heated Sq. Ft.:	3,264
Bedrooms: 3	Bathrooms: 3½
Exterior Walls:	2" x 6"
Foundation:	Crawl space

See index for more information

© Copyright by designer/architect

Images provided by designer/architect

Features

- This stunning modern home offers the open floor plan and high ceilings homeowners want today
- The split bedroom floor plan has the master suite tucked behind the kitchen and near a quiet study
- There are lovely outdoor spaces in the front and the back of the home
- The great room has a sleek fireplace that can also be seen by the kitchen and dining space
- 3-car side entry garage

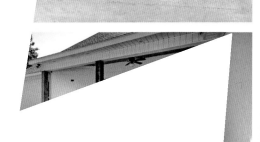

Plan #F09-170D-0004

Dimensions:	48'4" W x 66'4" D
Heated Sq. Ft.:	1,581
Bedrooms: 3	**Bathrooms:** 2

Foundation: Slab or monolithic slab standard; crawl space, basement or daylight basement for an additional fee

See index for more information

Features

- This modest sized one-story home offers many great features for today's family
- A side entry garage gives the exterior added curb appeal
- When entering from the garage you'll find lockers on the right and a utility room on the left
- The kitchen has a very open feel and includes an island with dining space
- The family room enjoys a cozy corner fireplace and an entire wall of windows that overlook the rear covered porch and beyond onto the patio
- The master bedroom and bath include a large walk-in closet
- Two secondary bedrooms share the full bath between them
- 2-car side entry garage

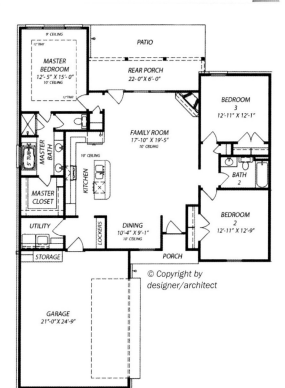

© Copyright by designer/architect

Images provided by designer/architect

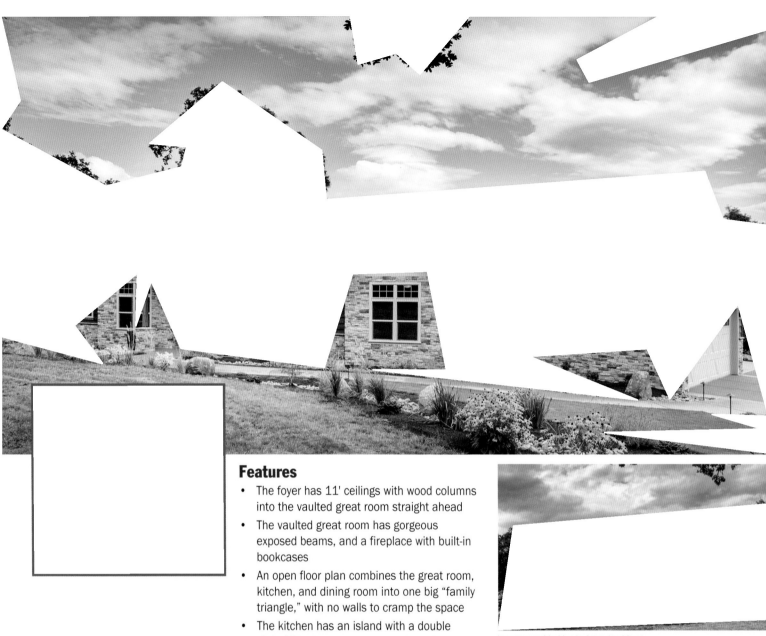

Features

- The foyer has 11' ceilings with wood columns into the vaulted great room straight ahead
- The vaulted great room has gorgeous exposed beams, and a fireplace with built-in bookcases
- An open floor plan combines the great room, kitchen, and dining room into one big "family triangle," with no walls to cramp the space
- The kitchen has an island with a double sink, 10' ceilings, and plenty of counterspace
- 3-car side entry garage

Images provided by designer/architect

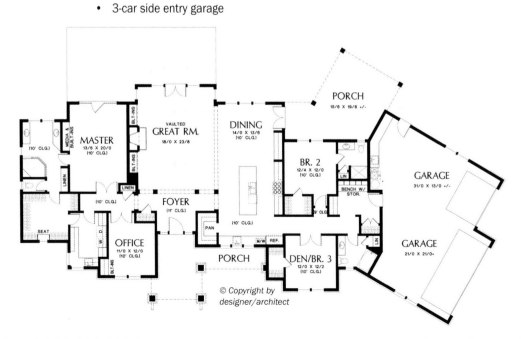

MASTER
13/6 X 20/0
(10' CLG.)

VAULTED
GREAT RM.
18/0 X 23/8

DINING
14/0 X 13/6
(10' CLG.)

PORCH
15/6 X 19/6 +/-

BR. 2
12/4 X 12/0
(10' CLG.)

GARAGE
31/0 X 13/0 +/-

FOYER
(11' CLG.)

GARAGE
21/0 X 21/0+

OFFICE
11/0 X 12/0
(10' CLG.)

PORCH

DEN/BR. 3
12/0 X 12/2
(10' CLG.)

BENCH W/
STOR.

PAN

M/W REF.

© Copyright by
designer/architect

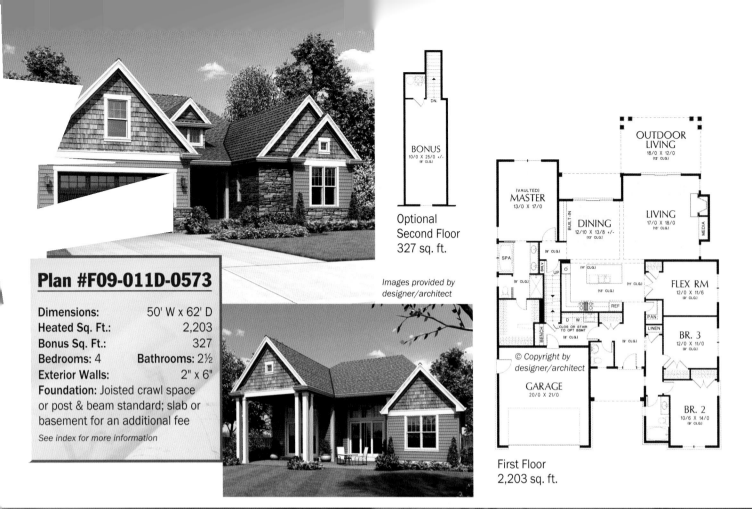

Plan #F09-011D-0573

Dimensions:	50' W x 62' D
Heated Sq. Ft.:	2,203
Bonus Sq. Ft.:	327
Bedrooms: 4	Bathrooms: 2½
Exterior Walls:	2" x 6"

Foundation: Joisted crawl space or post & beam standard; slab or basement for an additional fee

See index for more information

BONUS
10/0 X 25/0 +/-
(8' CLG)

Optional
Second Floor
327 sq. ft.

Images provided by designer/architect

© Copyright by designer/architect

First Floor
2,203 sq. ft.

OUTDOOR LIVING 18/0 X 12/0 (13' CLG)

(VAULTED) MASTER 13/0 X 17/0

DINING 12/10 X 13/8 +/- (13' CLG)

LIVING 17/0 X 18/0 (13' CLG)

FLEX RM 12/0 X 11/6 (8' CLG)

BR. 3 12/0 X 11/0 (8' CLG)

BR. 2 10/6 X 14/0 (8' CLG)

GARAGE 20/0 X 21/0

Plan #F09-130D-0336

Dimensions:	48' W x 55' D
Heated Sq. Ft.:	1,709
Bedrooms: 3	Bathrooms: 2½

Foundation: Slab standard; crawl space or basement for an additional fee

See index for more information

Images provided by designer/architect

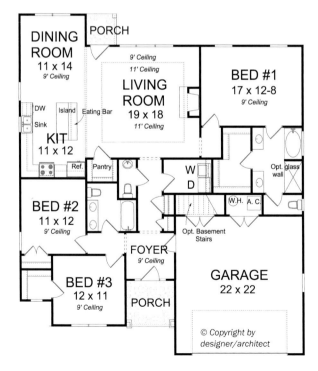

DINING ROOM 11 x 14 — 9' Ceiling

PORCH

LIVING ROOM 19 x 18 — 11' Ceiling

BED #1 17 x 12-8 — 9' Ceiling

KIT 11 x 12

BED #2 11 x 12 — 9' Ceiling

BED #3 12 x 11 — 9' Ceiling

FOYER — 9' Ceiling

GARAGE 22 x 22

PORCH

© Copyright by designer/architect

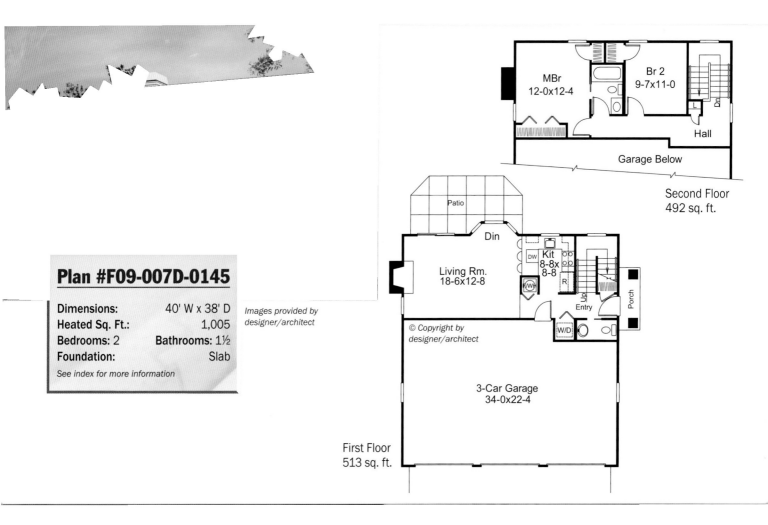

Plan #F09-007D-0145

Dimensions:	40' W x 38' D
Heated Sq. Ft.:	1,005
Bedrooms: 2	Bathrooms: 1½
Foundation:	Slab

See index for more information

Images provided by designer/architect

MBr
12-0x12-4

Br 2
9-7x11-0

Hall

Garage Below

Second Floor
492 sq. ft.

Patio

Din

Living Rm.
18-6x12-8

Kit
8-8x
8-8

DW

Up

Entry

Porch

W/D

© Copyright by
designer/architect

3-Car Garage
34-0x22-4

First Floor
513 sq. ft.

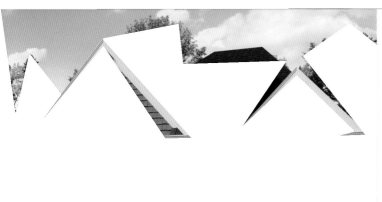

Plan #F09-121D-0048

Dimensions:	44' W x 53'4" D
Heated Sq. Ft.:	1,615
Bedrooms: 2	Bathrooms: 2

Foundation: Basement standard; crawl space or slab for an additional fee

See index for more information

Images provided by designer/architect

Patio

Brkfst/ Dining
12-8x14-11

MBr
12-8x14-6
Coffer Clg

Great Rm
16-9x21-11
12' Clg

DW

Kitchen
12-8x12-9

R

P

Dn

Garage
22-8x24-0

Foyer

Br 2
12-8x11-0

Porch

© Copyright by
designer/architect

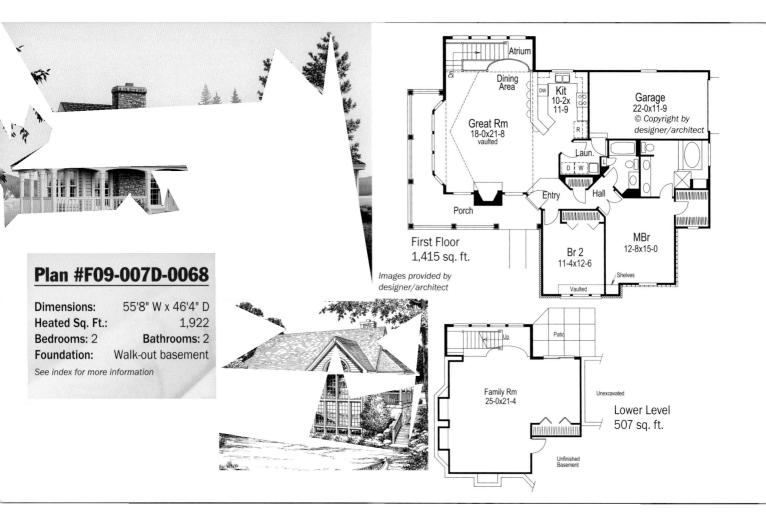

First Floor
1,415 sq. ft.

Images provided by designer/architect

Atrium

Dining Area

Great Rm
18-0x21-8
vaulted

Kit
10-2x
11-9

DW

Garage
22-0x11-9
© Copyright by designer/architect

Laun.

D W

Entry

Hall

Porch

MBr
12-8x15-0

Br 2
11-4x12-6

Shelves

Vaulted

Up

Patio

Family Rm
25-0x21-4

Unexcavated

Lower Level
507 sq. ft.

Unfinished Basement

Plan #F09-007D-0068

Dimensions:	55'8" W x 46'4" D
Heated Sq. Ft.:	1,922
Bedrooms: 2	Bathrooms: 2
Foundation:	Walk-out basement

See index for more information

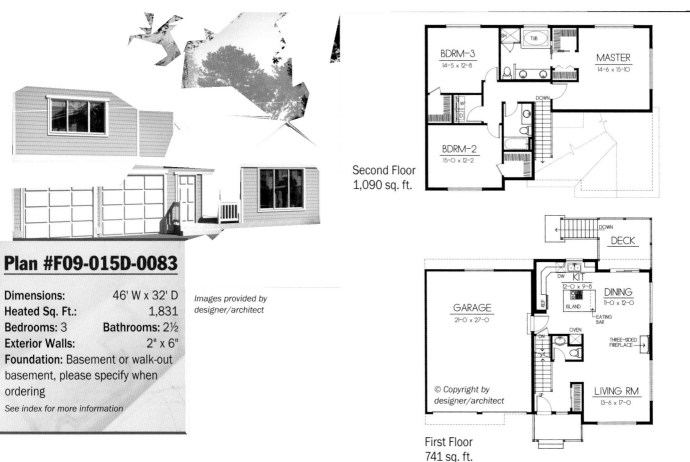

BDRM-3
14-5 x 12-8

TUB

MASTER
14-6 x 15-10

W D

DOWN

BDRM-2
15-0 x 12-2

Second Floor
1,090 sq. ft.

Images provided by designer/architect

DOWN

DECK

KIT
12-0 x 9-8

DW

DINING
11-0 x 12-0

ISLAND

EATING BAR

GARAGE
21-0 x 27-0

OVEN

THREE-SIDED FIREPLACE

DN

UP

LIVING RM
13-6 x 17-0

© Copyright by designer/architect

First Floor
741 sq. ft.

Plan #F09-015D-0083

Dimensions:	46' W x 32' D
Heated Sq. Ft.:	1,831
Bedrooms: 3	Bathrooms: 2½
Exterior Walls:	2" x 6"
Foundation:	Basement or walk-out basement, please specify when ordering

See index for more information

Plan #F09-058D-0247

Dimensions:	60' W x 36'4" D
Heated Sq. Ft.:	1,200
Bedrooms: 3	**Bathrooms:** 2
Foundation:	Basement

See index for more information

Images provided by designer/architect

Garage
19-8x23-4

Kit/Brk
16-4x15-1

Pantry

MBr
11-6x11-10

Dn

© Copyright by
designer/architect

16'x7' Door

Family
16-4x13-11

Bedrm 3
10-0x10-6

Bedrm 2
10-0x10-6

Lin

Porch
16-8x6-4

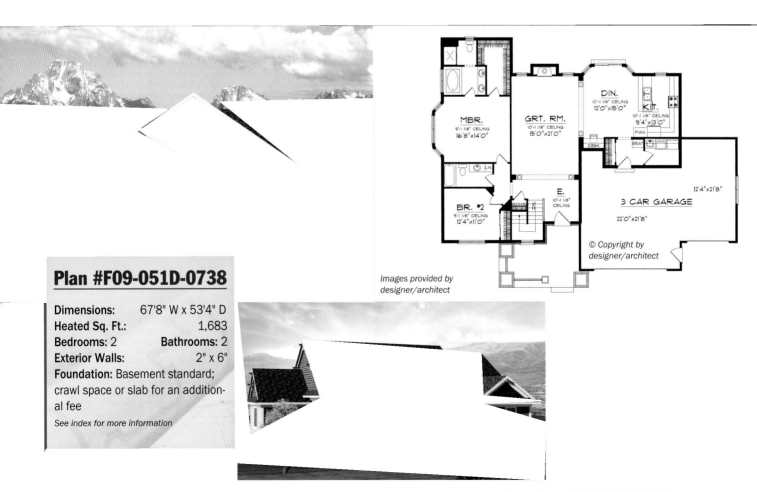

MBR.
9'-1 1/8" CEILING
16'8"x14'0"

GRT. RM.
10'-1 1/8" CEILING
15'0"x21'0"

DIN.
10'-1 1/8" CEILING
12'0"x15'0"

KIT.
10'-1 1/8" CEILING
9'4"x13'0"

PAN.

DESK

SEAT

BR. #2
9'-1 1/8" CEILING
12'4"x11'0"

E.
10'-1 1/8"
CEILING

3 CAR GARAGE
22'0"x21'8"

12'4"x21'8"

© Copyright by
designer/architect

Images provided by designer/architect

Plan #F09-051D-0738

Dimensions:	67'8" W x 53'4" D
Heated Sq. Ft.:	1,683
Bedrooms: 2	**Bathrooms:** 2
Exterior Walls:	2" x 6"

Foundation: Basement standard; crawl space or slab for an additional fee

See index for more information

Plan #F09-011S-0001

Dimensions:	130'3" W x 79'3" D
Heated Sq. Ft.:	4,732
Bedrooms:	4
Bathrooms:	3 full, 2 half
Exterior Walls:	2" x 6"
Foundation:	Walk-out basement

See index for more information

Images provided by designer/architect

© Copyright by designer/architect

Features

- This home's gourmet kitchen, accompanying nook and great room offer ample entertainment space, especially when utilized with the fully equipped outdoor kitchen

- An adjoining theater room and wet bar with separate wine cellar complements three lower level bedrooms perfectly

- The luxurious master bedroom has abundant his and hers closet space with built-in dressers

- 4-car front entry garage

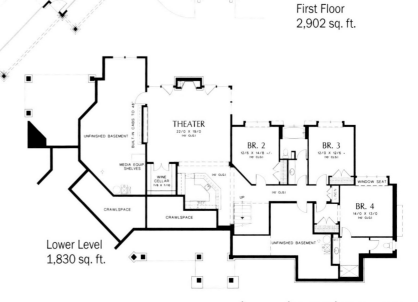

First Floor
2,902 sq. ft.

Lower Level
1,830 sq. ft.

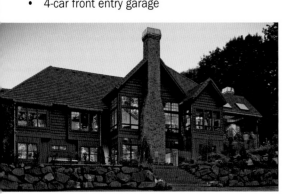

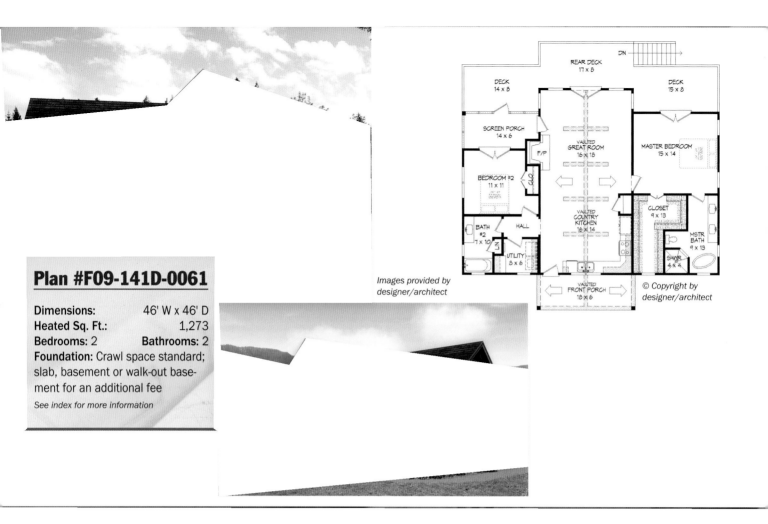

Plan #F09-141D-0061

Dimensions: 46' W x 46' D
Heated Sq. Ft.: 1,273
Bedrooms: 2 **Bathrooms:** 2
Foundation: Crawl space standard; slab, basement or walk-out basement for an additional fee

See index for more information

Images provided by designer/architect

© Copyright by designer/architect

Plan #F09-091D-0511

Dimensions: 78'11" W x 65'5" D
Heated Sq. Ft.: 2,150
Bonus Sq. Ft.: 733
Bedrooms: 4 **Bathrooms:** 3
Exterior Walls: 2" x 6"
Foundation: Basement or crawl space standard; slab, daylight basement or walk-out basement for an additional fee

See index for more information

Images provided by designer/architect

© Copyright by designer/architect

First Floor
2,150 sq. ft.

Optional Second Floor
733 sq. ft.

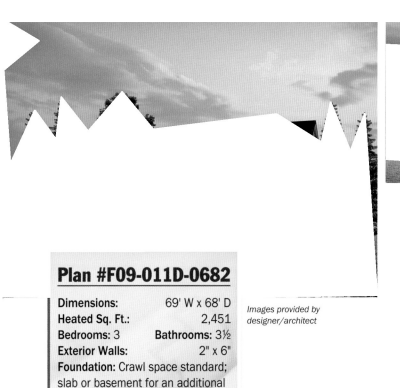

Plan #F09-011D-0682

Dimensions: 69' W x 68' D
Heated Sq. Ft.: 2,451
Bedrooms: 3   **Bathrooms:** 3½
Exterior Walls: 2" x 6"
Foundation: Crawl space standard; slab or basement for an additional fee

See index for more information

Images provided by designer/architect

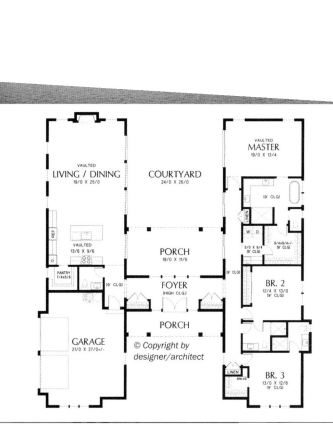

© Copyright by designer/architect

Plan #F09-152D-0134

Dimensions: 25' W x 25' D
Heated Sq. Ft.: 456
Bedrooms: 1   **Bathrooms:** 1
Exterior Walls: 2" x 6"
Foundation: Slab

See index for more information

Images provided by designer/architect

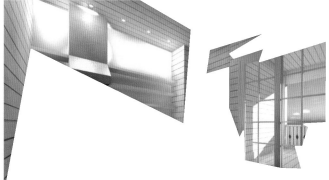

© Copyright by designer/architect

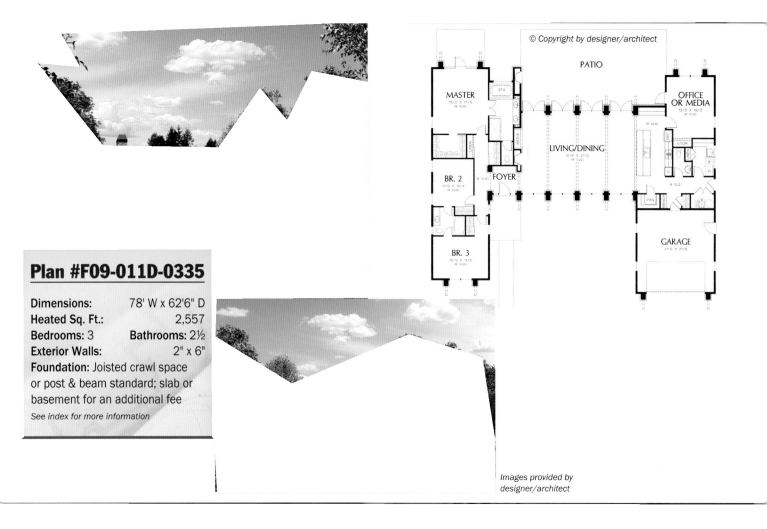

© Copyright by designer/architect

PATIO

MASTER
15'0 x 17'0
(9' CLG)

SPA

OFFICE
OR MEDIA
13'0 x 16'0
(9' CLG)

LIVING/DINING
31'6 X 21'0
(9' CLG)

BR. 2
15'0 x 12'4
(9' CLG)

FOYER

BR. 3
15'0 X 11'0
(9' CLG)

GARAGE
21'0 x 21'6

Plan #F09-011D-0335

Dimensions: 78' W x 62'6" D
Heated Sq. Ft.: 2,557
Bedrooms: 3   **Bathrooms:** 2½
Exterior Walls: 2" x 6"
Foundation: Joisted crawl space
or post & beam standard; slab or
basement for an additional fee
See index for more information

*Images provided by
designer/architect*

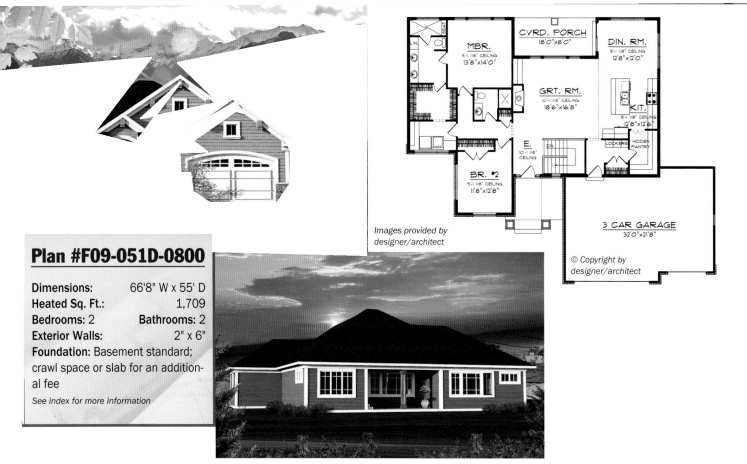

CVRD. PORCH
18'0"x8'0"

MBR.
9'-1 1/8" CEILING
13'8"x14'0"

DIN. RM.
9'-1 1/8" CEILING
12'8"x12'0"

GRT. RM.
10'-1 1/8" CEILING
18'6"x16'8"

KIT.
9'-1 1/8" CEILING
12'8"x12'8"

E.
10'-1 1/8"
CEILING

BR. #2
9'-1 1/8" CEILING
11'8"x12'8"

LOCKERS   HIDDEN
PANTRY

3 CAR GARAGE
32'0"x21'8"

*Images provided by
designer/architect*

© Copyright by
designer/architect

Plan #F09-051D-0800

Dimensions: 66'8" W x 55' D
Heated Sq. Ft.: 1,709
Bedrooms: 2   **Bathrooms:** 2
Exterior Walls: 2" x 6"
Foundation: Basement standard;
crawl space or slab for an addition-
al fee
See index for more information

houseplansandmore.com

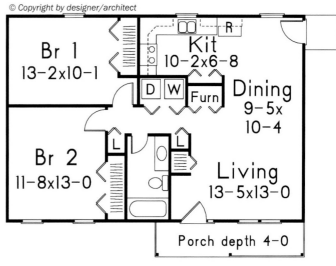

Br 1
13-2x10-1

Kit
10-2x6-8

R

D W Furn

Dining
9-5x
10-4

Br 2
11-8x13-0

L L

Living
13-5x13-0

Porch depth 4-0

Plan #F09-001D-0040

Images provided by designer/architect

Dimensions:	36' W x 28' D
Heated Sq. Ft.:	864
Bedrooms: 2	Bathrooms: 1

Foundation: Crawl space standard; basement or slab for an additional fee

See index for more information

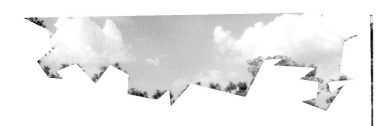

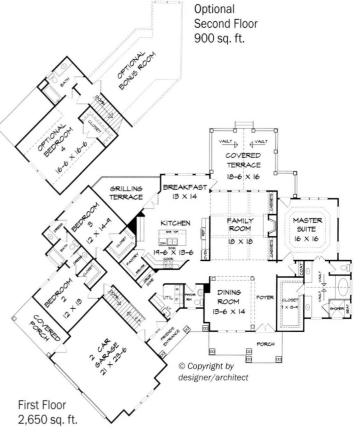

Optional
Second Floor
900 sq. ft.

First Floor
2,650 sq. ft.

Plan #F09-076D-0210

Images provided by designer/architect

Dimensions:	91'9" W x 76'4" D
Heated Sq. Ft.:	2,650
Bonus Sq. Ft.:	900
Bedrooms: 3	Bathrooms: 2½

Foundation: Basement, crawl space or slab, please specify when ordering

See index for more information

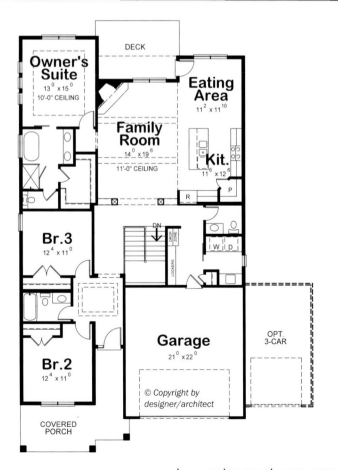

Second Floor
1,435 sq. ft.

VAULTED MASTER
15/2 X 17/0

BR. 2
13/10 X 10/0
(9' CLG.)

BR. 3
11/0 X 11/4+/-
(9' CLG.)

LAUNDRY
10/6 X 6/0

VAULTED BONUS/BR.4
14/0 X 12/0 +

PORCH

DINING
12/0 X 12/0+/-
(9' CLG.)

GREAT RM.
17/6 X 19/0+/-
(9' CLG.)

9/8 X 13/0
(9' CLG.)

10/0 X 13/0

GARAGE
20/0 X 22/6

2-STORY FOYER

DEN
10/6 X 11/0
(9' CLG.)

First Floor
1,142 sq. ft.

Plan #F09-011D-0681

Dimensions:	38' W x 55' D
Heated Sq. Ft.:	2,577
Bedrooms: 4	Bathrooms: 2½
Exterior Walls:	2" x 6"

Foundation: Crawl space standard; slab or basement for an additional fee

See index for more information

Owner's Suite
13⁰ x 15⁰
10'-0" CEILING

DECK

Eating Area
11² x 11¹⁰

Family Room
14⁰ x 19⁶
11'-0" CEILING

Kit.
11⁶ x 12⁶

Br.3
12⁴ x 11⁰

DN

DROP ZONE

LOCKERS

W D

Br.2
12⁴ x 11⁰

Garage
21⁰ x 22⁰

OPT. 3-CAR

COVERED PORCH

Plan #F09-026D-1985

Dimensions:	40' W x 70'8" D
Heated Sq. Ft.:	1,886
Bedrooms:3	Bathrooms: 2½
Exterior Walls:	2" x 6"

Foundation: Basement standard; crawl space, slab or walk-out basement for an additional fee

See index for more information

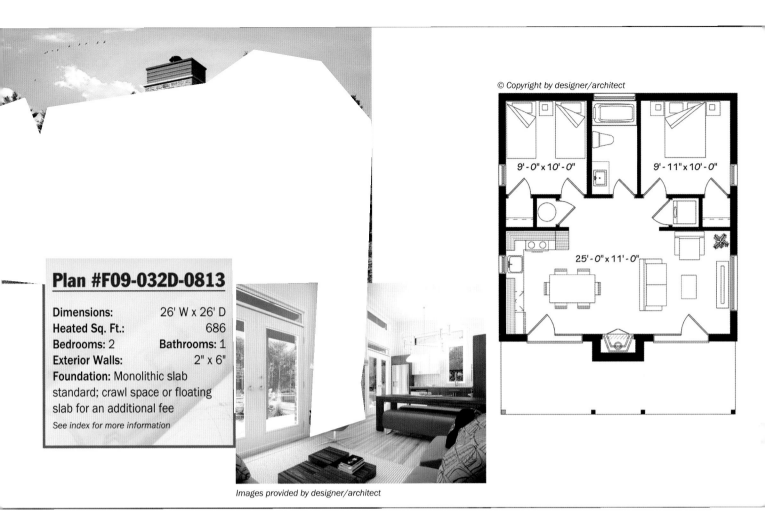

9'-0" x 10'-0"

9'-11" x 10'-0"

25'-0" x 11'-0"

Plan #F09-032D-0813

Dimensions:	26' W x 26' D
Heated Sq. Ft.:	686
Bedrooms: 2	**Bathrooms:** 1
Exterior Walls:	2" x 6"

Foundation: Monolithic slab
standard; crawl space or floating
slab for an additional fee

See index for more information

Images provided by designer/architect

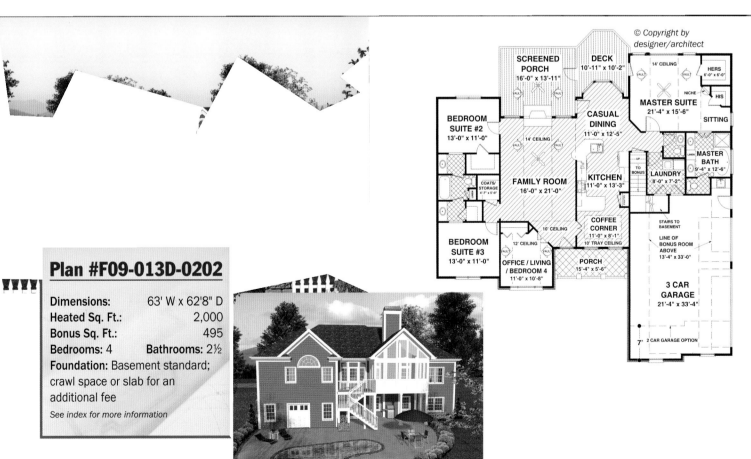

SCREENED PORCH
16'-0" x 13'-11"

DECK
10'-11" x 10'-2"

14' CEILING

HERS
6'-0" x 6'-0"

MASTER SUITE
21'-4" x 15'-6"

NICHE

HIS

SITTING

BEDROOM SUITE #2
13'-0" x 11'-0"

14' CEILING

CASUAL DINING
11'-0" x 12'-5"

MASTER BATH
9'-4" x 12'-6"

LINEN

FAMILY ROOM
16'-0" x 21'-0"

KITCHEN
11'-0" x 13'-3"

UP TO BONUS

LAUNDRY
8'-0" x 7'-2"

COATS/ STORAGE
4'-7" x 5'-0"

COFFEE CORNER
11'-0" x 8'-1"

STAIRS TO BASEMENT

LINE OF BONUS ROOM ABOVE
13'-4" x 33'-0"

10' CEILING

10' TRAY CEILING

BEDROOM SUITE #3
13'-0" x 11'-0"

12' CEILING

OFFICE / LIVING / BEDROOM 4
11'-0" x 10'-8"

PORCH
15'-4" x 5'-6"

3 CAR GARAGE
21'-4" x 33'-4"

7'

2 CAR GARAGE OPTION

Plan #F09-013D-0202

Dimensions:	63' W x 62'8" D
Heated Sq. Ft.:	2,000
Bonus Sq. Ft.:	495
Bedrooms: 4	**Bathrooms:** 2½

Foundation: Basement standard;
crawl space or slab for an
additional fee

See index for more information

Images provided by designer/architect

Plan #F09-001D-0043

Dimensions:	44' W x 26' D
Heated Sq. Ft.:	1,104
Bedrooms: 3	Bathrooms: 2

Foundation: Crawl space standard; basement or slab for an additional fee

See index for more information

Images provided by designer/architect

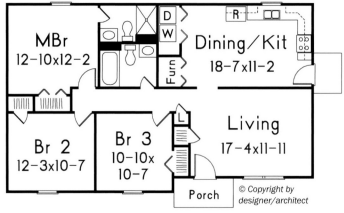

© Copyright by designer/architect

Plan #F09-065D-0315

Dimensions:	60' W x 49'6" D
Heated Sq. Ft.:	1,597
Bedrooms: 3	Bathrooms: 2

Foundation: Basement standard; crawl space for an additional fee

See index for more information

Images provided by designer/architect

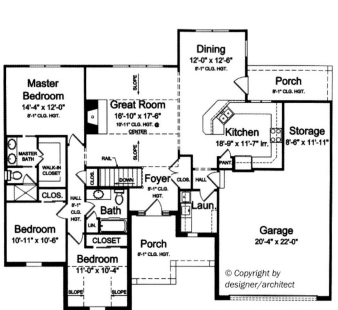

© Copyright by designer/architect

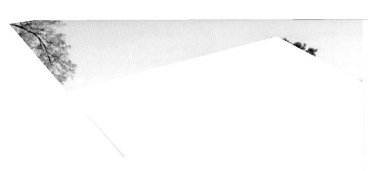

Plan #F09-139D-0044

Dimensions: 67'10" W x 70'4" D
Heated Sq. Ft.: 2,910
Bonus Sq. Ft.: 550
Bedrooms: 4 **Bathrooms:** 3½
Exterior Walls: 2" x 6"
Foundation: Crawl space standard; slab, basement, daylight basement or walk-out basement for an additional fee

See index for more information

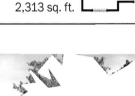

First Floor
2,313 sq. ft.

© Copyright by designer/architect

Second Floor
597 sq. ft.

Plan #F09-121D-0035

Dimensions: 45'8" W x 72'4" D
Heated Sq. Ft.: 1,759
Bedrooms: 3 **Bathrooms:** 2
Foundation: Basement standard; crawl space or slab for an additional fee

See index for more information

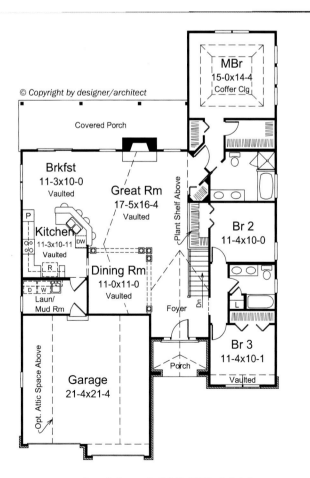

© Copyright by designer/architect

Plan #F09-155D-0047

Dimensions:	60' W x 80'4" D
Heated Sq. Ft.:	2,500
Bonus Sq. Ft.:	354
Bedrooms: 3	Bathrooms: 2½

Foundation: Crawl space or slab, please specify when ordering

See index for more information

Features

- Modern Farmhouse touches grace the interior of this attractive rustic-looking ranch home
- The vaulted great room has a centered fireplace directly across from the island in the kitchen creating an intimate and cozy feel
- The master suite boasts a bath with a free-standing tub, a separate shower, a double-sink vanity, and a huge walk-in closet with built-ins
- Two additional bedrooms share a full bath
- The optional second floor has an additional 354 square feet of living area
- 2-car front entry garage

Images provided by designer/architect

Optional
Second Floor
354 sq. ft.

First Floor
2,500 sq. ft.

© Copyright by designer/architect

Plan #F09-071S-0007

Dimensions:	71' W x 91'6" D
Heated Sq. Ft.:	5,250
Bedrooms: 4	Bathrooms: 4½
Exterior Walls:	2" x 6"
Foundation:	Crawl space

See index for more information

Images provided by designer/architect

Features

- An enormous wrap-around porch has plenty of room to sit and take in views of the outdoors

- A dramatic circular staircase is highlighted in the rotunda with a 27' ceiling

- The rear covered porch has an outdoor fireplace and built-in barbecue grill

- The master bath showcases an octagon-shaped space featuring a whirlpool tub

- 4-car side entry garage

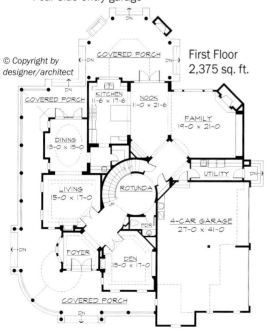

First Floor
2,375 sq. ft.

© Copyright by
designer/architect

Second Floor
2,875 sq. ft.

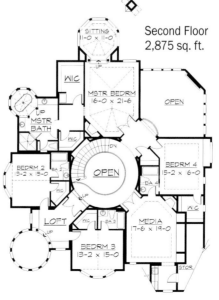

Plan #F09-155D-0100

Dimensions:	24' W x 56'6" D
Heated Sq. Ft.:	970
Bedrooms: 3	**Bathrooms:** 1

Foundation: Crawl space or slab, please specify when ordering

See index for more information

Images provided by designer/architect

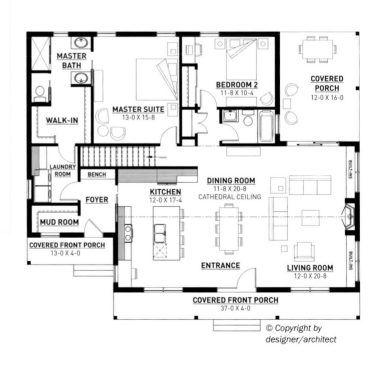

Plan #F09-032D-1081

Dimensions:	50' W x 38' D
Heated Sq. Ft.:	1,604
Bedrooms: 2	**Bathrooms:** 2
Exterior Walls:	2" x 6"

Foundation: Basement standard; crawl space, floating slab or monolithic slab for an additional fee

See index for more information

Images provided by designer/architect

Plan #F09-007D-0199

Dimensions:	39' W x 33' D
Heated Sq. Ft.:	496
Bedrooms: 1	Bathrooms: 1
Foundation:	Slab

See index for more information

Images provided by designer/architect

© Copyright by designer/architect

Plan #F09-058D-0053

Dimensions:	59' W x 44'4" D
Heated Sq. Ft.:	1,895
Bedrooms: 3	Bathrooms: 2
Foundation:	Basement

See the index for more information

Images provided by designer/architect

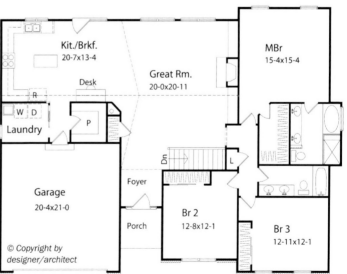

© Copyright by designer/architect

Plan #F09-055D-1004

Dimensions:	81'6" W x 61'3" D
Heated Sq. Ft.:	2,340
Bonus Sq. Ft.:	602
Bedrooms: 3	**Bathrooms:** 2½

Foundation: Crawl space or slab standard; basement or daylight basement for an additional fee

See index for more information

Images provided by designer/architect

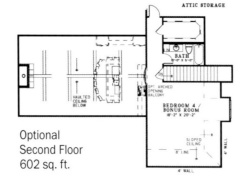

Optional
Second Floor
602 sq. ft.

Features

- The massive kitchen island has enough seating for six people, and doesn't miss the action in the great room
- An outdoor living/grilling porch has a vaulted ceiling and a cozy outdoor fireplace for those chilly nights
- Both informal and formal dining options are available in this floor plan
- The optional second floor has an additional 602 square feet of living area
- 2-car side entry garage, and a 1-car front entry garage

© Copyright by
designer/architect

First Floor
2,340 sq. ft.

Plan #F09-141D-0012

Dimensions:	47' W x 46'6" D
Heated Sq. Ft.:	1,972
Bedrooms: 3	Bathrooms: 3½

Foundation: Crawl space standard; slab, basement or walk-out basement for an additional fee

See index for more information

Features

- An open and airy vaulted family room is adorned with a rustic stone fireplace
- The kitchen is completely open to the dining area and the great room making the entire first floor feel spacious and comfortable even when entertaining
- Covered front and back porches create plenty of outdoor living space including the second floor covered porch
- There is a master suite on the first floor as well as two additional master suites on the second floor creating plenty of living spaces for a live-in parent, or adult child

Images provided by designer/architect

First Floor
1,199 sq. ft.

Second Floor
773 sq. ft.

Plan #F09-007D-0195

Dimensions: 17' W x 27' D
Heated Sq. Ft.: 342
Bedrooms: 1 **Bathrooms:** 1
Foundation: Slab

See index for more information

Images provided by designer/architect

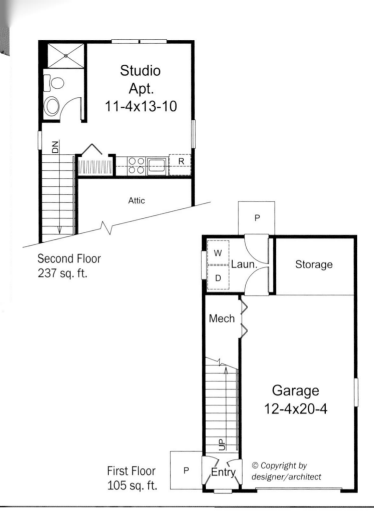

Studio Apt.
11-4x13-10

Attic

Second Floor
237 sq. ft.

P
W D Laun. Storage

Mech

Garage
12-4x20-4

First Floor
105 sq. ft.

P Entry

© Copyright by designer/architect

Plan #F09-121D-0040

Dimensions: 58' W x 58' D
Heated Sq. Ft.: 1,863
Bedrooms: 3 **Bathrooms:** 2½
Foundation: Basement standard; crawl space or slab for an additional fee

See index for more information

Images provided by designer/architect

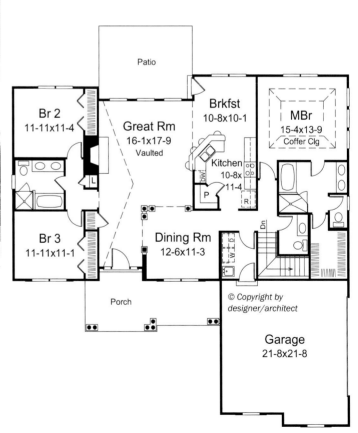

Patio

Br 2
11-11x11-4

Great Rm
16-1x17-9
Vaulted

Brkfst
10-8x10-1

MBr
15-4x13-9
Coffer Clg

Kitchen
10-8x 11-4

Br 3
11-11x11-1

Dining Rm
12-6x11-3

Porch

Garage
21-8x21-8

© Copyright by designer/architect

Floor plan labels (Plan #F09-148D-0050):

MASTER BEDROOM 13'-2" X 12'-2"
8'-0" HT. CEILING
COVERED BALCONY 20'-0" X 8'-0"
© Copyright by designer/architect
DINING ROOM 11'-2" X 14'-0"
KITCHEN 8'-6" X 12'-0"
BEDROOM #2 10'-6" X 10'-4"
8'-0" HT. CEILING
BATHROOM #1
WALK-IN 5'-0" X 8'-8"
REF
BATHROOM #2
GARAGE 13'-4" X 19'-0"
11'-0" HT. CEILING
BEDROOM #3 12'-4" X 9'-0"
DOWN UP
LIVING ROOM 13'-2" X 14'-6"

Plan #F09-148D-0050

Dimensions:	48' W x 40' D
Heated Sq. Ft.:	1,282
Bedrooms: 3	Bathrooms: 2
Exterior Walls:	2" x 6"
Foundation:	Basement

See index for more information

Images provided by designer/architect

Images provided by designer/architect

Plan #F09-130D-0365

Dimensions:	35'4" W x 64'8" D
Heated Sq. Ft.:	1,491
Bedrooms: 3	Bathrooms: 2

Foundation: Slab standard; crawl space or basement for an additional fee

See index for more information

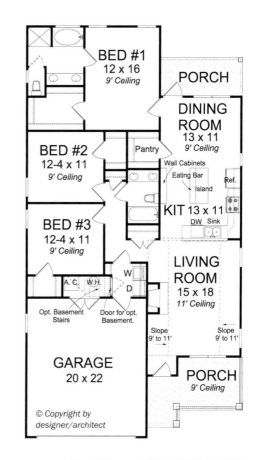

Floor plan labels (Plan #F09-130D-0365):

BED #1 12 x 16 9' Ceiling
PORCH
DINING ROOM 13 x 11 9' Ceiling
BED #2 12-4 x 11 9' Ceiling
Pantry
Wall Cabinets
Eating Bar
Island
Ref.
KIT 13 x 11
DW Sink
BED #3 12-4 x 11 9' Ceiling
A.C. W.H.
W D
Opt. Basement Stairs
Door for opt. Basement.
LIVING ROOM 15 x 18 11' Ceiling
Slope 9' to 11'
Slope 9' to 11'
GARAGE 20 x 22
PORCH 9' Ceiling
© Copyright by designer/architect

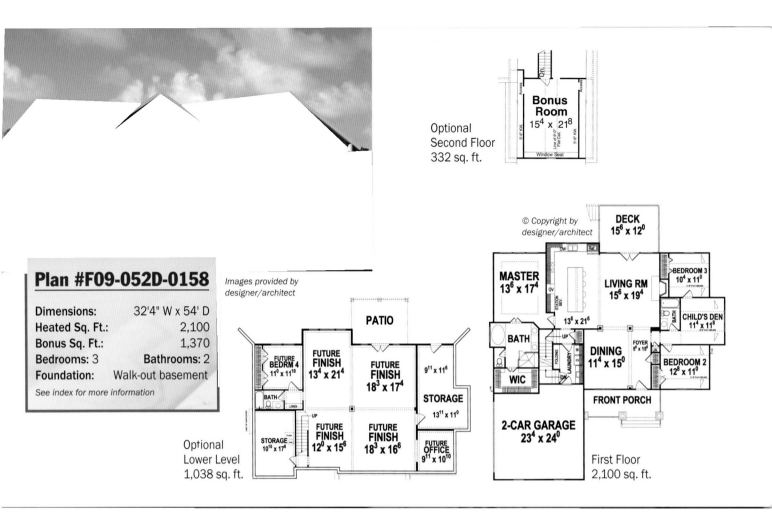

Optional Second Floor
332 sq. ft.

Bonus Room
15^4 x 21^8

© Copyright by designer/architect

Images provided by designer/architect

Plan #F09-052D-0158

Dimensions: 32'4" W x 54' D
Heated Sq. Ft.: 2,100
Bonus Sq. Ft.: 1,370
Bedrooms: 3   Bathrooms: 2
Foundation: Walk-out basement

See index for more information

Optional Lower Level
1,038 sq. ft.

PATIO

FUTURE BEDRM 4 11^0 x 11^{10}
FUTURE FINISH 13^4 x 21^4
FUTURE FINISH 18^3 x 17^4
9^{11} x 11^6
BATH
STORAGE 13^{11} x 11^0
LINEN
STORAGE 10^{10} x 17^6
UP
FUTURE FINISH 12^0 x 15^6
FUTURE FINISH 18^3 x 16^6
FUTURE OFFICE 9^{11} x 10^{10}

First Floor
2,100 sq. ft.

DECK 15^6 x 12^0
MASTER 13^6 x 17^4
LIVING RM 15^6 x 19^4
BEDROOM 3 10^4 x 11^0
13^6 x 21^6
CHILD'S DEN 11^4 x 11^8
BATH
BATH
WIC
FOLDING
LAUNDRY
DINING 11^4 x 15^0
FOYER 5^4 x 15^0
BEDROOM 2 12^8 x 11^0
FRONT PORCH
2-CAR GARAGE 23^4 x 24^0

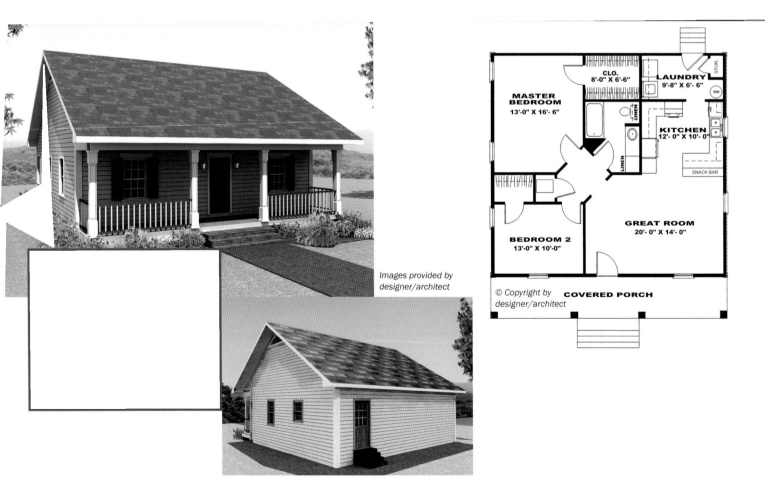

MASTER BEDROOM 13'-0" X 16'-6"
CLO. 8'-0" X 6'-6"
LAUNDRY 9'-8" X 6'-6"
STOR.
WH
LINEN
LINEN
KITCHEN 12'-0" X 10'-0"
SNACK BAR
BEDROOM 2 13'-0" X 10'-0"
GREAT ROOM 20'-0" X 14'-0"
© Copyright by designer/architect
COVERED PORCH

Images provided by designer/architect

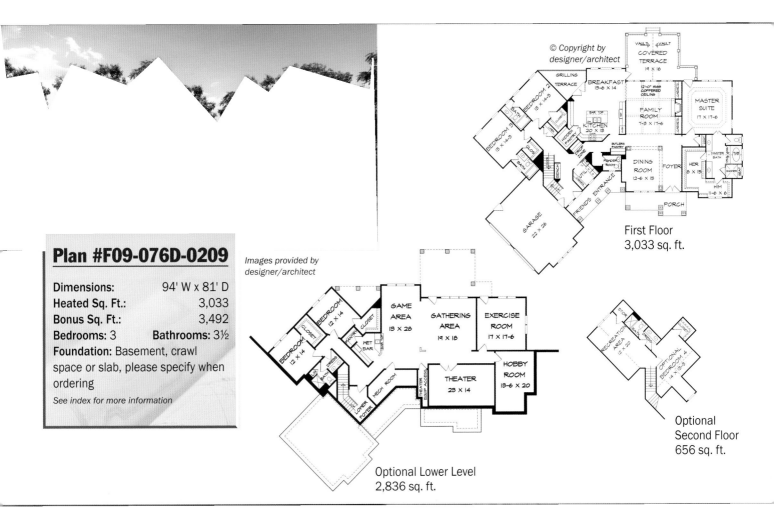

First Floor
3,033 sq. ft.

Plan #F09-076D-0209

Dimensions: 94' W x 81' D
Heated Sq. Ft.: 3,033
Bonus Sq. Ft.: 3,492
Bedrooms: 3   Bathrooms: 3½
Foundation: Basement, crawl space or slab, please specify when ordering

See index for more information

Images provided by designer/architect

Optional Lower Level
2,836 sq. ft.

Optional Second Floor
656 sq. ft.

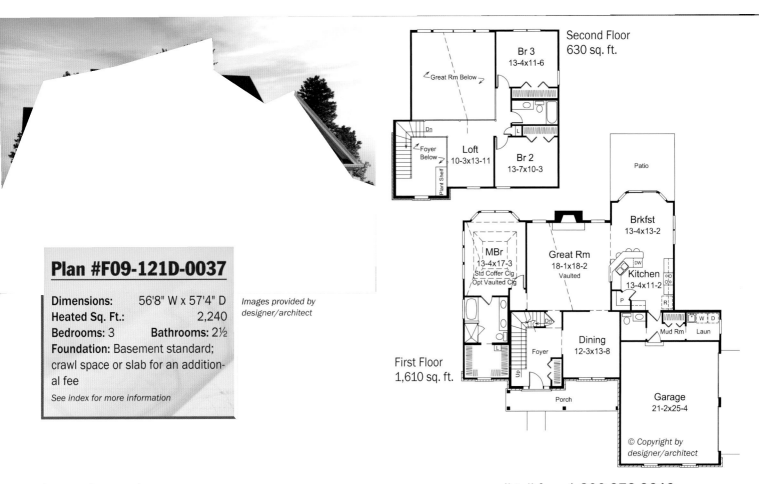

Second Floor
630 sq. ft.

Plan #F09-121D-0037

Dimensions: 56'8" W x 57'4" D
Heated Sq. Ft.: 2,240
Bedrooms: 3   Bathrooms: 2½
Foundation: Basement standard; crawl space or slab for an additional fee

See index for more information

Images provided by designer/architect

First Floor
1,610 sq. ft.

Plan #F09-011D-0662

Dimensions:	76' W x 62' D
Heated Sq. Ft.:	2,460
Bedrooms: 3	Bathrooms: 2½
Exterior Walls:	2" x 6"

Foundation: Joisted continuous footings

See index for more information

Images provided by designer/architect

Features

- Stunning curb appeal can be noted upon seeing this stylish one-story home
- The covered front porch welcomes you into the interior where you will find a formal dining room right off the foyer
- The vaulted great room enjoys direct access to the amazing vaulted outdoor living area with a fireplace, an outdoor kitchen and a sunny patio
- The bayed breakfast nook right off the kitchen will enjoy views of the outdoors
- The private master suite has a posh bath and a spacious walk-in closet with direct laundry room access
- Two additional bedrooms and a bath complete this home
- 2-car side entry garage

© Copyright by designer/architect

Plan #F09-084D-0086

Dimensions:	45'4" W x 76' D
Heated Sq. Ft.:	1,725
Bedrooms: 3	Bathrooms: 2
Foundation: Slab standard; crawl space for an additional fee	

See index for more information

Images provided by designer/architect

Features

- This stylish ranch home offers a great split bedroom layout for a more narrow lot
- The open living area enjoys beautiful views of the outdoor living space that features an outdoor fireplace
- The kitchen enjoys a snack bar, a center work island, tons of storage floor-to-ceiling and even a built-in desk
- A cheerful dining area is surrounded in windows
- The private master bedroom features a luxury bath with two walk-in closets, a double-bowl vanity, an oversized tub and walk-in easy access shower
- 2-car front entry garage

DINING
10-6 x 12-9
10' CEILING

LAUN.
5-4x8-4

MASTER BEDROOM
12-0 x 14-4
POP-UP TO 11' CEILING

POP-UP TO 11' CEILING

DESK

KITCHEN
11-8 x 17-8

PANTRY

M.BATH
16-4 x 12-6

SNACK BAR

GRILL   REF.

ISLAND SNACK BAR

OUTDOOR LIVING
14-6 x 23-6
VAULTED CLG.

LIVING
16-0 x 20-2
VAULTED CLG.

BEDROOM
12-0 x 11-0
10' CEILING

BATH

GARAGE
21-4 x 23-4
10' CEILING

FOYER

BEDROOM
12-0 x 11-4
10' CEILING

PORCH
19-6 x 8-2
10' CEILING

© Copyright by designer/architect

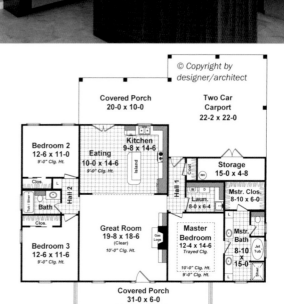

Plan #F09-077D-0216

Images provided by designer/architect

Dimensions: 55' W x 55' D
Heated Sq. Ft.: 1,640
Bedrooms: 3   Bathrooms: 2
Foundation: Crawl space or slab, please specify when ordering

See the index for more information

© Copyright by designer/architect

Covered Porch 20-0 x 10-0
Two Car Carport 22-2 x 22-0

Bedroom 2 12-6 x 11-0 9'-0" Clg. Ht.
Kitchen 9-8 x 14-6
Eating 10-0 x 14-6 9'-0" Clg. Ht.
Storage 15-0 x 4-8
Mstr. Clos. 8-10 x 6-0
Bath
Laun. 8-0 x 6-4
Mstr. Bath
Great Room 19-8 x 18-6 (Clear) 10'-0" Clg. Ht.
Bedroom 3 12-6 x 11-6 9'-0" Clg. Ht.
Master Bedroom 12-4 x 14-6 Trayed Clg. 10'-0" Clg. Ht. 9'-0" Clg. Ht.
8-10 x 15-0
Covered Porch 31-0 x 6-0

Plan #F09-070D-0749

Images provided by designer/architect

Dimensions: 67'4" W x 67' D
Heated Sq. Ft.: 2,167
Bedrooms: 3   Bathrooms: 2½
Exterior Walls: 2" x 6"
Foundation: Basement

See index for more information

COVERED PORCH 16-0 x 14-0
DINING 13-0 x 14-5
MASTER BDRM. step c'g. 13-0 x 16-0
BDRM. 2 11-2 x 12-0
GREAT RM. cath. c'g. 17-0 x 17-8
KIT. 14-0 x 14-3
W.I.C.
W.I.C. 7-0 x 10-2
MAS. BATH
GALLERY
FOYER step c'g.
GALLERY
ENTRY
LAUN.
BATH
BDRM. 3 11-0 x 11-8
PORCH
PWD.
GARAGE 24-0 x 22-0

© Copyright by designer/architect

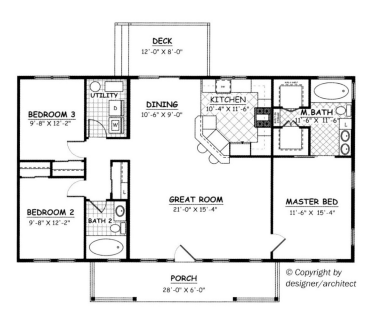

Plan #F09-0143-0006

Dimensions: 50' W x 28' D
Heated Sq. Ft.: 1,400
Bedrooms: 3   Bathrooms: 2
Exterior Walls: 2" x 6"
Foundation: Basement, crawl space or slab, please specify when ordering

See index for more information

Images provided by designer/architect

© Copyright by designer/architect

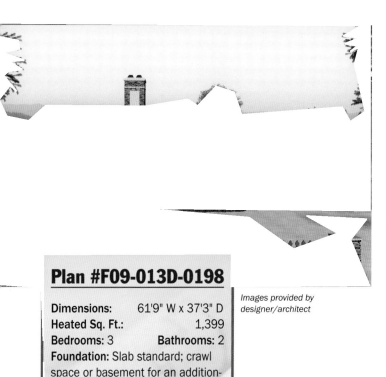

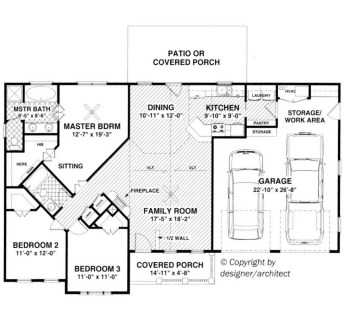

Plan #F09-013D-0198

Dimensions: 61'9" W x 37'3" D
Heated Sq. Ft.: 1,399
Bedrooms: 3   Bathrooms: 2
Foundation: Slab standard; crawl space or basement for an additional fee

See index for more information

Images provided by designer/architect

© Copyright by designer/architect

Plan #F09-065D-0041

Dimensions:	86'2" W x 63'8" D
Heated Sq. Ft.:	3,171
Bonus Sq. Ft.:	1,897
Bedrooms: 3	**Bathrooms:** 2½

Foundation: Walk-out basement standard; crawl space for an additional fee

See index for more information

Images provided by designer/architect

Features

- Beautiful columns define the living space and create a lovely entryway from the foyer into the great room
- The great room, breakfast area and kitchen combine with 12' ceilings to create an open feel
- The expansive kitchen has a lengthy peninsula that serves as both prep and dining space, while providing views of the great room
- A double door entrance into the master bedroom leads to an amazing retreat with a stepped ceiling and a luxury bath and an enormous walk-in closet
- The optional lower level has an additional 1,897 square feet of living area and is designed for entertaining featuring a wet bar with seating, a billiards room, a large media room, two bedrooms, and a full bath
- 3-car side entry garage

First Floor
3,171 sq. ft.

© Copyright by
designer/architect

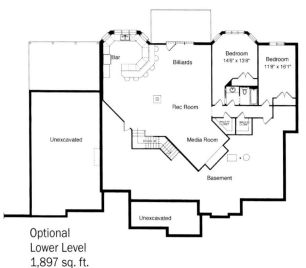

Optional
Lower Level
1,897 sq. ft.

Plan #F09-155D-0070

Dimensions:	60' W x 80'8" D
Heated Sq. Ft.:	2,464
Bonus Sq. Ft.:	758
Bedrooms: 4	**Bathrooms:** 3½

Foundation: Crawl space or slab standard; basement or daylight basement for an additional fee

See index for more information

Features

- The best in Farmhouse living, this home has a welcoming covered front porch and a rear grilling porch
- Decorative columns accent the private dining room, perfect for special events
- The combining of the great room, kitchen and breakfast room create a space that no doubt will be the central hub of this home
- The master suite offers all the amenities a homeowner needs including a private bath and walk-in closet
- The private bedroom 4 has its own bath and built-in desk
- The bonus area on the second floor has an additional 758 square feet of living area
- 2-car side entry garage

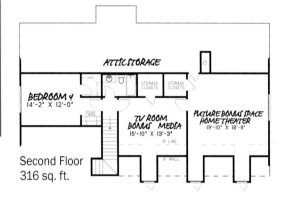

Second Floor
316 sq. ft.

First Floor
2,148 sq. ft.

© Copyright by designer/architect

Images provided by designer/architect

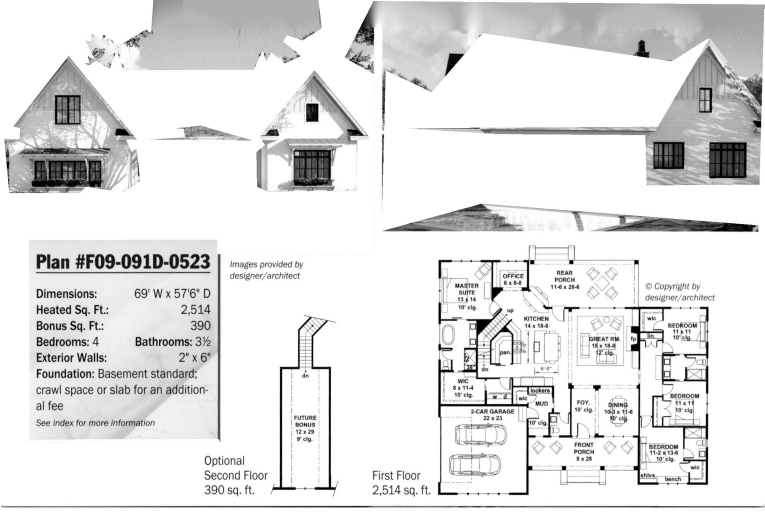

Plan #F09-091D-0523

Dimensions: 69' W x 57'6" D
Heated Sq. Ft.: 2,514
Bonus Sq. Ft.: 390
Bedrooms: 4 **Bathrooms:** 3½
Exterior Walls: 2" x 6"
Foundation: Basement standard; crawl space or slab for an additional fee

See index for more information

Images provided by designer/architect

Optional
Second Floor
390 sq. ft.

FUTURE BONUS
12 x 29
9' clg.

dn

First Floor
2,514 sq. ft.

© Copyright by designer/architect

MASTER SUITE
13 x 14
10' clg.

OFFICE
6 x 8-8

REAR PORCH
11-6 x 28-6

KITCHEN
14 x 18-8

GREAT RM.
18 x 18-8
12' clg.

up

pan.

WIC
8 x 11-4
10' clg.

lockers

MUD

BEDROOM
11 x 11
10' clg.

wic

lin.

2-CAR GARAGE
22 x 23

FOY.
10' clg.

DINING
10-3 x 11-6
10' clg.

BEDROOM
11 x 11
10' clg.

10' clg.

FRONT PORCH
8 x 28

BEDROOM
11-2 x 13-6
10' clg.

wic

shlvs.

bench

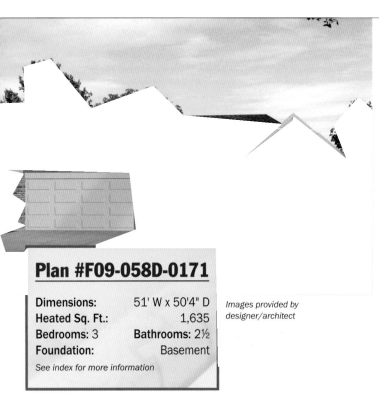

Plan #F09-058D-0171

Dimensions: 51' W x 50'4" D
Heated Sq. Ft.: 1,635
Bedrooms: 3 **Bathrooms:** 2½
Foundation: Basement

See index for more information

Images provided by designer/architect

Kitchen
11-7x10-0

Great Room
16-0x16-6

MBr
13-2x14-2

Dining
11-7x10-0

W
D
S Laun

P

Dn

Br 2
10-4x12-0

L

Garage
19-4x19-4

Covered Porch

Br 3
11-0x11-2

© Copyright by designer/architect

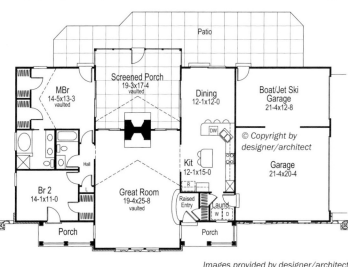

Plan #F09-007D-0137

Dimensions:	72'8" W x 44'4" D
Heated Sq. Ft.:	1,568
Bedrooms: 2	Bathrooms: 2

Foundation: Crawl space standard; slab for an additional fee

See index for more information

Images provided by designer/architect

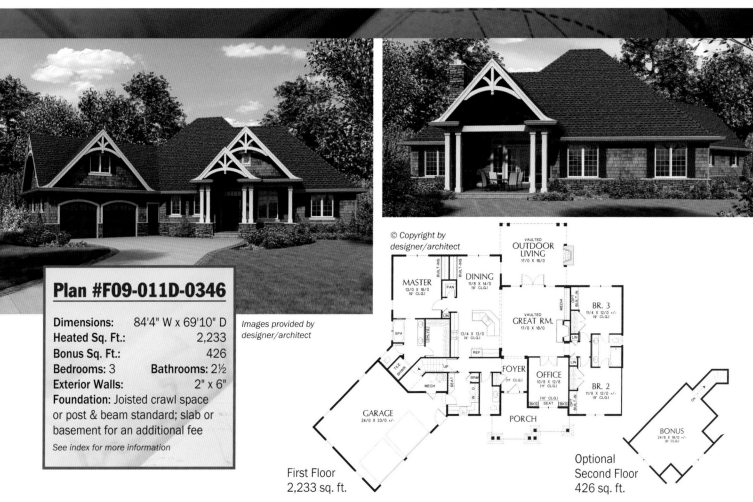

Plan #F09-011D-0346

Dimensions:	84'4" W x 69'10" D
Heated Sq. Ft.:	2,233
Bonus Sq. Ft.:	426
Bedrooms: 3	Bathrooms: 2½
Exterior Walls:	2" x 6"

Foundation: Joisted crawl space or post & beam standard; slab or basement for an additional fee

See index for more information

Images provided by designer/architect

First Floor
2,233 sq. ft.

Optional
Second Floor
426 sq. ft.

Plan #F09-011D-0342

Dimensions:	63' W x 61'6" D
Heated Sq. Ft.:	2,368
Bedrooms: 3	**Bathrooms:** 2½
Exterior Walls:	2" x 6"

Foundation: Joisted crawl space or post & beam standard; slab or basement for an additional fee

See index for more information

Features

- This Craftsman home's curb appeal will make it a standout in any neighborhood with its tasteful combination of stone, siding and gables
- The family chef will love the island kitchen, with its walk-in pantry and spacious snack bar
- The nearby laundry room is bright and cheerful, with plenty of counter space for folding clothes
- The secluded office could serve as a guest room, or a place for hobbies
- The well-appointed master suite features a vaulted ceiling, and a nice window arrangement with transoms overlooking the backyard
- A sit-down shower anchors the posh master bath, which also includes a private toilet, dual sinks and a walk-in closet
- 3-car front entry garage

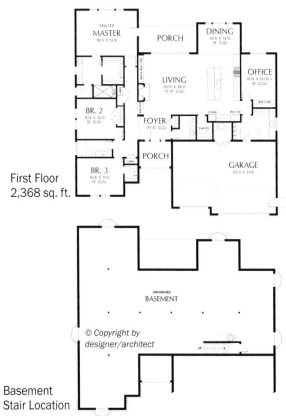

First Floor
2,368 sq. ft.

Basement
Stair Location

© Copyright by designer/architect

Images provided by designer/architect

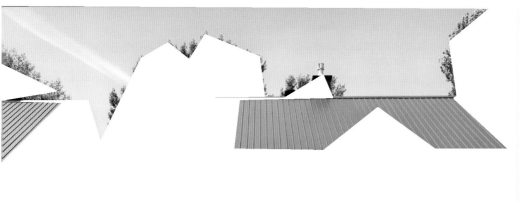

Plan #F09-032D-0887

Dimensions:	42' W x 40' D
Heated Sq. Ft.:	1,212
Bonus Sq. Ft.:	1,212
Bedrooms: 2	Bathrooms: 1
Exterior Walls:	2" x 6"

Foundation: Basement standard; crawl space, floating slab or monolithic slab for an additional fee

See index for more information

Features

- This highly efficient home offers an open floor plan with beamed ceilings above adding a tremendous amount of architectural interest to the interior
- A fireplace acts like a partition between the bedrooms and the gathering spaces
- The large covered porch is a wonderful extension of the interior living spaces
- The island in the kitchen includes casual dining space and a double basin sink and dishwasher
- The optional lower level has an additional 1,212 square feet of living area

26' - 0" x 10' - 0"   14' - 9" x 15' - 0"

25' - 8" x 20' - 9"

8' - 8" x 10' - 8"

First Floor
1,212 sq. ft.

© Copyright by designer/architect

Optional Lower Level
1,212 sq. ft.

Images provided by designer/architect

Creating Curb Appeal
making your home stand-out from the crowd

Everyone wants to own that home on a street that stops people in their tracks. No, that doesn't mean it has to be a huge mansion with jaw-dropping over-the-top features, it means it just has that "thing" called curb appeal that makes it feel warm and inviting, and seems to beg neighbors and friends to come on in. Below are some of the most popular ways to create that home "eye-candy" we all dream of.

exciting entries

Gone are the days of cookie-cutter front porch entries. Today's homeowners love showing off their personality and making front porches a precursor to what guests will find inside. These grand entrances often include statement lighting, custom doors, unique surrounding windows, luxurious plant holders and even furniture. Homeowners are really trying to pull you in and they are making these spaces comfortable for outdoor relaxation, too. Front doors

that are mostly glass, or that feature iron and glass are becoming more popular. Fun, playful colors are also being introduced. If you're building a European style home, then ornate iron and glass style doors are a beautiful option. For those building a Craftsman home, many front doors include glass windows in a variety of shapes and sizes traditional to the Arts & Crafts style movement. Another playful option is the Dutch door. A Dutch door allows half of the door to be open at anytime, whether it's the top, or the bottom. It's a great way to get some fresh air moving through your home on a nice day.

little extras = big impact

Just like it's being seen in the interior with statement lighting, there is a current statement being made on the exterior, too. Statement house numbers are all the rage and people are getting super creative in how they're displaying their home's address numbers. Adhered or added to modern planters, custom painted in a unique font on the front door, or positioned in a clever place on the front facade, house numbers are actually adding style to a home's exterior whatever its architectural style. No longer a necessity or eyesore, these numbers are enhancing the front of a home and are carefully taking homage to the home's architectural style. A thoughtfully selected style and finish can greatly enhance the authenticity of your home's architecture. Have fun, and be playful with it. It definitely allows you show off you and your home's personality and style.

bright is alright

Bright colors on home exteriors if they fit with the architectural style are still being seen. But, some styles like Craftsman, are still utilizing more neutral tones. Darker paint colors are also making a comeback on the exterior, and in complete contrast, off-white and white exteriors are also growing in popularity just like white has made a major comeback in interior home décor.

Unless noted, copyright by designer/architect; Page 235, left, top: Craftsman design carried through, Plan #F09-011D-0342 on page 232; left, bottom: Modern style is fresh and new again with its bright white exterior, Plan #152D-0004; Middle, top to bottom: Urban Green home, Sala Architects, Inc., sala-arc.com, Designed by Eric Odor with Chris Meyer, Construction by Knutson Custom Remodeling, Structure by Architstructures, Troy Thies, photographer; Playful Mid-Century modern entry, Destination Eichler, LLC, destinationeichler.com, Karen Nepacema, photographer; right, top to bottom: Stained glass house numbers, terrazastainedglass.com; Playful Craftsman design with statement house numbers, photo courtesy of House Beautiful®; Modern coastal getaway uses its home address to the fullest potential, Tongue & Groove - design-build by Mark Batson, tongue-and-groove.com. See additional photos and purchase plans at houseplansandmore.com.

custom doors, need we say more?

What used to be a pretty basic element to a home's front facade, the front door was often just a plain solid door meant for security purposes only. The doors homeowners are selecting today are thoughtful, well planned exterior ornamentation. Once again, they carry through with the home's architecture and often include many windows in unusual shapes, which add plenty of extra light to the interior. Take it one step further and paint the door (inside and out) in a vibrant color and add unique house numbers for the perfect expression that's friendly and inviting.

the vintage advantage

Vintage flair hasn't waned, either. Offering a casual and inviting element to a covered front porch, fun vintage pieces like re-purposed benches, antique watering cans, or planters offer a kitschy element that's fun, playful, and asks you to sit down and stay awhile.

nostalgic for front porches

Years ago, the front porch was the gathering place where people would mingle and socialize with neighbors. It was one of the only ways to stay connected with those around them and it provided a space for enjoying the outdoors. This trend is reappearing as lot sizes are becoming smaller and homeowners are interested more than ever in outdoor living spaces. Often, the covered front porch is one of the only outdoor spaces and because of this, people are using this space to the fullest by adding furniture, lighting, and other elements that make it feel comfortable and warm.

sidewalk talk

With all of the thought that goes into every little detail of your home's design, you would think by the time the landscaping and hardscapes have to be determined you can finally relax and not worry so much about the aesthetics of these elements. But, that truly isn't so! Sidewalk design is being carried through with a home's architectural style and color palette as it offers the initial welcome to guests. Don't get lazy when it comes to your sidewalk. You will see that a carefully designed walkway will pave the way for a major curb appeal moment. Today's homeowners are opting for pavers, stone, or other materials for their home's main entrance. And, due to the efficiency and affordability of LED light bulbs lining those paths and walkways with light add curb appeal at night for a very low cost.

sensing a pattern

Driveways, much like sidewalks can offer little or no added style to a home if you choose not to take them into account. But, homeowners today love the look of patterned driveways that either match the sidewalk or complement it. Have fun using textures and materials that complement your home's exterior and it will positively impact curb appeal.

Unless noted, copyright by designer/architect; Page 237, top, left: Plan #011D-0343; top, right: Plan #071S-0030; middle, left: Plan #106D-0051; middle, right: Plan #129S-0003; bottom, left: Plan #071S-0002; bottom, right: Plan #065S-0034. See additional photos and purchase plans at houseplansand-more.com.

lighter landscaping

Being paired down to reflect the less cluttered style of homes being designed today, landscaping especially in the front of a home is much less fussy than in previous years. Today, new homeowners are choosing not to over plant shrubs and trees. Think clean, well-manicured lawns, carefully selected bushes, and tree options that are well suited with the home's architecture. By reducing the amount of landscaping a yard has, homeowners are staying eco-friendly creating less erosion issues, too.

So, by using less, your choices are now more important in order to make an impact. Choose plants that complement the color scheme of your home. If your home is gray, then offset it with pinks and reds. Or, if you've chosen a dark blue or slate, then white and yellow can provide that pop of color, or brighten the exterior. Another fun option is to select edible landscape such as colorful pepper plants and herbs and suddenly your landscaping is working twice as hard as your own organic garden, too. This is especially a great idea if you lack backyard space, or the position of the front of your home has more sunlight, making it more suitable to successful gardening.

flora forever

Flowers and plants are more popular than ever for surrounding your home's facade and adding softness. Landscape designers of today are thoughtful in their plant choices. Native landscaping is the way to go. Selecting plants that naturally grow in your region allows for less watering and fertilization, which is better for the environment. Choosing native plants also goes in line with the trend that homeowners are pairing down their ecological footprint. Native plants require less water than what is already received in rainfall. Plus, less sprinkler time means lower water bills, less water waste, and all around happier plants.

more than just a pretty pot

The planters on the market today have really come a long way. These vessels that used to just hold flowers can now often upstage their contents. Uniquely shaped, and often in a style that complements a home's architecture, a well chosen and placed planter can add immense curb appeal.

let there be light

Transom windows are being added to the front exterior and around the entire perimeter of a home for several reasons. First, they add character to the facade in a clean, uncomplicated way, that is in line with Craftsman and Mid-Century modern style that is quite popular right now. They have a less formal feel, than an arched window design. And, they are adding additional light to the interior, which is a feature currently popular in interior home design. Open airy interiors are dictating home design, so the addition of larger windows makes an interior feel more open especially in homes with smaller square footages. Also, large picture windows are being seen in every style of home from Craftsman to Mid-Century Modern, and everything in between.

Exterior lighting adds drama once the sky goes dark. Even a solar light placed strategically on a unique ornamental tree can enhance your exterior and draw eyes to want to see more. Or, take it a step further and create a facade lit with soffit lighting, or light the bottom corners of the home for intensified drama. Many of these lighting systems can now be controlled right from your smart phone making it easy to use and creating added security when you're away.

the finish line

Depending on how luxurious the home is, those with larger budgets are using copper gutters to add curb appeal and style that truly stands out. Another interesting addition can be a unique fence that features an artistic pattern that basically becomes a work of art. Choosing a fence style with a similar architectural feel will make your home seem thoughtfully planned.

As homeowners tastes change, so do their ideas of what the ideal architectural style truly is. As their need for less complicated living, free of clutter and visual distractions becomes more important, the popular architectural styles reflect that. If they're craving a need to feel one with nature, then their desired style of home will turn to architecture that allows nature to be honored and respected. These constant shifts in tastes and trends in society are what make the landscape around us so colorful and interesting with glimpses of the past, present and future found all around us in any given city or neighborhood. Whatever style of architecture you choose, remember these curb appeal tips for optimizing the exterior style to the fullest and making your personality and home shine wherever it is that you live.

Unless noted, copyright by designer/architect; Page 238, top, left: Light up the night, Plan #013S-0014; top, middle: Easy to maintain native plants stay greener, Plan #106S-0070; top, right: Great use of native plants, Plan #011S-0003; middle: Less is more landscaping, Plan #101D-0061, Warren Diggles Photography; bottom, left: Planters that make an impact, Plan #101D-0059, Warren Diggles Photography; bottom, right: These planters steal the show, Plan #072S-0002; Page 239, bottom, left: Big windows and glass doors are in, Plan #091D-0028; top, left: Great door details, Plan #111D-0018; top, right: Unique large transom, Plan #011S-0003; bottom, right: Carefully determined decor, Plan #101D-0052, Damon Searles, photographer. See additional photos and purchase plans at houseplansandmore.com.

Style Seeker
the top architectural styles of today

New homeowners love the look and feel of many architectural styles somewhat new to them. Perhaps the Traditional homes of their past remind them of their parent's homes, but in reality, the interior layouts and finish preferences being demanded by new homeowners most likely are dictating the exterior style changes that are occurring, too. Homeowners want sleek interiors with modern furnishings, and the architectural styles being designed on the exterior today reflect that simpler interior style. These streamlined, less-cluttered, and informal interior spaces being requested by homeowners are definitely changing the style and feel of home exteriors. However, there is also no less of a desire for homes that feature front facades covered in stone and brick, so basically there's still something being built for everyone.

Here are some of the top architectural styles being designed today. Many you will see throughout the pages of this book. Some are timeless, some a little more trendy, but all display tons of personality and style.

mid-century modern

The Mid-Century Modern home features a steel structure that allows large floor-to-ceiling windows and doors to be supported. This style blurs the lines between indoor and outdoor spaces perfectly, which is a popular trend.

international modern

Stripped of any ornamentation on the exterior, this boxy, typically stucco home has a precise almost machine-like sleek style.

industrial modern

Using Industrial style, this style includes more texture and uses varied materials on the exterior such as corrugated metal, concrete, and exposed wood. It's becoming quite popular in urban developments.

georgian and federal

A Traditional symmetrical two-story style that is seen in every neighborhood across the country. It's a classic two-story that never seems to go out of style.

american farmhouse & modern farmhouse

This style ranges from small and simple to industrial or Traditional Victorian, but some newer versions have more streamlined exteriors.

cape cod

This distinctly American style was a result of the harsh weather conditions of the Northeast coast, but its classic look remains a mainstay throughout America.

french eclectic and european

These European styles evoke a vision of cottages and Chateaus often seen across the French and European countryside. Country French is another term associated with this style of home.

tudor

Based loosely off early English tradition, the distinctive features of Tudor style include exposed timber mixed with stucco. Many similar details have spread to Prairie and Craftsman style.

mission revival

Inspired by Spanish mission churches that appeared in California around the late 1800s, this style features stucco walls, and clay tile roofs with large arched openings.

spanish colonial

Seen throughout Florida and California in the early 1900s, there were several bathhouses and exhibit halls being designed in this style helping to spread the design across the country and especially the sunbelt region.

prairie

Popularized by Frank Lloyd Wright, Prairie Style homes embrace the belief that homes should appear as if they have grown from nature. They use horizontal bands of windows and trim to evoke a prairie landscape.

craftsman bungalow

Shallow roofs, exposed rafters, a mixture of brick, stone, shingles and siding give this style tons of personality. The addition of the term Bungalow means it's a 1 1/2 story Craftsman home with a deep covered front porch.

queen anne

This residential style, also referred to as Victorian displays an eclectic amount of details often with various colors and textures. Turrets, bay windows, and gables all contribute to their heavy ornamentation.

shingle

Shingle style homes were adopted as a way to move away from the heavily ornate Victorian and Queen Anne style. They feature shingle siding and are often seen in the rugged coastal towns of the Northeast and the Northwest.

ranch

Typically long and narrow one-story structures that spread out on their lot, ranch style homes can adopt any of the other styles mentioned previously for added character.

The exterior design of homes today is clearly changing from the past decades. As homeowners want less maintenance, they have shifted to yearning for a dwelling that requires little or no maintenance and fits their "paired down," less is more attitude and lifestyle. However, some architectural styles are always popular simply because their beauty can't be overlooked, so no matter what the trend may be certain styles will always remain popular even if they are deemed opulent for the times. The most popular styles of architecture remind us of our country's rich history, its diversity of cultures, and how they've collided to create the neighborhoods and landscapes full of history we're lucky enough to call "home."

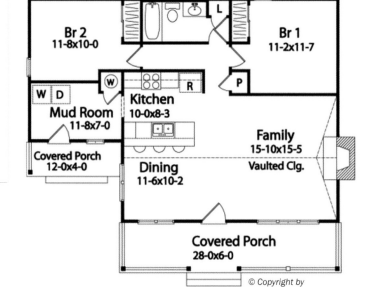

Plan #F09-058D-0029

Dimensions:	42' W x 34' D
Heated Sq. Ft.:	1,000
Bedrooms: 2	Bathrooms: 1
Foundation:	Crawl space

See index for more information

Images provided by designer/architect

Plan #F09-008D-0161

Dimensions:	20' W x 30' D
Heated Sq. Ft.:	618
Bedrooms: 1	Bathrooms: 1
Foundation:	Pier

See index for more information

Images provided by designer/architect

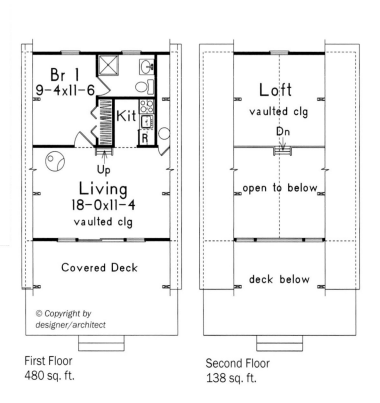

First Floor
480 sq. ft.

Second Floor
138 sq. ft.

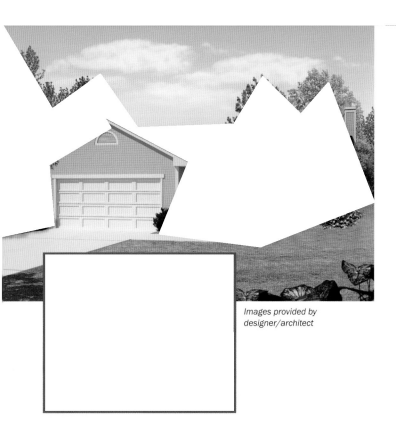

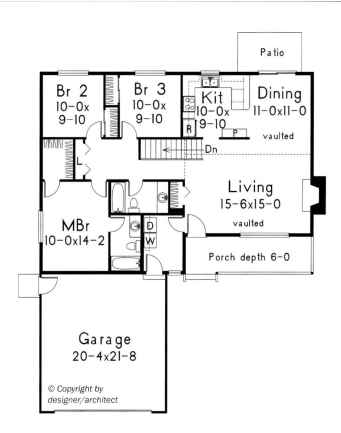

Images provided by
designer/architect

Patio

Br 2
10-0x
9-10

Br 3
10-0x
9-10

Kit
10-0x
9-10

Dining
11-0x11-0
vaulted

Dn

Living
15-6x15-0
vaulted

MBr
10-0x14-2

D
W

Porch depth 6-0

Garage
20-4x21-8

© Copyright by
designer/architect

Plan #F09-068D-0010

Dimensions:	74'6" W x 43' D
Heated Sq. Ft.:	1,849
Bedrooms: 3	**Bathrooms:** 2½

Foundation: Basement, crawl space or slab, please specify when ordering

See index for more information

Images provided by
designer/architect

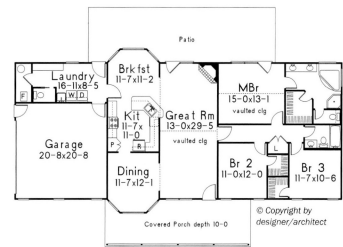

Patio

Laundry
16-11x8-5

Brkfst
11-7x11-2

MBr
15-0x13-1
vaulted clg

Kit
11-7x
11-0

Great Rm
13-0x29-5
vaulted clg

Garage
20-8x20-8

Dining
11-7x12-1

Br 2
11-0x12-0

Br 3
11-7x10-6

Covered Porch depth 10-0

© Copyright by
designer/architect

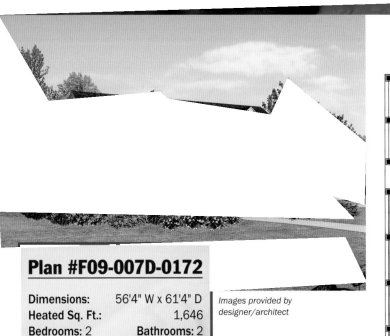

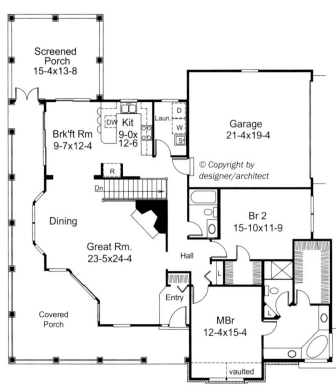

Images provided by designer/architect

Screened Porch
15-4x13-8

Brk'ft Rm
9-7x12-4

Kit
9-0x
12-6

DW

Laun.

D
W
S

Garage
21-4x19-4

© Copyright by designer/architect

Dining

Dn

Great Rm.
23-5x24-4

Hall

Br 2
15-10x11-9

Covered Porch

Entry

MBr
12-4x15-4

L

L

vaulted

Plan #F09-007D-0172

Dimensions: 56'4" W x 61'4" D
Heated Sq. Ft.: 1,646
Bedrooms: 2   **Bathrooms:** 2
Foundation: Basement standard; crawl space or slab for an additional fee

See index for more information

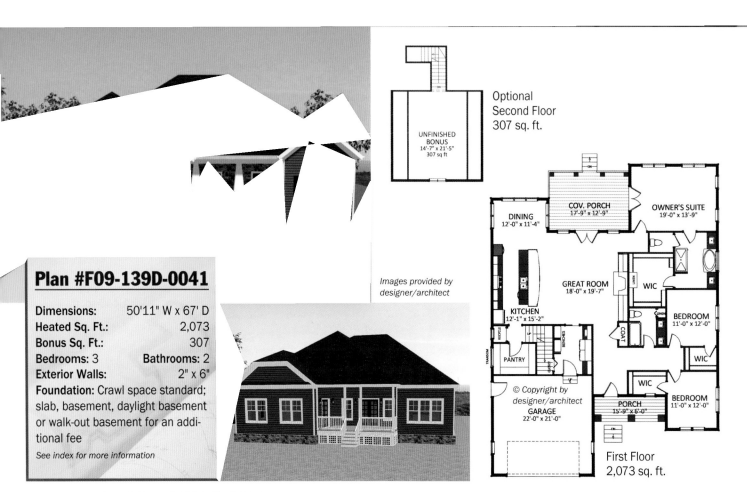

Optional
Second Floor
307 sq. ft.

UNFINISHED BONUS
14'-7" x 21'-5"
307 sq ft

Images provided by designer/architect

DINING
12'-0" x 11'-4"

COV. PORCH
17'-9" x 12'-9"

OWNER'S SUITE
19'-0" x 13'-9"

GREAT ROOM
18'-0" x 19'-7"

WIC

KITCHEN
12'-1" x 15'-2"

PANTRY

BENCHES

BEDROOM
11'-0" x 12'-0"

WIC

COAT

LINEN

WIC

© Copyright by designer/architect

GARAGE
22'-0" x 21'-0"

PORCH
15'-9" x 6'-0"

BEDROOM
11'-0" x 12'-0"

First Floor
2,073 sq. ft.

Plan #F09-139D-0041

Dimensions: 50'11" W x 67' D
Heated Sq. Ft.: 2,073
Bonus Sq. Ft.: 307
Bedrooms: 3   **Bathrooms:** 2
Exterior Walls: 2" x 6"
Foundation: Crawl space standard; slab, basement, daylight basement or walk-out basement for an additional fee

See index for more information

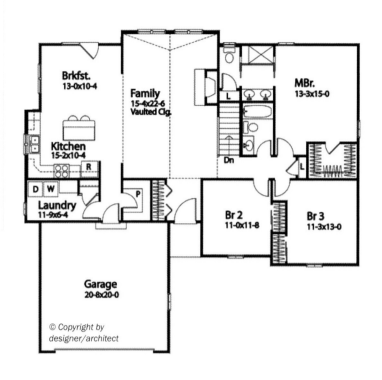

Plan #F09-058D-0219

Dimensions:	54'4" W x 50'4" D
Heated Sq. Ft.:	1,684
Bedrooms: 3	Bathrooms: 2
Foundation:	Basement

See index for more information

Images provided by designer/architect

© Copyright by designer/architect

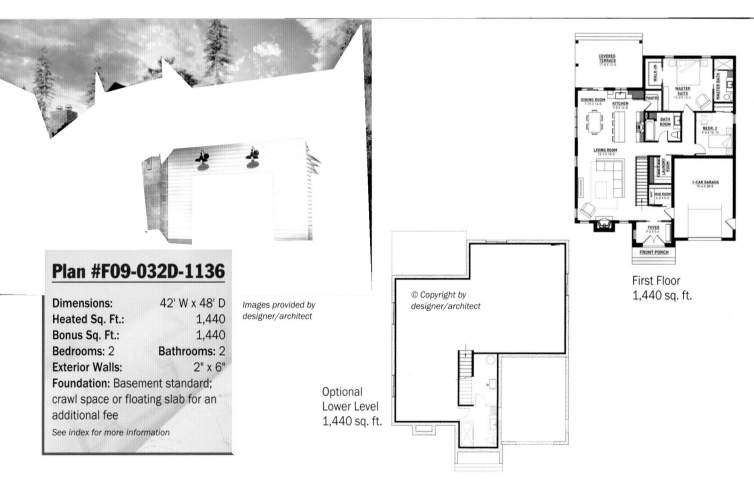

Plan #F09-032D-1136

Dimensions:	42' W x 48' D
Heated Sq. Ft.:	1,440
Bonus Sq. Ft.:	1,440
Bedrooms: 2	Bathrooms: 2
Exterior Walls:	2" x 6"

Foundation: Basement standard; crawl space or floating slab for an additional fee

See index for more information

Images provided by designer/architect

First Floor
1,440 sq. ft.

© Copyright by designer/architect

Optional
Lower Level
1,440 sq. ft.

DECK
12'-0" X 8'-0"

UTILITY

BEDROOM 3
9'-8" X 12'-2"

DINING
10'-6" X 9'-0"

KITCHEN
10'-4" X 11'-6"

M. BATH
11'-6" X 11'-6"

BEDROOM 2
9'-8" X 12'-2"

BATH 2

GREAT ROOM
21'-0" X 15'-4"

MASTER BED
11'-6" X 15'-4"

PORCH
28'-0" X 6'-0"

© Copyright by designer/architect

Plan #F09-143D-0015

Images provided by designer/architect

Dimensions:	50' W x 28' D
Heated Sq. Ft.:	1,400
Bedrooms: 3	Bathrooms: 2
Exterior Walls:	2" x 6"

Foundation: Basement, crawl space or slab, please specify when ordering

See index for more information

Loft
16-10x12-0

DN

Open to Below

Second Floor
327 sq. ft.

Br 1
10-10x12-0

Br 2
10-0x7-6

UP

DN

Living
13-6x11-2

Kit/Brk
10-0x13-10

First Floor
790 sq. ft.

Deck
19-0x10-0

© Copyright by designer/architect

Plan #F09-057D-0013

Dimensions:	36' W x 28' D
Heated Sq. Ft.:	1,117
Bedrooms: 2	Bathrooms: 1
Exterior Walls:	2" x 6"
Foundation:	Basement

Images provided by designer/architect

See index for more information

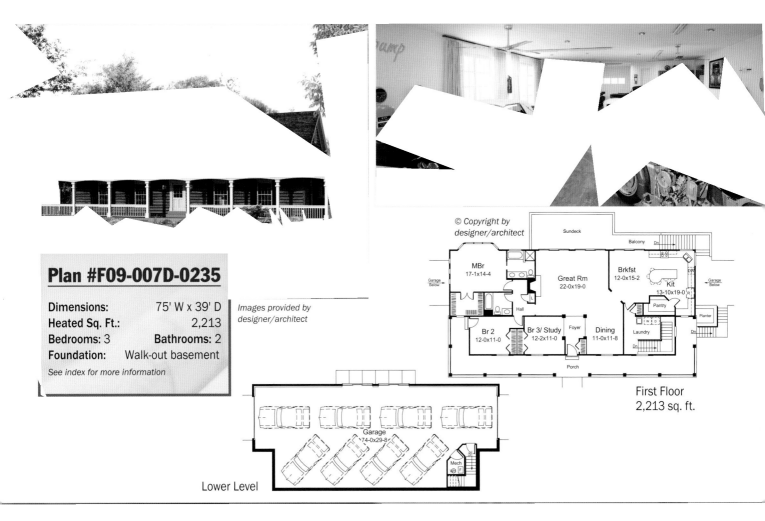

Plan #F09-007D-0235

Dimensions:	75' W x 39' D
Heated Sq. Ft.:	2,213
Bedrooms: 3	Bathrooms: 2
Foundation:	Walk-out basement

See index for more information

Images provided by designer/architect

First Floor
2,213 sq. ft.

Lower Level

Plan #F09-058D-0010

Dimensions:	26' W x 32' D
Heated Sq. Ft.:	676
Bedrooms: 1	Bathrooms: 1
Foundation:	Crawl space

See index for more information

Images provided by designer/architect

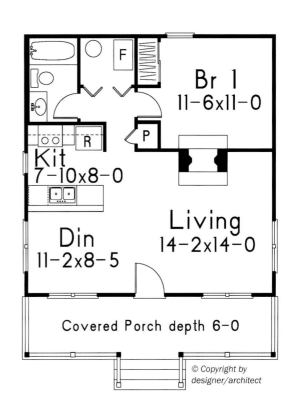

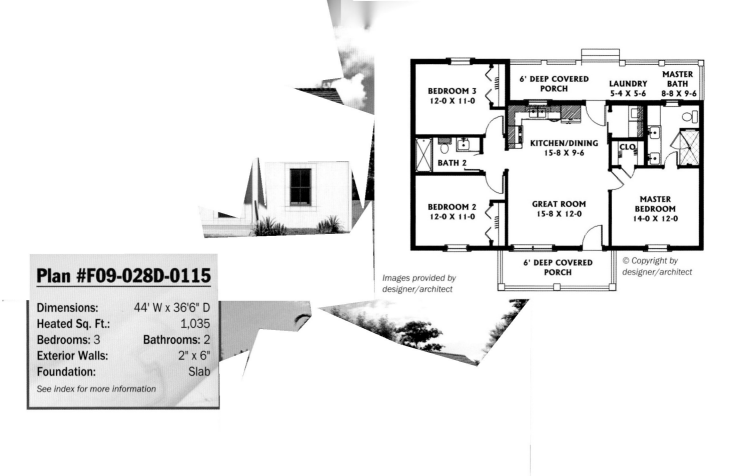

Plan #F09-028D-0115

Dimensions:	44' W x 36'6" D
Heated Sq. Ft.:	1,035
Bedrooms: 3	Bathrooms: 2
Exterior Walls:	2" x 6"
Foundation:	Slab

See index for more information

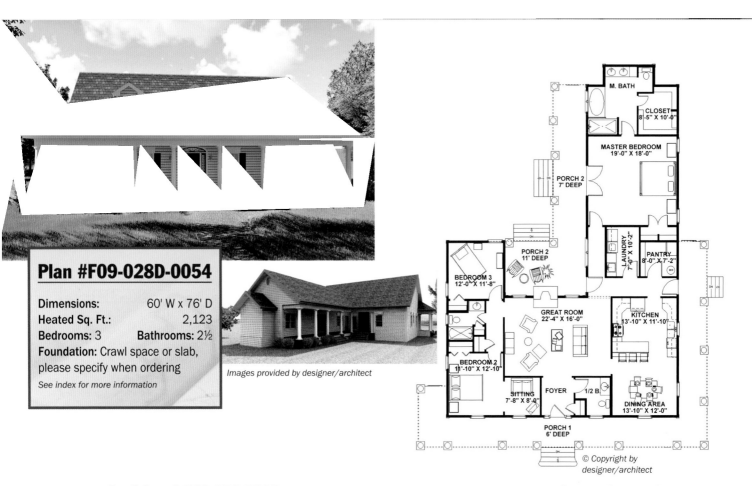

Plan #F09-028D-0054

Dimensions:	60' W x 76' D
Heated Sq. Ft.:	2,123
Bedrooms: 3	Bathrooms: 2½

Foundation: Crawl space or slab, please specify when ordering

See index for more information

Images provided by
designer/architect

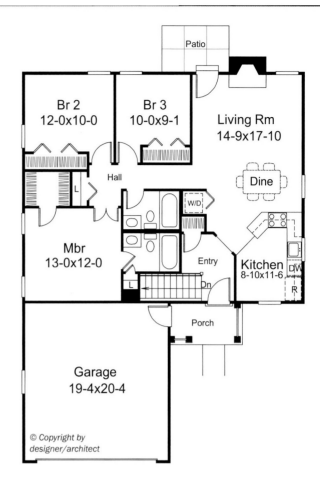

Br 2
12-0x10-0

Br 3
10-0x9-1

Living Rm
14-9x17-10

Patio

Hall

Dine

L

W/D

Mbr
13-0x12-0

Entry

Kitchen
8-10x11-6

DW

Dn

R

Porch

Garage
19-4x20-4

© Copyright by
designer/architect

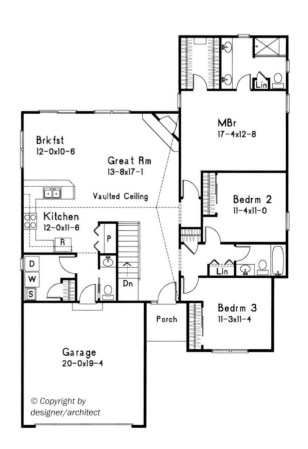

Plan #F09-058D-0232

Dimensions:	44' W x 62' D
Heated Sq. Ft.:	1,650
Bedrooms: 3	Bathrooms: 2½
Foundation:	Basement

See index for more information

Images provided by
designer/architect

MBr
17-4x12-8

Brkfst
12-0x10-6

Great Rm
13-8x17-1

Vaulted Ceiling

Bedrm 2
11-4x11-0

Kitchen
12-0x11-6

Lin

P

R

D

W

S

Dn

Lin

Bedrm 3
11-3x11-4

Porch

Garage
20-0x19-4

© Copyright by
designer/architect

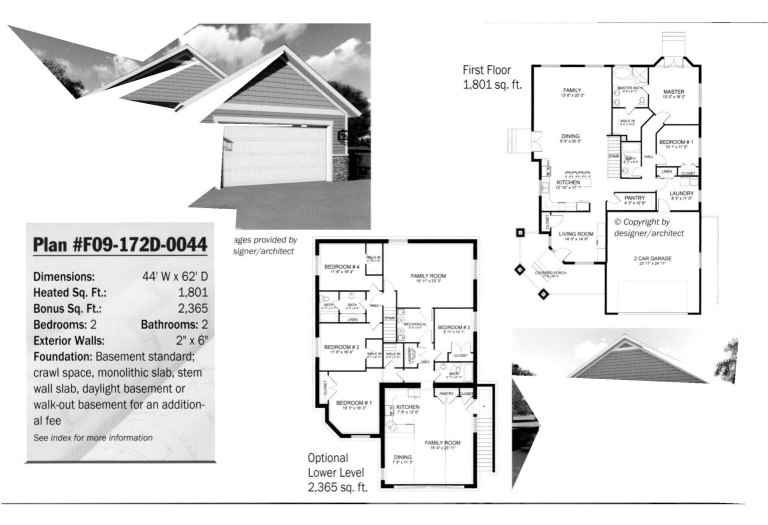

First Floor
1,801 sq. ft.

FAMILY
13' 6" x 20' 0"

MASTER BATH

MASTER
13' 0" x 16' 2"

DINING
9' 5" x 20' 0"

WALK IN

BEDROOM # 1
10' 1" x 11' 0"

STAIR

BATH

HALL

LINEN

CLOSET

KITCHEN
12' 10" x 17' 1"

PANTRY
4' 2" x 12' 6"

LAUNDRY
8' 3" x 11' 0"

CLOSET

LIVING ROOM
14' 0" x 14' 8"

© Copyright by
designer/architect

2 CAR GARAGE
23' 11" x 24' 11"

COVERED PORCH

Plan #F09-172D-0044

Dimensions:	44' W x 62' D
Heated Sq. Ft.:	1,801
Bonus Sq. Ft.:	2,365
Bedrooms: 2	Bathrooms: 2
Exterior Walls:	2" x 6"

Foundation: Basement standard; crawl space, monolithic slab, stem wall slab, daylight basement or walk-out basement for an additional fee

See index for more information

Images provided by designer/architect

BEDROOM # 4
11' 8" x 16' 4"

WALK IN

FAMILY ROOM
15' 11" x 23' 3"

BATH

BATH

HALL

LINEN

STAIR

MECHANICAL
8' 3" x 8' 1"

BEDROOM # 3
9' 11" x 13' 1"

BEDROOM # 2
11' 8" x 16' 4"

WALK IN

WALK IN

LAUNDRY

HALL

CLOSET

CLOSET

BEDROOM # 1
19' 3" x 16' 3"

KITCHEN
7' 8" x 12' 6"

PANTRY

CLOSET

BATH

DINING
7' 8" x 11' 5"

FAMILY ROOM
15' 4" x 23' 11"

Optional
Lower Level
2,365 sq. ft.

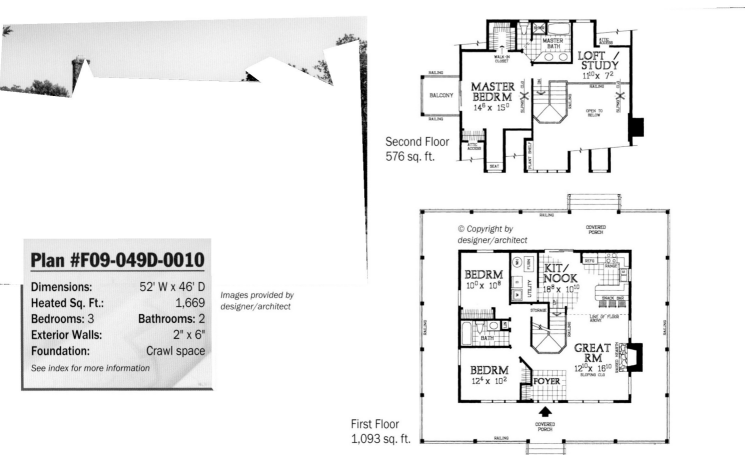

Second Floor
576 sq. ft.

MASTER BATH

ATTIC ACCESS

LOFT /
STUDY
11'10 x 7'2

WALK-IN CLOSET

RAILING

MASTER
BEDRM
14'8 x 15'0

BALCONY

RAILING

OPEN TO BELOW

RAILING

ATTIC ACCESS

SEAT

PLANT SHELF

Plan #F09-049D-0010

Dimensions:	52' W x 46' D
Heated Sq. Ft.:	1,669
Bedrooms: 3	Bathrooms: 2
Exterior Walls:	2" x 6"
Foundation:	Crawl space

See index for more information

Images provided by designer/architect

© Copyright by
designer/architect

COVERED PORCH

BEDRM
10'0 x 10'8

KIT /
NOOK
18'8 x 10'10

UTILITY

REFG

RANGE

SNACK BAR

STORAGE

BATH

LIN

LINE OF FLOOR ABOVE

GREAT
RM
12'10 x 16'10
SLOPING CLG

BEDRM
12'4 x 10'2

FOYER

RAISED HEARTH

First Floor
1,093 sq. ft.

COVERED PORCH

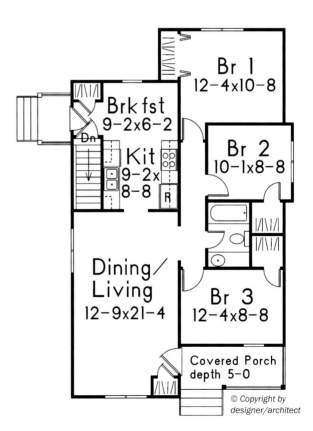

Plan #F09-167D-0007

Dimensions:	72' W x 76'9" D
Heated Sq. Ft.:	3,016
Bedrooms: 4	Bathrooms: 3
Exterior Walls:	2" x 6"

Foundation: Slab standard; crawl space for an additional fee

See index for more information

Images provided by designer/architect

Plan #F09-045D-0014

Dimensions:	27' W x 43' D
Heated Sq. Ft.:	987
Bedrooms: 3	Bathrooms: 1
Foundation:	Basement

See index for more information

Images provided by designer/architect

Plan #F09-121D-0021

Dimensions:	65' W x 46'4" D
Heated Sq. Ft.:	1,562
Bedrooms: 3	**Bathrooms:** 2

Foundation: Basement standard; crawl space or slab for an additional fee

See index for more information

Images provided by designer/architect

© Copyright by designer/architect

Plan #F09-051D-0696

Dimensions:	84'8" W x 50' D
Heated Sq. Ft.:	2,016
Bonus Sq. Ft.:	453
Bedrooms: 3	**Bathrooms:** 2
Exterior Walls:	2" x 6"

Foundation: Basement standard; crawl space or slab for an additional fee

See index for more information

Images provided by designer/architect

© Copyright by designer/architect

First Floor
2,016 sq. ft.

Optional
Second Floor
453 sq. ft.

Plan #F09-007D-0146

Dimensions: 68' W x 49'8" D
Heated Sq. Ft.: 1,929
Bedrooms: 4   **Bathrooms:** 3
Foundation: Crawl space standard; basement or slab for an additional fee

See index for more information

Images provided by designer/architect

© Copyright by designer/architect

Plan #F09-077D-0131

Dimensions: 69' W x 63'10" D
Heated Sq. Ft.: 2,021
Bonus Sq. Ft.: 354
Bedrooms: 3   **Bathrooms:** 2½
Foundation: Basement

See index for more information

Images provided by designer/architect

Optional Second Floor 354 sq. ft.

First Floor 2,021 sq. ft.

© Copyright by designer/architect

Plan #F09-051D-0981

Dimensions:	55'4" W x 71'8" D
Heated Sq. Ft.:	2,005
Bedrooms: 3	**Bathrooms:** 2
Exterior Walls:	2" x 6"

Foundation: Basement standard; crawl space or slab for an additional fee

See index for more information

Images provided by designer/architect

Features

- The master suite is located just off the great room and boasts dual sinks and a generously sized walk-in closet in its private bath

- There is easy access to the laundry room from the master closet which makes tackling dirty laundry a breeze

- The kitchen island looks out into the open great room and dining area giving a very open feeling

- The second and third bedrooms are situated in the front left side of the house, with the master bedroom in the back right side for privacy

- You can walk out onto the covered porch from the dining room for a view of the backyard

- 3-car front entry garage

Floor Plan:

- CVRD. PORCH 14'0"x12'0"
- DECK
- DIN. RM. 9'-1 1/8" CEILING 11'0"x10'6"
- GRT. RM. 10'-1 1/8" STEP CEILING 19'8"x22'0"
- MBR. 10'-1 1/8" STEP CEILING 15'4"x14'0"
- KIT. 9'-1 1/8" CEILING 11'0"x14'6"
- PAN.
- E. 10'-1 1/8" STEP CEILING
- BENCH
- STOR. 9'0"x10'0"
- BR. #2 9'-1 1/8" CEILING 12'0"x11'4"
- BR. #3 9'-1 1/8" CEILING 13'4"x10'0"
- 3 CAR GARAGE 30'8"x24'0"

© Copyright by designer/architect

Plan #F09-101D-0089

Dimensions:	70' W x 77'9" D
Heated Sq. Ft.:	2,509
Bonus Sq. Ft.:	1,645
Bedrooms: 4	Bathrooms: 2½
Exterior Walls:	2" x 6"
Foundation:	Basement

See index for more information

Images provided by designer/architect

Features

- The wrap-around porch welcomes you into this beautiful airy home designed with a popular Modern Farmhouse flair
- Expansive windows bring so much natural light into every room
- The desirable split bedroom layout of this home is perfect for families
- The dining, kitchen and great room are all open, creating one large open family area
- With a walk-in closet, dual sinks and generously sized bedroom, the master suite makes for a perfect place to retire for the evening
- The optional lower level has an additional 1,645 square feet of living area including a recreation room with a wet bar, two bedrooms and a bath
- 3-car side entry garage

Optional
Lower Level
1,645 sq. ft.

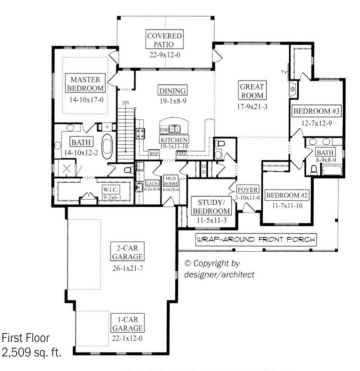

First Floor
2,509 sq. ft.

© Copyright by
designer/architect

Plan #F09-144D-0005

Dimensions:	48' W x 58' D
Heated Sq. Ft.:	1,506
Bedrooms: 3	Bathrooms: 2
Exterior Walls:	2" x 6"

Foundation: Basement standard; crawl space or slab for an additional fee

See index for more information

Images provided by designer/architect

Covered Deck

Whirlpool

Master Suite
16-0 x 12-0

Ens

French Doors

lin

Dining
10-0 x 14-4

Kitchen
10-8 x 14-0

WIC

Br 2
10-0 x 10-0

raised snack bar

F

Bath

lin

P

1/2 wall

DN

3-sided Gas FP

railing

Great Room
18-0 x 17-6

Hall

niche

Br 3
10-0 x 10-0

Util.

W

French Doors

Foyer

D

Gazebo

Double Garage
19-4 x 21-8

Porch

© Copyright by designer/architect

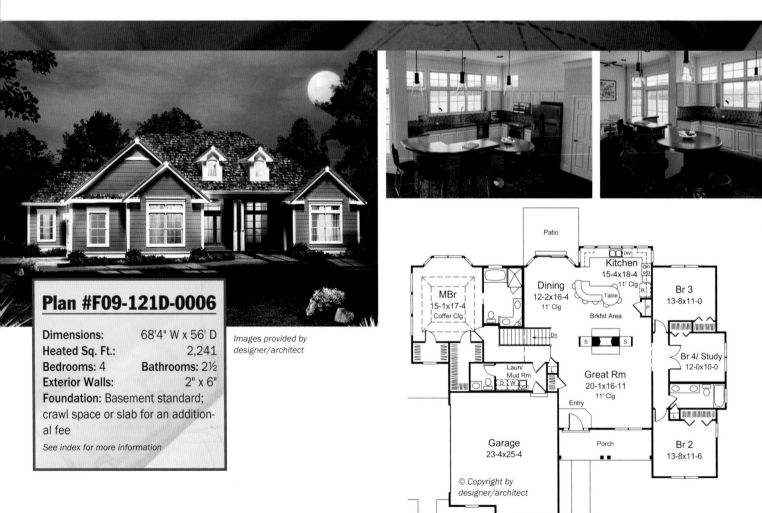

Plan #F09-121D-0006

Dimensions:	68'4" W x 56' D
Heated Sq. Ft.:	2,241
Bedrooms: 4	Bathrooms: 2½
Exterior Walls:	2" x 6"

Foundation: Basement standard; crawl space or slab for an additional fee

See index for more information

Images provided by designer/architect

Patio

MBr
15-1x17-4
Coffer Clg

Kitchen
15-4x18-4
11' Clg

Dining
12-2x16-4
11' Clg

Br 3
13-8x11-0

Table

Brkfst Area

Dn

Br 4/ Study
12-0x10-0

Laun/
Mud Rm

Great Rm
20-1x16-11
11' Clg

Entry

Garage
23-4x25-4

Porch

Br 2
13-8x11-6

© Copyright by designer/architect

Plan #F09-007D-0163

Dimensions: 50'8" W x 50'4" D
Heated Sq. Ft.: 1,580
Bedrooms: 3   **Bathrooms:** 2
Foundation: Crawl space standard; basement or slab for an additional fee

See index for more information

Images provided by designer/architect

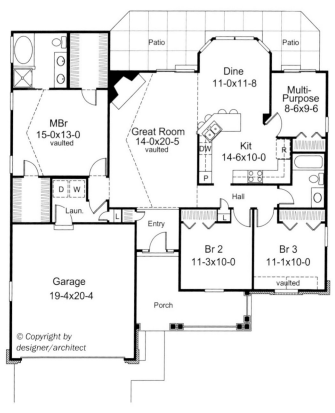

MBr
15-0x13-0
vaulted

Patio   Patio

Dine
11-0x11-8

Multi-Purpose
8-6x9-6

Great Room
14-0x20-5
vaulted

Kit
14-6x10-0

DW

P

R

D   W

Laun.

L

Entry

Hall

L

Br 2
11-3x10-0

Br 3
11-1x10-0

vaulted

Garage
19-4x20-4

Porch

© Copyright by designer/architect

Plan #F09-126D-1049

Dimensions: 26' W x 30' D
Heated Sq. Ft.: 1,083
Bedrooms: 3   **Bathrooms:** 1
Exterior Walls: 2" x 6"
Foundation: Walk-out basement

See index for more information

Images provided by designer/architect

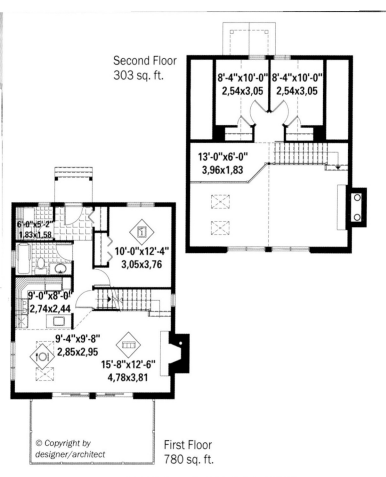

Second Floor
303 sq. ft.

8'-4"x10'-0"
2,54x3,05

8'-4"x10'-0"
2,54x3,05

13'-0"x6'-0"
3,96x1,83

6'-0"x5'-2"
1,83x1,58

10'-0"x12'-4"
3,05x3,76

9'-0"x8'-0"
2,74x2,44

9'-4"x9'-8"
2,85x2,95

15'-8"x12'-6"
4,78x3,81

© Copyright by designer/architect

First Floor
780 sq. ft.

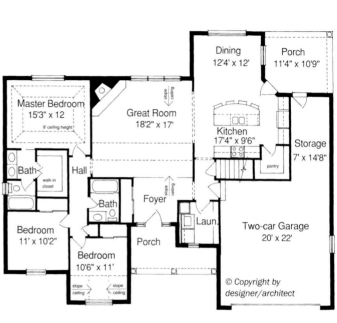

Plan #F09-065D-0022

Dimensions: 60' W x 48'10" D
Heated Sq. Ft.: 1,593
Bedrooms: 3 **Bathrooms:** 2
Foundation: Basement standard; slab or walk-out basement for an additional fee

Please see the index for more information

Images provided by designer/architect

© Copyright by designer/architect

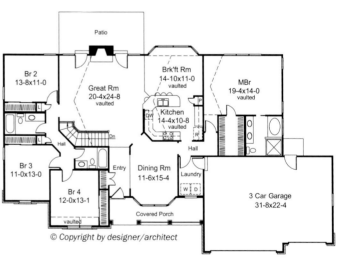

Plan #F09-007D-0174

Dimensions: 82'4" W x 49'4" D
Heated Sq. Ft.: 2,322
Bedrooms: 4 **Bathrooms:** 3
Foundation: Basement standard; crawl space or slab for an additional fee

See index for more information

Images provided by designer/architect

© Copyright by designer/architect

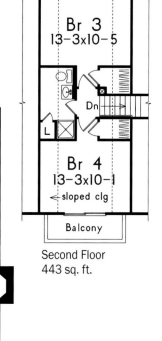

Br 3
13-3x10-5

Dn

Br 4
13-3x10-1
← sloped clg

Balcony

Second Floor
443 sq. ft.

Br 1
10-1x9-2

Br 2
10-1x11-7

Kit
10-0x8-9

Dn

Up

Dining
10-4x10-8

Living
15-0x13-3

Deck

© Copyright by
designer/architect

First Floor
832 sq. ft.

Plan #F09-008D-0134

Dimensions: 28' W x 32' D
Heated Sq. Ft.:   1,275
Bedrooms: 4   Bathrooms: 2
Foundation: Basement standard;
crawl space or slab for an addition-
al fee

See index for more information

*Images provided by
designer/architect*

Plan #F09-128D-0159

Dimensions: 71'2" W x 62'2" D
Heated Sq. Ft.:   2,533
Bonus Sq. Ft.:   623
Bedrooms: 4   Bathrooms: 3½
Foundation: Basement

See index for more information

*Images provided by
designer/architect*

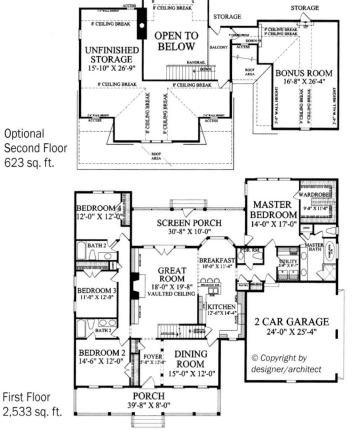

ACCESS

8' CEILING BREAK

STORAGE

STORAGE

8' CEILING BREAK

OPEN TO
BELOW

BALCONY

DOWN

UNFINISHED
STORAGE
15'-10" X 26'-9"

HANDRAIL

ROOF
AREA

BONUS ROOM
16'-8" X 26'-4"

8' CEILING BREAK

8' CEILING BREAK

ROOF
AREA

Optional
Second Floor
623 sq. ft.

WARDROBE
9'-8" X 11'-0"

BEDROOM 4
12'-0" X 12'-0"

SCREEN PORCH
30'-8" X 10'-0"

MASTER
BEDROOM
14'-0" X 17'-0"

BATH 2

BREAKFAST
10'-0" X 11'-4"

PDR RM

MASTER
BATH

BEDROOM 3
11'-0" X 12'-0"

GREAT
ROOM
18'-0" X 19'-8"
VAULTED CEILING

UTILITY

LINEN

KITCHEN
12'-6" X 14'-4"

BATH 2

2 CAR GARAGE
24'-0" X 25'-4"

BEDROOM 2
14'-6" X 12'-0"

FOYER
5'-8" X 12'-0"

DINING
ROOM
15'-0" X 12'-0"

© Copyright by
designer/architect

First Floor
2,533 sq. ft.

PORCH
39'-8" X 8'-0"

Plan #F09-007D-0151

Dimensions:	70'4" W x 35'8" D
Heated Sq. Ft.:	1,941
Bedrooms: 5	**Bathrooms:** 3
Foundation:	Walk-out basement

See index for more information

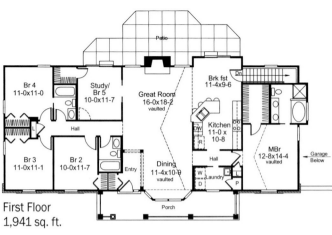

Images provided by designer/architect

First Floor
1,941 sq. ft.

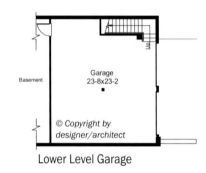

Lower Level Garage

© Copyright by designer/architect

Plan #F09-051D-0652

Dimensions:	60' W x 56'4" D
Heated Sq. Ft.:	1,884
Bedrooms: 3	**Bathrooms:** 2
Exterior Walls:	2" x 6"
Foundation:	Basement standard; crawl space or slab for an additional fee

See index for more information

Images provided by designer/architect

© Copyright by designer/architect

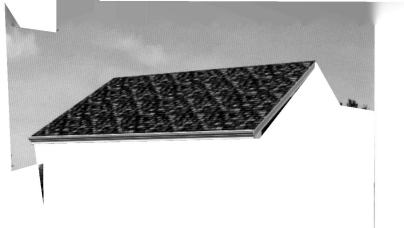

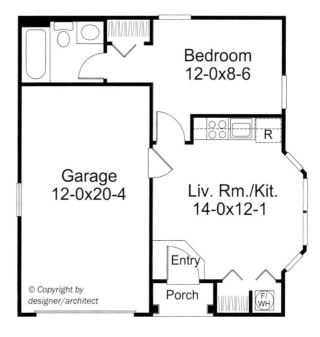

Plan #F09-007D-0196

Dimensions: 27' W x 27' D
Heated Sq. Ft.: 421
Bedrooms: 1   **Bathrooms:** 1
Foundation: Slab

See index for more information

Images provided by designer/architect

Bedroom
12-0x8-6

Garage
12-0x20-4

Liv. Rm./Kit.
14-0x12-1

R

Entry

Porch

F/WH

© Copyright by designer/architect

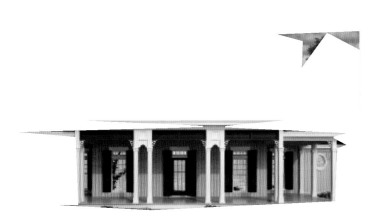

Plan #F09-020D-0363

Dimensions: 63' W x 51' D
Heated Sq. Ft.: 1,832
Bedrooms: 3   **Bathrooms:** 2½
Exterior Walls: 2" x 6"
Foundation: Crawl space standard; slab for an additional fee

See index for more information

porch
44 x 8

liv kit & eating
24 x 30

util
5x8

br
11 x 12

bath

mbr
18 x 18

bath

br
13 x 12

ent
13x4

dining
13 x 12

sitting

porch
54 x 10

coffee bar

stor
11x6

stor
11x6

locate door where best suited

garage
22 x 22

© Copyright by designer/architect

Images provided by designer/architect

GLASS BLOCKS

GRILLING PORCH
10'-6" X 9'-2"

COVERED PORCH
13'-2" X 9'-2"

WHP TUB

DINING ROOM
11'-0" X 9'-6"

M.BATH
16'-0" X 12'-0"

BRKFAST ROOM
10'-0" X 8'-0"

COMPUTER DESK

GAS FIREPLACE

OPEN BAR

MASTER SUITE
15'-8" X 12'-0"

9' BOXED CEILING

KITCHEN
15'-2" X 11'-0"

RG

REF

DW

GREAT ROOM
13'-6" X 19'-8"

PANTRY

9' BOXED CEILING

D

W

LIN

OPT DOOR

BEDROOM 2
10'-2" X 10'-8"

BEDROOM 3 / STUDY
10'-0" X 10'-8"

FOYER

GARAGE
20'-10" X 20'-0"

COVERED PORCH
16'-6" X 5'-0"

10" BOXED COLUMNS

Images provided by designer/architect

© Copyright by designer/architect

Plan #F09-055D-0017

Dimensions: 51'6" W x 49'10" D
Heated Sq. Ft.: 1,525
Bedrooms: 3 **Bathrooms:** 2
Foundation: Slab or crawl space standard; basement or daylight basement for an additional fee

See index for more information

Garage Below

Deck

Kit
11-0x9-6

Din
10-4x11-0

MBr
13-4x10-8

DW

R

P

Dn

L

Hall

Living
19-0x13-4

Br 2
10-0x8-9

Br 3
9-1x10-0

Entry

Porch

Images provided by designer/architect

© Copyright by designer/architect

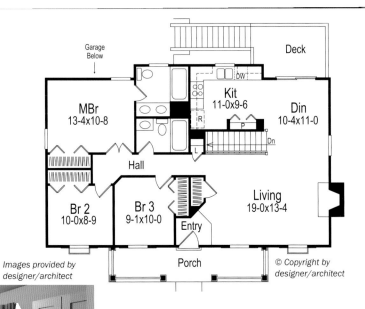

Plan #F09-007D-0030

Dimensions: 46' W x 32' D
Heated Sq. Ft.: 1,140
Bedrooms: 3 **Bathrooms:** 2
Foundation: Basement standard; crawl space or slab for an additional fee

See index for more information

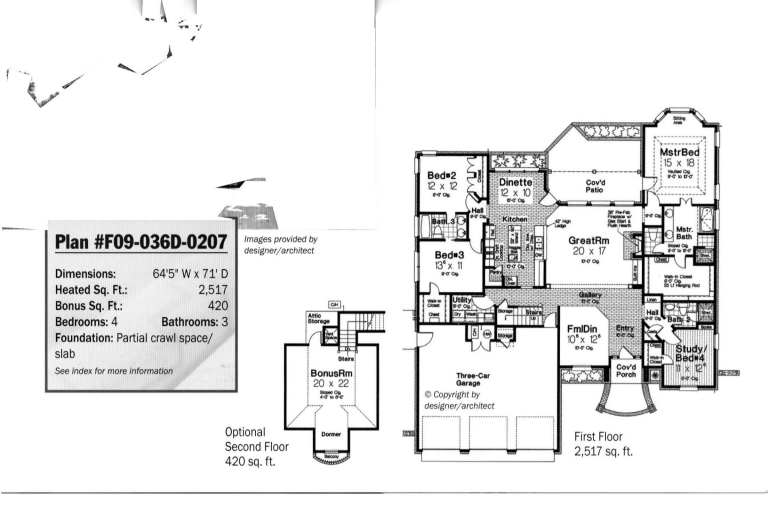

Plan #F09-036D-0207

Dimensions: 64'5" W x 71' D
Heated Sq. Ft.: 2,517
Bonus Sq. Ft.: 420
Bedrooms: 4   **Bathrooms:** 3
Foundation: Partial crawl space/ slab

See index for more information

Images provided by designer/architect

Optional Second Floor
420 sq. ft.

© Copyright by designer/architect

First Floor
2,517 sq. ft.

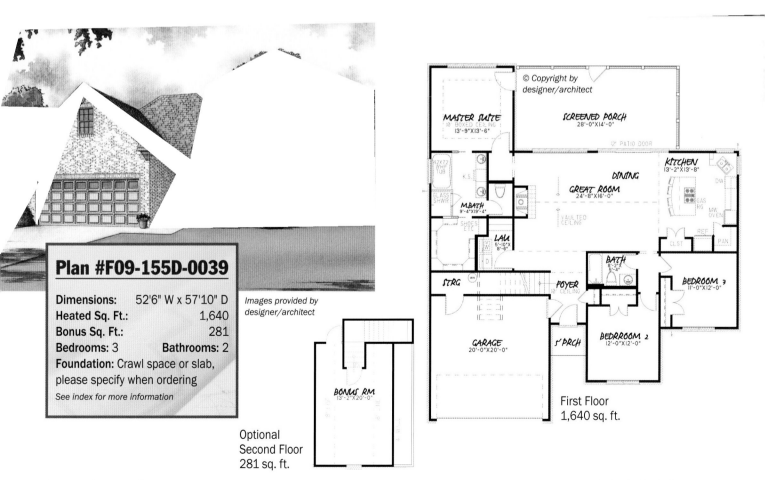

Plan #F09-155D-0039

Dimensions: 52'6" W x 57'10" D
Heated Sq. Ft.: 1,640
Bonus Sq. Ft.: 281
Bedrooms: 3   **Bathrooms:** 2
Foundation: Crawl space or slab, please specify when ordering

See index for more information

Images provided by designer/architect

© Copyright by designer/architect

Optional Second Floor
281 sq. ft.

First Floor
1,640 sq. ft.

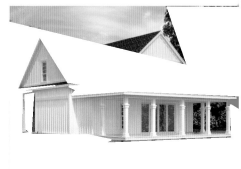

Plan #F09-020D-0393

Dimensions:	36' W x 44' D
Heated Sq. Ft.:	1,370
Bedrooms: 3	Bathrooms: 2½
Exterior Walls:	2" x 6"
Foundation:	Crawl space

See index for more information

Images provided by designer/architect

Features

- This Southern style cottage offers relaxed and comfortable living thanks to its open floor plan, multiple covered porches for outdoor enjoyment and well positioned sleeping spaces
- The kitchen features an island and the living area boasts tall ceilings for an even more spacious feel
- There's a handy utility room right off the kitchen, too

Second Floor
468 sq. ft.

© Copyright by designer/architect

First Floor
902 sq. ft.

Plan #F09-019S-0004

Dimensions: 81'3" W x 101'4" D
Heated Sq. Ft.: 3,381
Bedrooms: 3 **Bathrooms:** 4
Foundation: Slab standard; crawl space or basement for an additional fee

See index for more information

Features

- This luxury one-story home offers ultra private bedrooms and plenty of spaces for entertaining in style
- As you enter the foyer you are greeted by a wine bar to the left
- The spacious great room enjoys covered porch views and a cozy corner fireplace
- The open kitchen has an island with a breakfast bar extension, a drop zone from the garage and a walk-in pantry
- A friend's entry off the side of the home has the office steps away creating an easy way for clients or business partners to access the office space
- The master suite enjoys an oversized bath with all of the amenities, a huge walk-in closet with utility room access and a nearby exercise room
- A fun game room is near the secondary bedrooms and offers plenty of space for billiards, a gaming area or a card table
- 3-car side entry garage

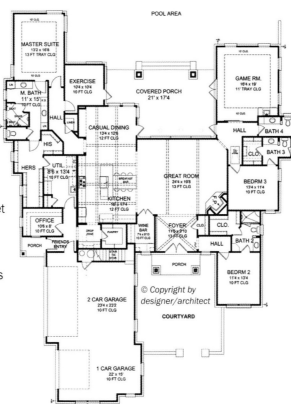

Images provided by designer/architect

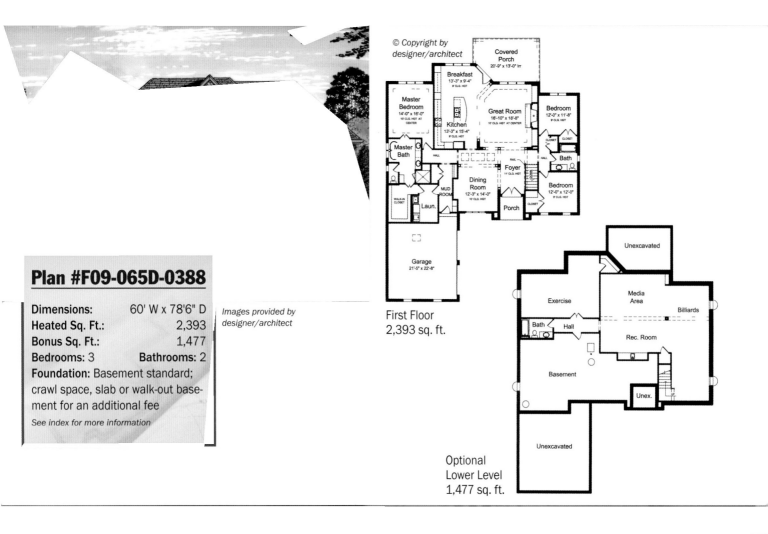

© Copyright by designer/architect

Covered Porch
20'-9" x 13'-0" Irr

Breakfast
13'-3" x 9'-4"

Master Bedroom
14'-0" x 16'-0"
10' CLG. HGT AT CENTER

Great Room
16'-10" x 18'-8"
10' CLG. HGT AT CENTER

Bedroom
12'-0" x 11'-8"
8' CLG. HGT

Kitchen
13'-3" x 15'-4"
9' CLG. HGT

Master Bath

WALK-IN CLOSET

HALL

Foyer
11' CLG. HGT

Bath

Dining Room
12'-3" x 14'-0"
10' CLG. HGT

Bedroom
12'-0" x 12'-0"
8' CLG. HGT

MUD ROOM

Laun.

Porch

Garage
21'-6" x 22'-8"

First Floor
2,393 sq. ft.

Unexcavated

Exercise

Media Area

Billiards

Bath

Hall

Rec. Room

Basement

Unex.

Unexcavated

Optional Lower Level
1,477 sq. ft.

Plan #F09-065D-0388

Dimensions:	60' W x 78'6" D
Heated Sq. Ft.:	2,393
Bonus Sq. Ft.:	1,477
Bedrooms: 3	Bathrooms: 2

Foundation: Basement standard; crawl space, slab or walk-out basement for an additional fee

See index for more information

Images provided by designer/architect

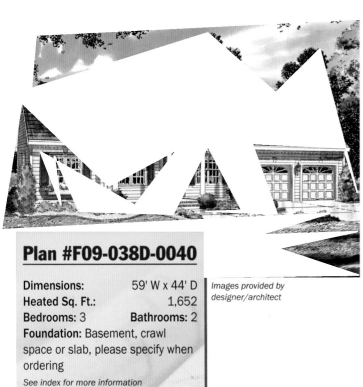

Plan #F09-038D-0040

Dimensions:	59' W x 44' D
Heated Sq. Ft.:	1,652
Bedrooms: 3	Bathrooms: 2

Foundation: Basement, crawl space or slab, please specify when ordering

See index for more information

Images provided by designer/architect

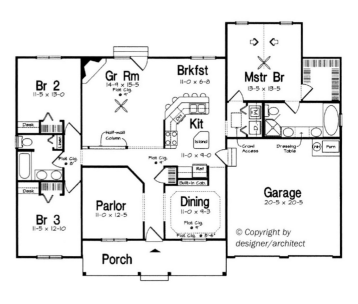

Br 2
11-5 x 13-0

Desk

Gr Rm
14-9 x 15-5
Flat Clg.

Brkfst
11-0 x 6-8

Mstr Br
13-5 x 13-5

Half-wall Column

Kit
11-0 x 9-0

Island

Crawl Access

Dressing Table

Fum

Flat Clg.
8"

Desk

Built-in Cab.

Ref

Br 3
11-5 x 12-10

Parlor
11-0 x 12-5

Dining
11-0 x 9-3
Flat Clg.
8'

Garage
20-5 x 20-5

Flat Clg.
8'-6"

Porch

© Copyright by designer/architect

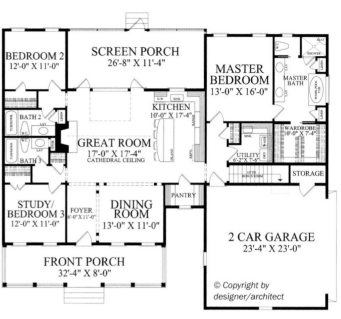

Plan #F09-128D-0313

Dimensions: 64'2" W x 52'2" D
Heated Sq. Ft.: 1,903
Bedrooms: 3   Bathrooms: 3
Foundation: Basement or crawl space, please specify when ordering

See index for more information

Images provided by designer/architect

Floor plan labels:
- BEDROOM 2 12'-0" X 11'-0"
- SCREEN PORCH 26'-8" X 11'-4"
- MASTER BEDROOM 13'-0" X 16'-0"
- MASTER BATH
- BATH 2
- KITCHEN 10'-0" X 17'-4"
- WARDROBE 10'-0" X 7'-4"
- GREAT ROOM 17'-0" X 17'-4" CATHEDRAL CEILING
- BATH 3
- UTILITY 6'-2" X 7'-6"
- STORAGE
- STUDY/BEDROOM 3 12'-0" X 11'-0"
- FOYER 6'-0" X 11'-0"
- DINING ROOM 13'-0" X 11'-0"
- PANTRY
- 2 CAR GARAGE 23'-4" X 23'-0"
- FRONT PORCH 32'-4" X 8'-0"

© Copyright by designer/architect

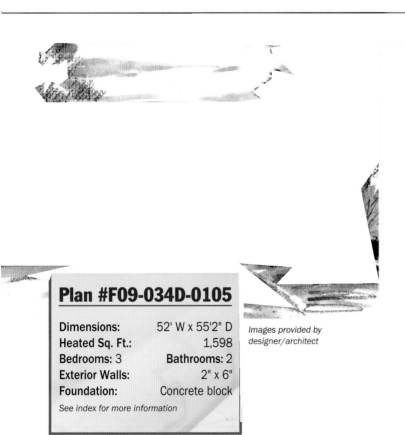

Plan #F09-034D-0105

Dimensions: 52' W x 55'2" D
Heated Sq. Ft.: 1,598
Bedrooms: 3   Bathrooms: 2
Exterior Walls: 2" x 6"
Foundation: Concrete block

See index for more information

Images provided by designer/architect

© Copyright by designer/architect

Floor plan labels:
- MBR 14' x 15' tray cl'g
- MBATH
- WIC
- Covered Porch 16'8 x 9'
- DIN RM 12' x 12'4
- Entry
- Laun
- GREAT RM 19'8 x 16'
- KIT 9' x 12'8
- TWO-CAR GARAGE 20'2 x 19'8
- BATH2
- FOYER
- STUDY/BR3 10' x 10' plus
- BR2 11' x 11'6
- Covered Porch

Plan #F09-101D-0050

Dimensions:	110'6" W x 84' D
Heated Sq. Ft.:	4,784
Bonus Sq. Ft.:	1,926
Bedrooms: 5	Bathrooms: 4½
Exterior Walls:	2" x 6"
Foundation:	Walk-out basement

Please see the index for more information

Features

- Rustic beams above the entry give this home a lodge feel
- The first floor enjoys an open floor plan that has the kitchen in the center of activity surrounded by the great room and casual dining area with a fireplace
- The private master bedroom and bath enjoy covered deck access and double walk-in closets
- A quiet home office is hidden behind the kitchen
- The second floor loft is a nice place to hang-out, and the laundry room is located near the second floor bedrooms for ease with this ongoing chore
- The optional lower level has an additional 1,926 square feet of living area and enjoys a wet bar and family room for entertaining, and for hobbies there's a climbing room and craft room
- 2-car side entry garage, and a 1-car front entry garage

Images provided by designer/architect

Second Floor
1,753 sq. ft.

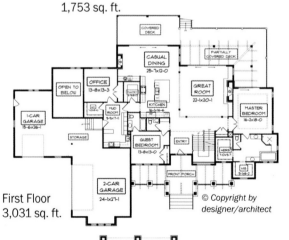

First Floor
3,031 sq. ft.

© Copyright by designer/architect

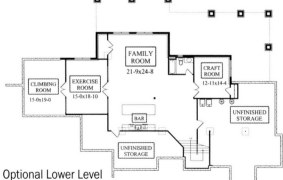

Optional Lower Level
1,926 sq. ft.

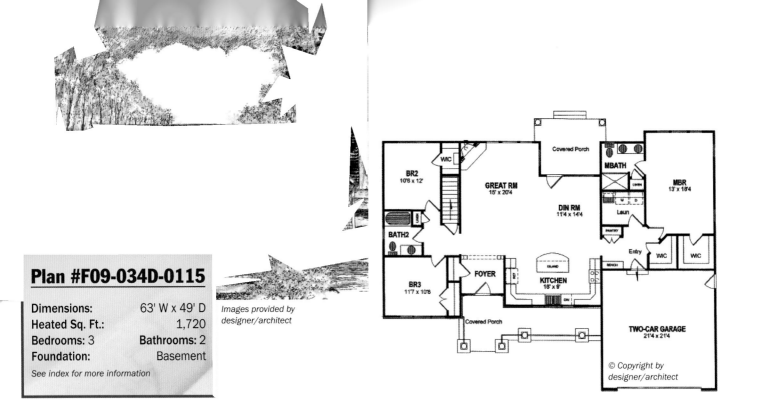

Plan #F09-034D-0115

Dimensions:	63' W x 49' D
Heated Sq. Ft.:	1,720
Bedrooms: 3	Bathrooms: 2
Foundation:	Basement

See index for more information

Images provided by designer/architect

© Copyright by designer/architect

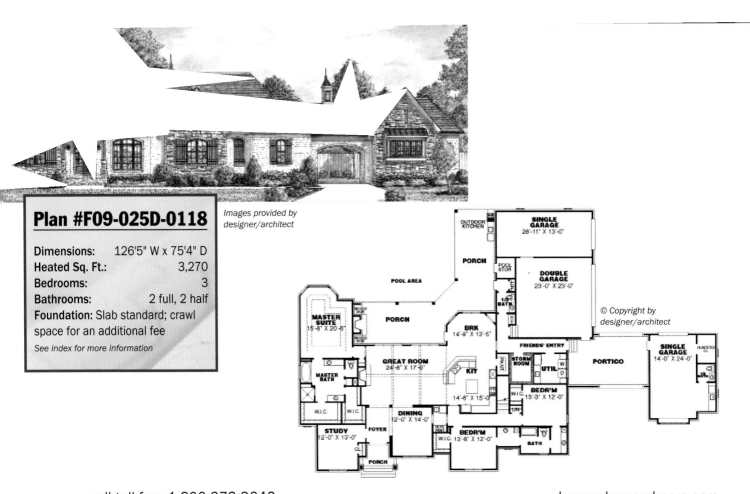

Plan #F09-025D-0118

Images provided by designer/architect

Dimensions:	126'5" W x 75'4" D
Heated Sq. Ft.:	3,270
Bedrooms:	3
Bathrooms:	2 full, 2 half
Foundation:	Slab standard; crawl space for an additional fee

See index for more information

© Copyright by designer/architect

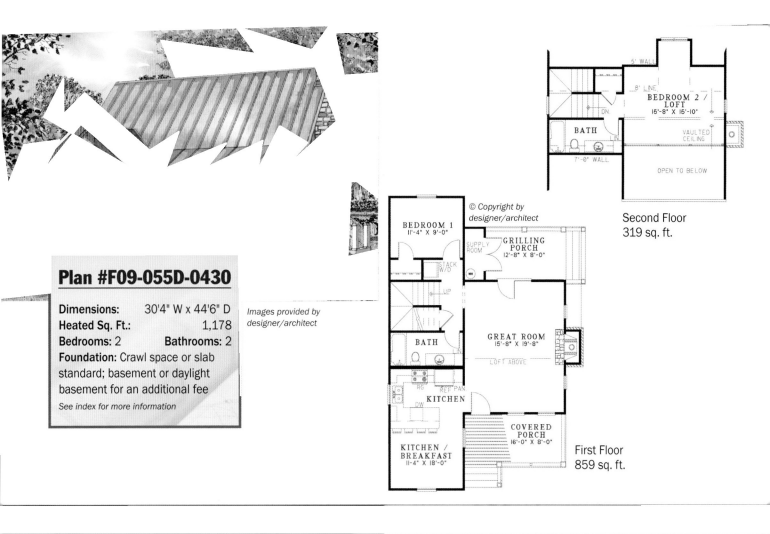

Second Floor
319 sq. ft.

First Floor
859 sq. ft.

© Copyright by designer/architect

Images provided by designer/architect

Second Floor (plan labels):
BEDROOM 2 / LOFT 16'-8" X 15'-10"
BATH
VAULTED CEILING
OPEN TO BELOW
5' WALL
8' LINE
7'-0" WALL
DN

First Floor (plan labels):
BEDROOM 1 11'-4" X 9'-0"
GRILLING PORCH 12'-8" X 8'-0"
SUPPLY ROOM
STACK W/D
BATH
GREAT ROOM 15'-8" X 19'-8"
LOFT ABOVE
KITCHEN
KITCHEN / BREAKFAST 11'-4" X 18'-0"
COVERED PORCH 16'-0" X 8'-0"
UP

Plan #F09-055D-0430

Dimensions: 30'4" W x 44'6" D
Heated Sq. Ft.: 1,178
Bedrooms: 2   Bathrooms: 2
Foundation: Crawl space or slab standard; basement or daylight basement for an additional fee

See index for more information

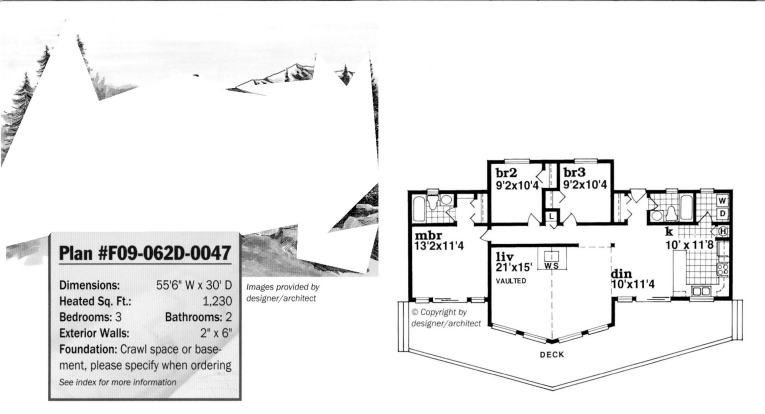

© Copyright by designer/architect

Images provided by designer/architect

(plan labels):
br2 9'2"x10'4"
br3 9'2"x10'4"
mbr 13'2"x11'4"
liv 21'x15' VAULTED
din 10'x11'4"
k 10' x 11'8"
W D
H
DECK

Plan #F09-062D-0047

Dimensions: 55'6" W x 30' D
Heated Sq. Ft.: 1,230
Bedrooms: 3   Bathrooms: 2
Exterior Walls: 2" x 6"
Foundation: Crawl space or basement, please specify when ordering

See index for more information

Plan #F09-055D-0651

Dimensions: 89' W x 49'4" D
Heated Sq. Ft.: 1,800
Bedrooms: 3 **Bathrooms:** 2
Foundation: Slab or crawl space standard; basement or walk-out basement for an additional fee

See index for more information

Images provided by designer/architect

© Copyright by designer/architect

Plan #F09-034D-0104

Dimensions: 52' W x 55'2" D
Heated Sq. Ft.: 1,598
Bedrooms: 3 **Bathrooms:** 2
Exterior Walls: 2" x 6"
Foundation: Concrete block

See index for more information

Images provided by designer/architect

© Copyright by designer/architect

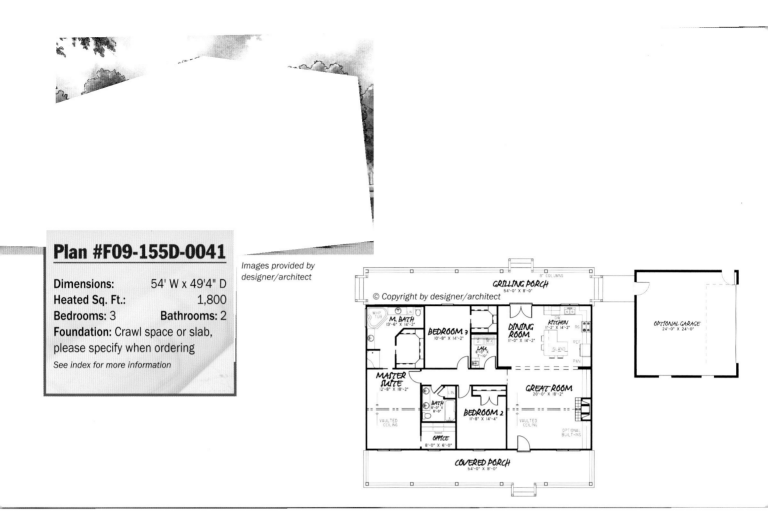

Plan #F09-155D-0041

Dimensions: 54' W x 49'4" D
Heated Sq. Ft.: 1,800
Bedrooms: 3   Bathrooms: 2
Foundation: Crawl space or slab,
please specify when ordering

See index for more information

Images provided by
designer/architect

© Copyright by designer/architect

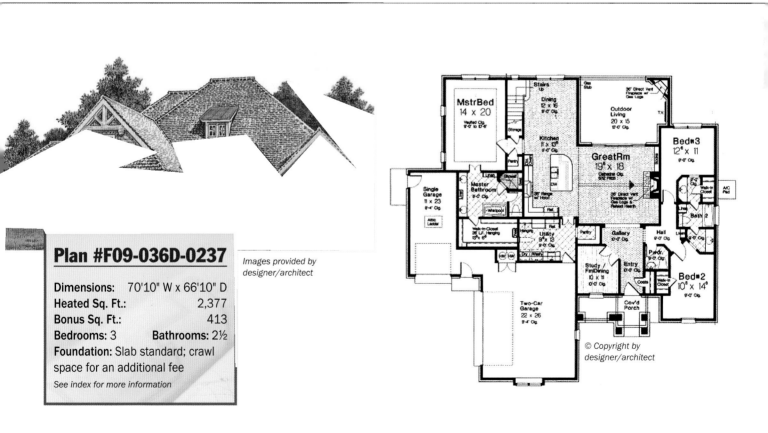

Plan #F09-036D-0237

Dimensions: 70'10" W x 66'10" D
Heated Sq. Ft.: 2,377
Bonus Sq. Ft.: 413
Bedrooms: 3   Bathrooms: 2½
Foundation: Slab standard; crawl
space for an additional fee

See index for more information

Images provided by
designer/architect

© Copyright by
designer/architect

Home Plans Index

Plan Number	Square Feet	PDF File	5-Sets	CAD File	Material List	Page	Plan Number	Square Feet	PDF File	5-Sets	CAD File	Material List	Page
F09-001D-0013	1,882	$989	$989	$1,589	$125	31	F09-008D-0134	1,275	$889	$889	$1,389	$125	261
F09-001D-0024	1,360	$889	$889	$1,389	$125	164	F09-008D-0153	792	$589	$589	$989	$125	155
F09-001D-0031	1,501	$989	$989	$1,589	$125	121	F09-008D-0161	618	589	589	-	$125	244
F09-001D-0040	864	$789	$789	$1,239	$125	209	F09-011D-0006	1,873	$1,263	$1,438	$2,526	$170	21
F09-001D-0041	1,000	$789	$789	$1,239	$125	166	F09-011D-0007	1,580	$1,119	$1,294	$2,238	$170	145
F09-001D-0043	1,104	$889	$889	$1,389	$125	212	F09-011D-0008	1,728	$1,178	$1,353	$2,356	$170	30
F09-001D-0067	1,285	$889	$889	$1,389	$125	72	F09-011D-0013	2,001	$1,288	$1,463	$2,576	$170	109
F09-001D-0085	720	$589	$589	$989	$125	161	F09-011D-0091	2,650	$1,506	$1,681	$3,012	$170	32
F09-001D-0086	1,154	$889	$889	$1,389	$125	158	F09-011D-0225	1,891	$1,211	$1,386	$2,422	$170	28
F09-001D-0088	800	$589	$589	$989	$125	165	F09-011D-0307	1,529	$1,126	$1,301	$2,252	$170	118
F09-005D-0001	1,400	$889	$889	$1,389	$125	146	F09-011D-0335	2,557	$1,465	$1,640	$2,930	$170	208
F09-007D-0010	1,845	$989	$989	$1,589	$125	151	F09-011D-0342	2,368	$1,430	$1,605	$2,860	$170	232
F09-007D-0029	576	$589	$589	$989	$125	166	F09-011D-0346	2,233	$1,587	$1,762	$3,174	$170	231
F09-007D-0030	1,140	$889	$889	$1,389	$125	264	F09-011D-0347	2,910	$1,619	$1,794	$3,238	$170	198
F09-007D-0040	632	$575	$625	$1,025	$125	150	F09-011D-0351	3,242	$1,697	$1,872	$3,394	$220	44
F09-007D-0049	1,791	$989	$989	$1,589	$125	27	F09-011D-0396	2,577	$1,479	$1,654	$2,958	$220	63
F09-007D-0055	2,029	$1,089	$1,089	$1,789	$125	155	F09-011D-0526	2,735	$1,662	$1,837	$3,324	$170	50
F09-007D-0060	1,268	$889	$889	$1,389	$125	144	F09-011D-0573	2,203	$1,429	$1,604	$2,858	$170	200
F09-007D-0068	1,922	$989	$989	$1,589	$125	202	F09-011D-0606	2,301	$1,587	$1,762	$3,174	$170	105
F09-007D-0085	1,787	$989	$989	$1,589	$125	172	F09-011D-0617	2,104	$1,201	$1,351	$2,402	$170	73
F09-007D-0105	1,084	$789	$789	$1,239	$125	158	F09-011D-0627	1,878	$1,256	$1,431	$2,512	$170	95
F09-007D-0108	983	$789	$789	$1,239	$125	163	F09-011D-0630	2,495	$1,450	$1,625	$2,900	$170	122
F09-007D-0113	2,547	$1,189	$1,189	$1,989	$125	167	F09-011D-0650	2,213	$1,499	$1,674	$2,998	$170	91
F09-007D-0114	1,671	$989	$989	$1,589	$125	153	F09-011D-0657	1,394	$1,068	$1,243	$2,136	$220	88
F09-007D-0124	1,944	$989	$989	$1,589	$125	147	F09-011D-0658	2,618	$1,490	$1,665	$2,980	$220	179
F09-007D-0134	1,310	$889	$889	$1,389	$125	86	F09-011D-0660	1,704	$1,213	$1,388	$2,426	$170	93
F09-007D-0136	1,532	$989	$989	$1,589	$125	148	F09-011D-0661	2,508	$1,472	$1,647	$2,944	$170	181
F09-007D-0137	1,568	$989	$989	$1,589	$125	231	F09-011D-0662	2,460	$1,453	$1,628	$2,906	$170	224
F09-007D-0140	1,591	$989	$989	$1,589	$125	152	F09-011D-0674	1,552	$1,119	$1,294	$2,238	$170	96
F09-007D-0145	1,005	$789	$789	$1,239	$125	201	F09-011D-0676	1,196	$999	$1,174	$1,998	$170	67
F09-007D-0146	1,929	$989	$989	$1,589	$125	255	F09-011D-0677	1,922	$1,221	$1,396	$2,442	$170	129
F09-007D-0151	1,941	$989	$989	$1,589	$125	262	F09-011D-0679	1,821	$1,219	$1,394	$2,438	$170	173
F09-007D-0159	615	$575	$625	$1,025	$125	107	F09-011D-0681	2,577	$1,434	$1,609	$2,868	$220	210
F09-007D-0161	1,480	$889	$889	$1,389	$125	174	F09-011D-0682	2,451	$1,390	$1,565	$2,780	$170	207
F09-007D-0162	1,519	$989	$989	$1,589	$125	154	F09-011D-0683	944	$883	$1,058	$1,766	$220	121
F09-007D-0163	1,580	$989	$989	$1,589	$125	259	F09-011S-0001	4,732	$2,203	$2,378	$4,406	$220	204
F09-007D-0172	1,646	$989	$989	$1,589	$125	246	F09-013D-0022	1,992	$1,045	$1,145	$1,595	$195	12
F09-007D-0181	1,140	$889	$889	$1,389	$125	251	F09-013D-0025	2,097	$1,195	$1,245	$1,695	$195	29
F09-007D-0195	342	$575	$625	$1,025	$125	220	F09-013D-0027	2,184	$1,195	$1,245	$1,695	$195	168
F09-007D-0196	421	$349	$349	$699	$125	263	F09-013D-0048	2,071	$1,195	$1,245	$1,695	$195	72
F09-007D-0199	496	$349	$349	$699	$125	217	F09-013D-0053	2,461	$1,195	$1,245	$1,695	$195	16
F09-007D-0235	2,213	$1,089	$1,089	$1,789	$125	249	F09-013D-0133	953	$895	$945	$1,295	$195	162
F09-007D-5060	1,344	$889	$889	$1,389	$125	159	F09-013D-0134	1,496	$945	$1,045	$1,395	$195	167
F09-008D-0016	768	$589	$589	$989	$125	124	F09-013D-0156	1,800	$1,045	$1,145	$1,595	$195	78
F09-008D-0133	624	$589	$589	-	$125	125	F09-013D-0198	1,399	$945	$1,045	$1,395	$195	227
							F09-013D-0200	4,508	$1,195	$1,245	$1,695	$195	69

Home Plans Index

Plan Number	Square Feet	PDF File	5-Sets	CAD File	Material List	Page	Plan Number	Square Feet	PDF File	5-Sets	CAD File	Material List	Page
F09-013D-0202	2,000	$1,195	$1,245	$1,695	$195	211	F09-032D-1124	2,117	$1,195	$1,320	$1,795	-	116
F09-013D-0235	2,140	$1,195	$1,245	$1,695	$195	120	F09-032D-1134	2,652	$1,320	$1,445	$1,920	-	10
F09-014D-0005	1,314	$775	$825	$1,300	$125	245	F09-032D-1135	1,788	$1,130	$1,255	$1,730	-	94
F09-015D-0083	1,831	$800	$850	$1,400	-	202	F09-032D-1136	1,440	$1,055	$1,180	$1,655	-	247
F09-016D-0049	1,793	$965	$1,055	$1,895	$95	17	F09-033D-0012	1,546	$1,510	$850	-	-	161
F09-016D-0062	1,380	$840	$930	$1,695	$95	156	F09-034D-0104	1,598	$1,210	$825	-	-	274
F09-016D-0105	2,065	$1,010	$1,100	$1,995	-	100	F09-034D-0105	1,598	$1,210	$825	-	-	269
F09-016D-0106	2,233	$1,010	$1,100	$1,995	-	195	F09-034D-0115	1,720	$1,210	$825	-	-	272
F09-017D-0010	1,660	$910	$1,000	-	$95	65	F09-036D-0207	2,517	$1,485	$1,195	$2,610	-	265
F09-019D-0046	2,413	$1,995	-	$2,995	-	40	F09-036D-0219	2,503	$1,485	$1,195	-	-	20
F09-019S-0004	3,381	$1,995	-	$2,995	-	267	F09-036D-0237	2,377	$1,335	$1,045	-	-	275
F09-019S-0007	3,886	$1,995	-	$2,995	-	76	F09-038D-0040	1,652	$895	$715	$1,345	$75	268
F09-019S-0008	4,420	$1,995	-	$2,995	-	104	F09-041D-0006	1,189	$889	$889	-	$125	48
F09-020D-0015	1,191	$800	$950	$1,500	$90	66	F09-045D-0014	987	$789	$789	$1,239	$125	253
F09-020D-0363	1,832	$900	$1,030	$1,700	-	263	F09-045D-0018	858	$789	$789	$1,239	$125	195
F09-020D-0365	1,976	$900	$1,030	$1,700	-	87	F09-047D-0056	3,424	$1,450	$1,650	$2,900	-	38
F09-020D-0393	1,370	$800	$950	$1,500	-	266	F09-049D-0010	1,669	$840	$945	$1,680	$85	252
F09-020D-0397	1,608	$900	$1,030	$1,700	-	105	F09-051D-0652	1,884	$1,188	$949	$1,887	-	262
F09-022D-0002	1,246	$889	$889	-	$125	174	F09-051D-0670	3,109	$1,397	$1,112	$2,224	-	28
F09-024S-0021	5,862	$3,025	-	$3,025	-	113	F09-051D-0696	2,016	$1,234	$979	$1,953	-	254
F09-025D-0118	3,270	$1,600	$1,100	-	-	272	F09-051D-0738	1,683	$1,148	$918	$1,811	-	203
F09-026D-0175	3,094	$1,155	-	$2,000	$125	32	F09-051D-0757	1,501	$1,148	$918	$1,811	-	160
F09-026D-1871	1,945	$1,005	-	$1,740	$125	63	F09-051D-0800	1,709	$1,148	$918	$1,811	-	208
F09-026D-1890	2,449	$1,055	-	$1,830	$125	48	F09-051D-0850	1,334	$1,107	$882	$1,744	-	173
F09-026D-1985	1,886	$1,005	-	$1,740	-	210	F09-051D-0859	1,850	$1,188	$949	$1,887	-	119
F09-026D-1989	1,452	$955	-	$1,650	-	194	F09-051D-0960	2,784	$1,352	$1,081	$2,162	-	36
F09-026D-2051	1,511	$1,005	-	$1,740	-	110	F09-051D-0970	1,354	$1,107	$882	$1,744	-	108
F09-026D-2102	2,155	$1,055	-	$1,830	$125	47	F09-051D-0977	1,837	$1,188	$949	$1,887	-	33
F09-027D-0005	2,135	$1,089	$1,089	$1,789	$125	43	F09-051D-0981	2,005	$1,234	$979	$1,953	-	256
F09-028D-0022	3,029	$1,200	$1,320	-	-	178	F09-051D-1006	3,235	$1,397	$1,112	$2,224	-	81
F09-028D-0054	2,123	$1,000	$1,110	-	-	250	F09-052D-0158	2,100	$989	$989	$1,589	-	222
F09-028D-0057	1,007	$795	$910	-	-	222	F09-053D-0002	1,668	$989	$989	-	$125	26
F09-028D-0064	1,292	$795	$910	-	-	16	F09-055D-0017	1,525	$1,100	$1,200	$2,200	-	264
F09-028D-0097	1,908	$920	$1,020	-	-	13	F09-055D-0030	2,107	$1,100	$1,200	$2,200	-	42
F09-028D-0100	1,311	$795	$910	-	$100	123	F09-055D-0031	2,133	$1,000	$1,100	$2,000	-	35
F09-028D-0112	1,611	$920	$1,020	-	-	18	F09-055D-0162	1,921	$1,100	$1,200	$2,200	-	157
F09-028D-0115	1,035	$795	$910	-	-	250	F09-055D-0192	2,096	$1,200	$1,300	$2,400	-	49
F09-028D-0120	2,096	$1,000	$1,110	-	-	64	F09-055D-0193	2,131	$1,100	$1,200	$2,200	-	154
F09-030D-0018	1,250	$889	$889	$1,389	-	259	F09-055D-0194	1,379	$800	$900	$1,600	-	42
F09-032D-0368	1,625	$1,130	$1,255	$1,730	-	45	F09-055D-0211	2,405	$1,200	$1,300	$2,400	-	12
F09-032D-0656	1,184	$970	$1,095	$1,570	-	46	F09-055D-0212	2,603	$1,100	$1,200	$2,200	-	20
F09-032D-0813	686	$845	$970	$1,445	-	211	F09-055D-0430	1,178	$700	$800	$1,400	-	273
F09-032D-0887	1,212	$1,055	$1,180	$1,655	-	233	F09-055D-0651	1,800	$800	$900	$1,600	-	274
F09-032D-0932	1,102	$970	$1,095	$1,570	-	177	F09-055D-0748	2,525	$1,100	$1,200	$2,200	-	25
F09-032D-0935	1,050	$970	$1,095	$1,570	-	82	F09-055D-0976	2,180	$1,550	$1,650	$3,100	-	164
F09-032D-1081	1,604	$1,130	$1,255	$1,730	-	216							

Home Plans Index

Home Plans Index

Plan Number	Square Feet	PDF File	5-Sets	CAD File	Material List	Page	Plan Number	Square Feet	PDF File	5-Sets	CAD File	Material List	Page
F09-126D-1049	1,083	$875	$716	$1,463	$105	259	F09-155D-0101	2,072	$1,650	$1,750	$3,300	-	180
F09-126D-1167	1,022	$875	$716	$1,463	$105	180	F09-155D-0134	2,031	$1,200	$1,300	$2,400	-	17
F09-128D-0017	2,568	$1,100	$800		-	62	F09-155D-0136	1,438	$1,200	$1,300	$2,400	-	131
F09-128D-0159	2,533	$1,100	$800	-	-	261	F09-155D-0147	2,073	$1,350	$1,450	$2,700	-	179
F09-128D-0313	1,903	$1,100	$800	-	-	269	F09-156D-0006	550	$675	$775	$1,475	-	65
F09-130D-0336	1,709	$985	-	$1,280	-	200	F09-156D-0014	551	$675	$775	$1,475	-	97
F09-130D-0337	2,107	$1,025	-	$1,320	-	114	F09-157D-0010	3,287	$1,029	$1,134	$2,058	-	87
F09-130D-0364	1,492	$965	-	$1,260	-	175	F09-157D-0023	2,873	$1,029	$1,134	$2,058	-	128
F09-130D-0365	1,491	$965	-	$1,260	-	221	F09-159D-0007	1,850	$1,100	$1,000	$2,000	-	76
F09-130D-0366	1,720	$985	-	$1,280	-	1123	F09-159D-0017	1,200	$800	$700	$1,600	-	172
F09-130D-0367	1,277	$945	-	$1,240	-	93	F09-159D-0018	1,818	$1,100	$1,000	$2,000	-	92
F09-130D-0396	1,420	$965	-	$1,260	-	181	F09-161D-0001	4,036	$2,095	$2,295	$2,895	-	170
F09-139D-0041	2,073	$1,495	$1,620	$2,995	-	246	F09-161D-0013	3,264	$1,995	$2,145	$2,595	-	196
F09-139D-0044	2,910	$1,495	$1,620	$2,995	-	213	F09-161D-0022	3,338	$1,795	$1,895	$2,595	-	14
F09-139D-0070	2,928	$1,495	$1,620	$2,995	-	90	F09-163D-0003	1,416	$1,250	-	$1,550	-	112
F09-141D-0012	1,972	$1,393	$1,533	$2,163	-	219	F09-163D-0013	1,676	$1,575	-	$1,775	-	125
F09-141D-0013	1,200	$1,043	$1,183	$1,673	-	119	F09-163D-0016	1,825	$1,575	-	$1,775	-	78
F09-141D-0026	1,500	$1,253	$1,393	$1,953	-	77	F09-164D-0004	3,273	$2,128	-	$3,110	-	83
F09-141D-0061	1,273	$1,113	$1,253	$1,813	-	206	F09-166D-0004	2,512	$1,189	$1,189	$1,989	-	131
F09-141D-0066	1,050	$1,043	$1,183	$1,673	-	79	F09-167D-0001	2,017	$1,089	$1,089	$1,789	-	124
F09-141D-0233	1,835	$1,393	$1,533	$2,163	-	110	F09-167D-0002	2,063	$1,089	$1,089	$1,789	-	101
F09-141D-0235	1,452	$1,113	$1,253	$1,813	-	111	F09-167D-0004	2,589	$1,189	$1,189	$1,989	-	111
F09-143D-0003	1,324	$1,010	$925	$1,700	-	100	F09-167D-0006	2,939	$1,189	$1,189	$1,989	-	83
F09-143D-0006	1,400	$1,010	$925	$1,700	-	227	F09-167D-0007	3,016	$1,289	$1,289	$2,189	-	253
F09-143D-0007	1,380	$1,010	$925	$1,700	-	106	F09-167D-0008	3,328	$1,289	$1,289	$2,189	-	8
F09-143D-0008	1,704	$1,025	$950	$1,850	-	129	F09-169D-0001	1,400	$889	$889	$1,389	-	96
F09-143D-0015	1,400	$1,010	$925	$1,700	-	248	F09-169D-0002	1,762	$989	$989	$1,589	-	68
F09-144D-0005	1,506	$1,150	$1,275	$1,645	$95	258	F09-169D-0003	1,762	$989	$989	$1,589	-	62
F09-144D-0023	928	$1,040	$1,165	$1,535	$85	61	F09-170D-0003	2,672	$945	$995	$1,795	-	49
F09-147D-0001	1,472	$889	$889	-	-	175	F09-170D-0004	1,581	$845	$895	$1,650	-	197
F09-148D-0047	720	$1,273	$892	$1,897	-	90	F09-170D-0005	1,422	$745	$795	$1,350	-	34
F09-148D-0048	1,217	$1,273	$892	$1,897	-	169	F09-170D-0007	2,323	$945	$995	$1,795	-	27
F09-148D-0050	1,282	$1,273	$892	$1,897	-	221	F09-170D-0010	1,824	$845	$895	$1,650	-	30
F09-149D-0007	2,381	$1,100	$875	$1,875	-	24	F09-170D-0012	2,605	$945	$995	$1,795	-	29
F09-150D-0007	2,901	$1,150	$880	-	-	99	F09-170D-0014	2,292	$945	$995	$1,795	-	21
F09-152D-0060	1,581	$1,026	-	$1,026	-	60	F09-170D-0015	2,694	$945	$995	$1,795	-	13
F09-152D-0079	361	$267	-	$267	-	107	F09-172D-0004	2,710	$1,150	$1,075	$2,000	-	64
F09-152D-0115	750	$465	-	$465	-	68	F09-172D-0008	3,016	$1,350	$1,200	$2,200	-	66
F09-152D-0134	456	$312	-	$312	-	207	F09-172D-0021	2,050	$1,050	$995	$1,850	-	71
F09-155D-0027	2,513	$1,550	$1,650	$3,100	-	31	F09-172D-0023	1,069	$850	$800	$1,500	-	91
F09-155D-0039	1,640	$1,100	$1,200	$2,200	-	265	F09-172D-0044	1,801	$950	$900	$1,675	-	252
F09-155D-0041	1,800	$1,100	$1,200	$2,200	-	275	F09-172D-0045	1,972	$950	$900	$1,675	-	130
F09-155D-0047	2,500	$1,650	$1,750	$3,300	-	214	F09-172D-0050	1,709	$950	$900	$1,675	-	126
F09-155D-0070	2,464	$1,550	$1,650	$3,100	-	229	F09-172S-0003	4,658	$1,500	$1,300	$2,300	-	19
F09-155D-0073	2,199	$1,350	$1,450	$2,700	-	43							
F09-155D-0100	970	$1,100	$1,200	$2,200	-	216							

why buy stock plans?

Building a home yourself presents many opportunities to showcase your creativity, individuality, and dreams turned into reality. With these opportunities, many challenges and questions will crop up. Location, size, and budget are all important to consider, as well as special features and amenities. When you begin to examine everything, it can become overwhelming to search for your dream home. But, before you get too anxious, start the search process an easier way and choose a home design that's a stock home plan.

Custom home plans, as well as stock home plans, offer positives and negatives; what is "best" can only be determined by your lifestyle, budget, and time. A customized home plan is one that a homeowner and designer or architect work together to develop from scratch, taking ideas and putting them down on paper. These plans require extra patience, as it may be months before the architect has them drawn and ready. A stock plan is a pre-developed plan that fits the needs and desires of a group of people, or the general population. These are often available within days of purchasing and typically cost up to one-tenth of the price of customized home plans. They still have all of the amenities you were looking for in a home, and usually at a much more affordable price than having custom plans drawn for you.

When compared to a customized plan, some homeowners fear that a stock home will be a carbon copy home, taking away the opportunity for individualism and creating a unique design. This is a common misconception that can waste a lot of money and time!

As you can see from the home designs throughout this book, the variety of stock plans available is truly impressive, encompassing the most up-to-date features and amenities. With a little patience, browse the numerous available stock plans available throughout this book, and easily purchase a plan and be ready to build almost immediately.

Plus, stock plans can be customized. For example, perhaps you see a stock plan that is just about perfect, but you wish the mud room was a tad larger. Rather than go through the cost and time of having a custom home design drawn, you could have our customizing service modify the stock home plan and have your new dream plan ready to go in no time. Also, stock home plans often have a material list available, helping to eliminate unknown costs from developing during construction.

It's often a good idea to speak with someone who has recently built. Did they use stock or custom plans? What would they recommend you do, or do not undertake? Can they recommend professionals that will help you narrow down your options? As you take a look at plans throughout this publication, don't hesitate to take notes, or write down questions. Also, take advantage of our website, houseplansandmore.com. This website is very user-friendly, allowing you to search for the perfect house design by style, size, budget, and a home's features. With all of these tools readily available to you, you'll find the home design of your dreams in no time at all, thanks to the innovative stock plans readily available today that take into account your wishes in a floor plan as well as your wallet.

how can I find out if I can **afford** to build a home?

The most important question for someone wanting to build a new home is, "How much is it going to cost?" Obviously, you must have an accurate budget set before ordering house plans and beginning construction, or your dream home will quickly turn into a nightmare. We make building your dream home a much simpler reality thanks to the estimated cost-to-build report available for all of the home plans in this book and on our website, houseplansandmore.com.

Price is always the number one factor when choosing a new home. Price dictates the size and the quality of materials you will use. So, it comes as no surprise that having an accurate building estimate prior to making your final decision on a home plan quite possibly is the most important step.

If you feel you've found "the" home, then before buying the plans, order a cost-to-build report for the zip code where you want to build. This report is created specifically for you when ordered, and it will educate you on all costs associated with building the home. Simply order the cost-to-build report on houseplansandmore.com for the home design you want to build and gain knowledge of the material and labor cost. Not only does the report allow you to choose the quality of the materials, you can also select from various options from lot condition to contractor fees. Successfully manage your construction budget in all areas, clearly see where the majority of the costs lie, and save money from start to finish.

Listed to the right are the categories included in a cost-to-build report. Each category breaks down labor cost, material cost, funds needed, and the report offers the ability to manipulate over/under adjustments if necessary.

BASIC INFORMATION includes your contact information, the state and zip code where you intend to build and material class. This section also includes: square footage, number of windows, fireplaces, balconies, baths, garage location and size, decks, foundation type, and bonus room square footage.

GENERAL SOFT COSTS include cost for plans, customizing (if applicable), building permits, pre-construction services, and planning expenses.

SITE WORK & UTILITIES include water, sewer, electric, and gas. Choose the type of site work and if you'll need a driveway.

FOUNDATION includes a menu that lists the most common types.

FRAMING ROUGH SHELL calculates rough framing costs including framing for fireplaces, balconies, decks, porches, basements and bonus rooms.

ROOFING includes several common options.

DRY OUT SHELL allows you to select doors, windows, and siding.

ELECTRICAL includes wiring and the quality of the light fixtures.

PLUMBING includes labor costs, plumbing materials, plumbing fixtures, and fire proofing materials.

HVAC includes costs for both labor and materials.

INSULATION includes costs for both labor and materials.

FINISH SHELL includes drywall, interior doors and trim, stairs, shower doors, mirrors, bath accessories, and labor costs.

CABINETS & VANITIES select the grade of your cabinets, vanities, kitchen countertops, and bathroom vanity materials, as well as appliances.

PAINTING includes all painting materials, paint quality, and labor.

FLOORING includes over a dozen flooring material options.

SPECIAL EQUIPMENT NEEDS calculate cost for unforeseen expenses.

CONTRACTOR FEE / PROJECT MANAGER includes the cost of your cost-to-build report, project manager and/or general contractor fees. If you're doing the managing yourself, your costs will be tremendously lower in this section.

LAND PAYOFF includes the cost of your land.

RESERVES / CLOSING COSTS includes interest, contingency reserves, and closing costs.

We've taken the guesswork out of figuring out what your new home is going to cost. Take control of construction, determine the major expenses, and save money. Supervise all costs, from labor to materials and manage construction with confidence, which allows you to avoid costly mistakes and unforeseen expenses. To order a Cost-To-Build Report, visit houseplansandmore.com and search for the specific plan. Then, look for the button that says, "Request Your Report" and get started.

what kind of
plan package do I need?

5-SET PLAN PACKAGE includes five complete sets of construction drawings. Besides one set for yourself, additional sets of blueprints will be required for your lender, your local building department, your contractor, and any other tradespeople working on your project. Please note: These 5 sets of plans are copyrighted, so they can't be altered or copied.

8-SET PLAN PACKAGE includes eight complete sets of construction drawings. Besides one set for yourself, additional sets of blueprints will be required for your lender, your local building department, your contractor, and any other tradespeople working on your project. Please note: These 8 sets of plans are copyrighted, so they can't be altered or copied.

REPRODUCIBLE MASTERS is one complete paper set of construction drawings that can be modified. They include a one-time build copyright release that allows you to draw changes on the plans. This allows you, your builder, or local design professional to make the necessary drawing changes without the major expense of entirely redrawing the plans. Easily make minor drawing changes by using correction fluid to cover up small areas of the existing drawing, then draw in your modifications. Once the plan has been altered to fit your needs, you have the right to copy, or reproduce the modified plans as needed for building your home. Please note: The right of building only one home from these plans is li-censed exclusively to the buyer. You may not use this design to build a second or multiple dwelling(s) without purchasing a multi-build license (see page 287 for more information).

PDF FILE FORMAT is our most popular plan package option because of how fast you can receive them your blueprints (usually within 24 to 48 hours Monday through Friday), and their ability to be easily shared via email with your contractor, subcontractors, and local building officials. The PDF file format is a complete set of construction drawings in an electronic file format. It includes a one-time build copyright release that allows you to make changes and copies of the plans. Typically you will receive a PDF file via email within 24-48 hours (Mon-Fri, 7:30am-4:30pm CST) allowing you to save money on shipping. Upon receiving, visit a local copy or print shop and print the number of plans you need to build your home, or print one and alter the plan by using correction fluid and drawing in your modifications. Please note: These are flat image files and cannot be altered electronically. PDF files are non-refundable and not returnable.

CAD FILE FORMAT is the actual computer files for a plan directly from Auto-CAD, or another computer aided design program. CAD files are the best option if you have a significant amount of changes to make to the plan, or if you need to make the plan fit your local codes. If you purchase a CAD File, it allows you, or a local design professional the ability to modify the plans electronically in a CAD program, so making changes to the plan is easier and less expensive than using a paper set of plans when modifying. A CAD package also includes a one-time build copyright release that allows you to legally make your changes, and print multiple copies of the plan. See the specific plan page for availability and pricing. Please note: CAD files are non-refundable and not returnable.

MIRROR REVERSE SETS Sometimes a home fits a site better if it is flipped left to right. A mirror reverse set of plans is simply a mirror image of the original drawings causing the lettering and dimensions to read backwards. Therefore, when ordering a mirror reverse set of plans, you must purchase at least one set of the original plans to read from, and use the mirror reverse set for construction. Some plans offer right reading reverse for an additional fee. This means the plan has been redrawn by the designer as the mirrored version and can easily be read.

ADDITIONAL SETS You can order extra plan sets of a plan for an additional fee. A 5-set, 8-set, or reproducible master must have been previously purchased. Please note: Only available within 90 days after purchase of a plan package.

2" X 6" EXTERIOR WALLS 2" x 6" exterior walls can be purchased for some plans for an additional fee (see houseplansandmore. com for availability and pricing).

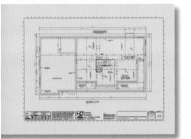

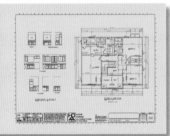

our
plan packages include...

Quality plans for building your future, with extras that provide unsurpassed value, ensure good construction and long-term enjoyment. A quality home - one that looks good, functions well, and provides years of enjoyment - is a product of many things - design, materials, and craftsmanship. But it's also the result of outstanding blueprints - the actual plans and specifications that tell the builder exactly how to build your home.

And with our BLUEPRINT PACKAGES you get the absolute best. A complete set of blueprints is available for every design in this book. These "working drawings" are highly detailed, resulting in two key benefits:

- **BETTER UNDERSTANDING BY THE CONTRACTOR OF HOW TO BUILD YOUR HOME AND...**
- **MORE ACCURATE CONSTRUCTION ESTIMATES THAT WILL SAVE YOU TIME AND MONEY.**

Below is a sample of the plan information included for most of the designs in this book. Specific details may vary with each designer's plan. While this information is typical for most plans, we cannot assure the inclusion of all the following referenced items. Please contact us at 1-800-373-2646 for a plan's specific information, including which of the following items are included.

1 cover sheet
is included with many of the plans, the cover sheet is the artist's rendering of the exterior of the home. It will give you an idea of how your home will look when completed and landscaped.

2 foundation
plan shows the layout of the basement, walk-out basement, crawl space, slab or pier foundation. All necessary notations and dimensions are included. See plan page for the foundation types included. If the home plan you choose does not have your desired foundation type, our Customer Service Representatives can advise you on how to customize your foundation to suit your specific needs or site conditions.

3 floor plans
show the placement of walls, doors, closets, plumbing fixtures, electrical outlets, columns, and beams for each level of the home.

4 interior elevations
provide views of special interior elements such as fireplaces, kitchen cabinets, built-in units and other features of the home.

5 exterior elevations
illustrate the front, rear and both sides of the house, with all details of exterior materials and the required dimensions.

6 sections
show detail views of the home or portions of the home as if it were sliced from the roof to the foundation. This sheet shows important areas such as load-bearing walls, stairs, joists, trusses and other structural elements, which are critical for proper construction.

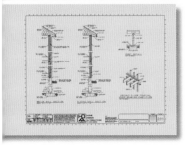

7 details
show how to construct certain components of your home, such as the roof system, stairs, deck, etc.

do you want to make
changes to your plan?

We understand that sometimes it is difficult to find blueprints that meet all of your specific needs.
That is why we offer home plan modification services so you can build a home exactly the way you want it!

ARE YOU THINKING ABOUT CUSTOMIZING A PLAN?

If you're like many customers, you may want to make changes to your home plan to make it the dream home you've always wanted. That's where our expert design and modification partners come in. You won't find a more efficient and economic way to get your changes done than by using our home plan customizing services.

Whether it's enlarging a kitchen, adding a porch, or converting a crawl space to a basement, we can customize any plan and make it perfect for your needs. Simply create your wish list and let us go to work. Soon you'll have the blueprints for your new home, and at a fraction of the cost of hiring a local architect!

IT'S EASY!

- We can customize any of the plans in this book, or on houseplansandmore.com.
- We provide a FREE cost estimate for your home plan modifications within 24-48 hours (Monday-Friday, 7:30am-4:30pm CST).
- Average turn-around time to complete the modifications is typically 2-3 weeks.
- You will receive one-on-one design consultations.

CUSTOMIZING FACTS

- The average cost to have a house plan customized is typically less than 1 percent of the building costs — compare that to the national average of 7 percent of building costs.
- The average modification cost for a home is typically $800 to $1,500. This does not include the cost of purchasing the PDF file format of the blueprints, which is required to legally make plan changes.

OTHER HELPFUL INFORMATION

- Sketch, or make a specific list of changes you'd like to make on the Home Plan Modification Request Form.
- A home plan modification specialist will contact you within 24-48 hours with your free estimate.
- Upon accepting the estimate, you will need to purchase the PDF or CAD file format.
- A contract, which includes a specific list of changes and fees will be sent to you prior for your approval.
- Upon approving the contract, our design partners will keep you up to date by emailing sketches throughout the project.
- Plans can be converted to metric, or to a Barrier-free layout (also referred to as a universal home design, which allows easy mobility for an individual with limitations of any kind).

2 easy steps

1 visit

houseplansandmore.com
and click on the Resources tab at the top of the home page, then click "How to Customize Your House Plan," or scan the QR code here to download the Home Plan Modification Request Form.

2 email

your completed form to:
customizehpm@designamerica.com,
or fax it to: 651-602-5050.

If you are not able to access the Internet, please call 1-800-373-2646
(Monday - Friday, 7:30am - 4:30 pm CST).

helpful **building aids**

Your Blueprint Package will contain all of the necessary construction information you need to build your home. But, we also offer the following products and services to save you time and money during the building process.

MATERIAL LIST Many of the home plans in this book have a material list available for purchase that gives you the quantity, dimensions, and description of the building materials needed to construct the home (see the index on pages 276-279 for availability and pricing). Keep in mind, due to variations in local building code requirements, exact material quantities cannot be guaranteed. Note: Material lists are created with the standard foundation type only. Please review the material list and the construction drawings with your material supplier to verify measurements and quantities of the materials listed before ordering supplies.

THE LEGAL KIT Avoid many legal pitfalls and build your home with confidence using the forms and contracts featured in this kit. Included are request for proposal documents, various fixed price and cost plus contracts, instructions on how and when to use each form, warranty statements and more. Save time and money before you break ground on your new home or start a remodeling project. All forms are reproducible. This kit is ideal for homebuilders and contractors. Cost: $35.00

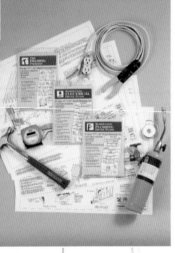

DETAIL PLAN PACKAGES - ELECTRICAL, FRAMING & PLUMBING Three separate packages offer homebuilders details for constructing various foundations; numerous floor, wall and roof framing techniques; simple to complex residential wiring; sump and water softener hookups; plumbing connection methods; installation of septic systems, and more. Each package includes three dimensional illustrations and a glossary of terms. Purchase one or all three. Please note: These drawings do not pertain to a specific home plan, but they include general guidelines and tips for construction in all 3 of these trades. Cost: $20.00 each or all three for $40.00

EXPRESS DELIVERY Most orders are processed within 24 hours of receipt. Please allow 7-10 business days for standard delivery. If you need to place a rush order, please call us by 11:00 am Monday through Friday CST and ask for express service (allow 1-2 business days). Please see page 287 for all shipping and handling charges.

TECHNICAL ASSISTANCE If you have questions about your blueprints, we offer technical assistance by calling 1-314-770-2228 between 7:30 am and 4:30 pm Monday through Friday CST. Whether it involves design modifications or field assistance, our home plans team is extremely familiar with all of our home designs and will be happy to help. We want your home to be everything you expect it to be.

before you **order**

Please note: Plan pricing is subject to change without notice.
For current pricing, visit houseplansandmore.com, or call us at 1-800-373-2646.

BUILDING CODE REQUIREMENTS At the time the construction drawings were prepared, every effort was made to ensure that these plans and specifications met nationally recognized codes. These plans conform to most national building codes. Because building codes vary from area to area, some drawing modifications and/or the assistance of a professional designer or architect may be necessary to comply with your local codes, or to accommodate your specific building site conditions. We advise you to consult with your local building official, or a local builder for information regarding codes governing your area prior to ordering blueprints.

COPYRIGHT Plans are protected under Copyright Law. Reproduction by any means is strictly prohibited. The right of building only one structure from all plan packages is licensed exclusively to the buyer and the plans may not be resold unless by express written authorization from the home designer, or architect. You may not use this plan to build a second or multiple structure(s) without purchasing a multi-build license. Each violation of the Copyright Law is punishable in a fine.

LICENSE TO BUILD When you purchase a "full set of construction drawings" from Design America, Inc., you are purchasing an exclusive one-time "License to Build," not the rights to the design. Design America, Inc. is granting you permission on behalf of the plan's designer or architect to use the construction drawings one-time for the building of the home. The construction drawings (also referred to as blueprints/plans and any derivative of that plan whether extensive or minor) are still owned and protected under copyright laws by the original designer. The blueprints/plans cannot be resold, transferred, rented, loaned or used by anyone other than the original purchaser of the "License to Build" without written consent from Design America, Inc., or the plan designer. If you are interested in building the plan more than once, please call 1-800-373-2646 and inquire about purchasing a Multi-Build License that will allow you to build a home design more than one time. Please note: A multi-build license can only be purchased if a CAD file or PDF file were initially purchased.

EXCHANGE POLICY Since blueprints are printed in response to your order, we cannot honor requests for refunds.

SHIPPING & HANDLING CHARGES

U.S. SHIPPING -
(AK and HI express only)

Regular (allow 7-10 business days)	$30.00
Priority (allow 3-5 business days)	$50.00
Express* (allow 1-2 business days)	$70.00

CANADA SHIPPING**

Regular (allow 8-12 business days)	$50.00
Express* (allow 3-5 business days)	$100.00

OVERSEAS SHIPPING/INTERNATIONAL
Call, fax, or e-mail (customerservice@designamerica.com) for shipping costs.

*   For express delivery please call us by 11:00 am Monday-Friday CST

**   Orders may be subject to custom's fees and or duties/taxes.

Note: Shipping and handling does not apply on PDF and CAD File orders. PDF and CAD File orders will be emailed within 24-48 hours (Monday - Friday, 7:30 am - 4:30 pm CST) of purchase.

Please send me the following:

Plan Number: F09-_____

Select Foundation Type: (Select ONE- see plan page for available options).

❏ Slab   ❏ Crawl space   ❏ Basement

❏ Walk-out basement   ❏ Pier

❏ Optional Foundation for an additional fee

   Enter foundation cost here $ _____

Plan Package   Cost

❏ CAD File $ _____

❏ PDF File Format (recommended) $ _____

❏ Reproducible Masters $ _____

❏ 8-Set Plan Package $ _____

❏ 5-Set Plan Package $ _____

See the index on pages 276-279 for the most commonly ordered plan packages, or visit houseplansandmore.com to see current pricing and all plan package options available.

Important Extras

For pricing and Material List availability, see the index on pages 276-279. For the other plan options listed below, visit houseplansandmore.com, or call 1-800-373-2646.

❏ Additional plan sets*:

   _____ set(s) at $_____ per set $ _____

❏ Print in right-reading reverse:

   one-time additional fee of $_____ $ _____

❏ Print in mirror reverse:

   _____ set(s) at $_____ per set $ _____

   (where right reading reverse is not available)

❏ Material list (see the index on pages 276-279) $ _____

Shipping (see page 287) $ _____

SUBTOTAL $ _____

Sales Tax (MO residents only, add 8.113%) $ _____

TOTAL $ _____

*Available only within 90 days after purchase of plan.

HELPFUL TIPS

■ You can upgrade to a different plan package within 90 days of your original plan purchase.

■ Additional sets cannot be ordered without the purchase of a 5-Set, 8-Set, or Reproducible Masters.

Name _____

(Please print or type)

Street _____

(Please do not use a P.O. Box)

City _____ State _____

Country _____ Zip _____

Daytime telephone   (_____) _____

E-Mail _____

(For invoice and tracking information)

Payment   ❏ Bank check/money order. No personal checks.
           Make checks payable to Design America, Inc.

❏ MasterCard   ❏ VISA   ❏ DISCOVER   ❏ American Express Cards

Credit card number _____

Expiration date (mm/yy) _____ CID _____

Signature _____

❏ I hereby authorize Design America, Inc. to charge this purchase to my credit card.

Please check the appropriate box:

❏ Building home for myself

❏ Building home for someone else

ORDER ONLINE

houseplansandmore.com

ORDER TOLL-FREE BY PHONE

1-800-373-2646

Fax: 314-770-2226

EXPRESS DELIVERY

Most orders are processed within 24 hours of receipt. If you need to place a rush order, please call us by 11:00 am CST and ask for express service.

Business Hours: Monday - Friday (7:30 am - 4:30 pm CST)

MAIL YOUR ORDER

Design America, Inc.

734 West Port Plaza, Suite #208

St. Louis, MO 63146

Best-Selling House Plans

SOURCE CODE **F09**